D1105465

ALLAN SHIVERS: The Pied Piper
Of Texas Politics

ALLAN SHIVERS: The Pied Piper Of Texas Politics

Sam Kinch

and

Stuart Long

SHOAL CREEK PUBLISHERS, INC.
P.O. Box 968
Austin, Texas 78767

Library of Congress No. 73-86925
ISBN 0-88319-017-6

Lithographed and bound in the United States of America
by Steck-Warlick, Austin, Texas

Foreword

It was the last Texas governor's staff small enough to be intimately acquainted with one another. This sparse crowd of a dozen or so formed the changeover when Governor Beauford Jester was found dead in his berth on the morning train to Houston and Allan Shivers, the handsome 42-year-old lieutenant governor, was catapulted into an eventful walk with destiny. That date was July 11, 1949.

Survivors recall it well: writers, secretaries and clerks quickly learned that the new man hadn't come to town on a load of green wood. Shivers operated quietly, quickly, calmly, positively, and with a confident air that proved well justified. He had, obviously, a keen administrative talent, a business mind. During the record seven-and-a-half years he was to occupy the governor's chair, he created records for something more than longevity.

The Shivers tools of government and politics were forged in a legislative furnace. He was a state senator twelve years and, as the saying went, never quite got over it. Briefly as lieutenant governor and longer as governor, he never forgot who he was—or who the legislators were, individually and collectively. The result was a productive working relationship between the executive and legislative branches—although not necessarily a sweet one. Shivers could and did hit hard when circumstances warranted and opportunity presented itself.

His Deep East Texas birthright included a pleasant personality for a political figure. It helped overcome any resentment the electorate might feel toward a person of wealth and substantial business ties. Never a favorite of professional-type leaders with labor or racial group connections, and definitely at arms-length with the type a U.S. vice president was to describe as "effete intellectual snobs," Shivers managed to keep animosity at a low level. An admirer termed him a typical East Texan who "never comes out of the same hole he went in."

However, his courage to risk political fights was never questioned. As a leader who rarely hesitated or backed away, Shivers attracted friends and followers of a fiercely faithful order. He gradually acquired an almost equal number of tireless enemies. The attrition of the years, a dubious episode or two involving associates, and his own controversial party record finally led to a bristling third-term race in 1954. There was a run off, and an unfamiliarly close (53 percent) final verdict. His opponent for the second time was Ralph Yarborough, who became the symbol of dissent from Shivers' role as a political kingpin and a substantially effective governor.

Party loyalty became a hot issue in 1952, the "Year of Decision," when Shivers badgered the "Truman Democrats" most of the year and then led Texas "Democrats for Eisenhower" in an October strike that carried the state for "Ike" and the Republicans. It was a revolt of spectacular proportions, even more so than Eisenhower's 1956 victory by nearly twice the margin. Shivers led that one, too, his Last Hurrah as a practicing politician. The congressional issue, particularly in the first campaign, was a "tidelands" claim that Texas and friends finally won.

Political thunder in '56 was rolling on both sides and all around as Senator Lyndon B. Johnson gave Shivers his first and only political defeat in the party conventions. The enigmatic relationship between Shivers and Johnson, close personally but sometimes violent politically, draws the somewhat perplexed attention of the authors of this book.

These authors, more than incidentally, are contemporaries who watched and weighed Shivers throughout his 22-year public career. Stuart Long and Sam Kinch are good newspapermen, which fact helps a political book. They are both admirers of the Shivers technique, which does not particularly help their objectivity. In personal politics one was a Shivercrat and the other wasn't, which ought to help their credibility. Their differences, if any, do not show between the lines of this conscientious, meticulous joint endeavor.

Weldon Hart

Acknowledgments

A far better writer than either of us should have written this book. Read again the foreword by Weldon Hart, and you'll see what we mean. But Hart felt that folks wouldn't really believe his version of Shivers, and didn't write it. Instead, he encouraged us to, helped us a lot with recollections, suggestions and corrections of recollections which had dimmed even though they seemed unforgettable at the time.

So we want to acknowledge Weldon Hart's help, first among many. Allan and Marialice Shivers were very generous of their time and their memories, and without their help, much of the real inside of their political career could not have been told.

We hope fellow senators will forgive James E. Taylor for his story of what sometimes happens in a Senate executive session which has nothing to do with nominees of the Governor. We acknowledge his help in putting together the decision-making process by which Allan Shivers became lieutenant governor.

We have drawn, usually with credit, on news stories by our colleagues of the Capitol Press Corps in those days—Dawson Duncan, Traxel Stevens, Dave Cheavens, Roy Grimes, Bill Gardner, Garth Jones, Richard Morehead, John McCully, Margaret Mayer, Sam Wood and others—and upon those ever-helpful librarians like Jim Sanders of the Legislative Reference Library, Harry Middleton of the Lyndon B. Johnson Library and Mrs. Quaidie Sullivan of the Allan Shivers Library at Woodville. Joe B. Frantz, the amiable University of Texas historian, helped us with his Oral History project. The North Texas State University Oral History project also was valuable.

Jimmy Banks and the late Wick Fowler, press secretaries to Shivers, were invaluable in their recollections of Shivers during their terms with him.

Banks, as president of Texas Publishing Company, originally contracted to publish this manuscript, but a desire to return to his own writing interests and to political activity prompted him to sell his firm.

Demp Toney and Mrs. Alice Meeks of Governor Shivers' "civilian" office staff, aided greatly in that most invaluable job of finding files. The Staff of the Chamber of Commerce of the United States supplied valuable documentation for the period when Shivers was No. 1 U.S. Businessman.

The late President Lyndon B. Johnson and his then-assistant, Bob

Hardesty, graciously spent about two hours helping us decipher the relationship between Shivers and Johnson, as well, we hope, as anyone can explain the attraction and cooperation between two such similar but unlike men.

The *Dallas Morning News, Washington Star-News, Houston Chronicle, Fort Worth Star-Telegram* and *Newsweek* were kind enough to allow us to use illustrations which helped catch the spirit of the times. Mrs. Eva Hardeman's cover catches the spark, too.

Mrs. Helen Rugeley, our editor, was merciless in correcting our grammar, demanding consistency and eliminating repetitiveness. A.J. Lerager, our publisher, made deadlines seem possible, even when they weren't.

But we also must give our thanks to the fascinating bunch of Texans who occupied the Capitol during those years from 1935 to 1957, who made all this possible, and to our editors like the late James R. Record and Dwight Allison, who made it possible for us to be there and to write about the Shivers Era.

Sam Kinch
Stuart Long

Table of Contents

Preface

One of the authors, researching one day, suddenly realized that no one had ever put together the story of Allan Shivers, the most important governor Texas has ever had, from both Texas and National viewpoints.

To fill this real gap in the history of Texas, the other author was enlisted, since both had been State Capitol newsmen through most of the twenty-two years Allan Shivers was a holder of State office in Texas, and the years thereafter during which he played an important role in the political, financial and social life of Texas.

The two of us struck up a bargain, to which Governor Shivers agreed. He would make his recollections available to us, to be blended into our own. Our effort was to produce as factual as possible a recounting of this remarkable man's political career. We agreed that it would neither be an effort to prove he had a halo, nor one to prove he had horns and a tail, but a story as near as two newspaper reporters could make it along the line of truth and fact. Oddly, while we agreed that any of the three could file a dissent on any part, none has chosen to do so.

It is easy to see that the foes of this controversial man will criticize us for failure to indict, while Shivers' friends will criticize us for failure to return a no bill. Both of us accept these complaints. We just tried to tell it like it was and let folks decide, as they did at the polls.

But everyone will agree that Allan Shivers is a man whose impact on Texas was tremendous and whose impact on national politics was, at the very least, great. Indeed, who but Allan Shivers drew the blueprint which enables Richard Nixon to carry much of the formerly Solid South in 1968, and all of it in 1972?

So, here is our version of what we found when we tried to put together the first real accounting of the story of Allan and Marialice Shivers. We respect your right to disagree. The Lord knows that our wives, who tolerated us during three years of gestation, both disagree with some of it. But in spite of that, we dedicate it to Totsy and Emma, who spared us the time to write it.

Sam Kinch and Stuart Long

"Besides, our losses have made us thrifty;
 "A thousand guilders! Come, take fifty."

   "And folks who put me in a passion
       "May find me pipe to another fashion."

          "You threaten us, fellow? Do your worst,
          "Blow your pipe there till you burst!"

                        From *The Pied Piper of Hamelin*
                        By Robert Browning

Chapter 1

A Piper of
Paradox

"Governor, I think somebody's pulling our leg," the nervous Freddie Smith blurted, as he quietly entered the dining room at Magnolia Hills (the historic Shivers family home near Woodville in Tyler County, Texas) where Allan and Marialice Shivers and five old friends were having breakfast.

"What's the problem, Freddie?" Shivers asked his long-time, loyal employee.

"The operator says the President of the United States wants to talk to you," Smith said, motioning toward the telephone.

"I'll answer it," Shivers replied, still in a mellow mood after the previous night's double observance of his 65th birthday and 35th wedding anniversary.

Shivers pushed back his chair from the marvelous maple table Mrs. Shivers had had made to fit that room—a table that revolves like a Lazy Susan. He took four steps to the phone and, sure enough, it was President Richard M. Nixon, calling a few weeks before his 1972 re-election to add his congratulations on the double celebration.

"I remember that both you and Governor Jimmy Byrnes were married on your birthdays," the President told Shivers. "That seems to be a wonderful idea, because both you couples have enjoyed such wholesome lives."

Shivers then put Nixon to a test.

"Mr. President, do you know which one of my birthdays this happens to be?" he inquired.

Nixon replied that he did, saying: "I promise you I am going to take good care of both Social Security and Medicare."

"I appreciate that, Mr. President, and I hope you'll see to it that Social Security is increased right along," Shivers said.

This light banter was vastly different from the tone of a previous call from President Nixon when, right after the 1968 election, he offered the Texan a place in the cabinet.

That was the third time Allan Shivers had been offered a place in a national administration. Both President Dwight D. Eisenhower and President Lyndon B. Johnson had wanted Shivers in their cabinets. He had declined the Eisenhower offers, and could not get away to Washington to discuss the Johnson tender. In 1968, his answer to Nixon had been that he simply could not spare the time from his business to take any other job.

Shivers' long association with Eisenhower led to his association with Nixon. And, like so many other things, his first meeting with Eisenhower was all but a military accident.

There was nothing about that cold morning of Dec. 22, 1943, to indicate to Captain Robert A. Shivers that the day was to produce a meeting which would write political history in his native Texas and drastically affect his own role in it. In fact, Shivers, like many another GI, was devoting full time to wishing he were at home in Texas, instead of in Italy, for Christmas.

But before the day was over, he had met General Dwight D. Eisenhower, commander of Allied Forces in Europe, and started a personal and political friendship that twice put Texas in the Republican presidential column and gave Shivers the first of several opportunities to serve in a national administration.

Shivers, a Port Arthur lawyer, had left his place in the Texas Senate to join the Army's military government branch. At the time he was aide to Maj. Gen. Leslie Kincaid of New York, who was military governor of Naples.

The general and his British counterpart received orders to arrange an honor guard and transportation for some VIPs who wanted to go to the Isle of Capri. Shivers had no word about the identity of the visitors. But when he was assigned to the detail by Kincaid, he knew that if they were important enough to rate an honor guard, he'd better not make any mistakes. He got to the port two hours ahead of time.

Not until he saw General Eisenhower and Major Elliott Roosevelt, son of the President, get out of their vehicle did he realize who the VIPs were.

"Ike was just as affable as always," Shivers afterwards recalled. "He remembered the meeting later, as of course I did."

It was really no surprise that Major Roosevelt was General Eisenhower's aide. After he and Eisenhower met on a train going from

Texas to Washington in 1939, the major had introduced Eisenhower to President Roosevelt. This meeting probably contributed to President Roosevelt's decision to give Eisenhower the supreme command job in Western Europe, elevating him over scores of military men with "lower numbers."

About a year after the Isle of Capri trip, Shivers and Eisenhower renewed their acquaintanceship. At a station in Ireland, Shivers was duty officer one night when word came that Eisenhower would be there in a few days on an inspection trip. Shivers, fearing he was risking court-martial, woke the commanding officer; as he had expected, preparations for the inspection began at once.

During that inspection Ike found a GI working under a truck as he made his rounds, and in typical Eisenhower fashion called the GI out to shake hands. "And he wasn't even running for office then," Shivers says of the man who was to become his close personal friend and golfing companion in later years.

Through his later work for Eisenhower, Shivers was to meet Richard M. Nixon, help him stay on the ticket with Ike in 1952 when many wanted him removed, work for Nixon in Nixon's three presidential campaigns—and get cabinet offers from him as he had from Ike and from President Lyndon B. Johnson's staff members.

Shivers led the fight to put Texas behind the Eisenhower-Nixon tickets in 1952 and 1956 and helped Nixon's drives in 1960, 1968 and 1972. So it is only natural that he was one of a tiny group of Americans who got a call from Nixon that November morning in 1968 after the election. Shivers was one of an even smaller number who got offers of places in the upcoming Republican cabinet; certainly the only Democrat.

"Mr. President," the then Austin National Bank board chairman told him, "there's no possible way I could at this time. I just can't become involved in a full-time place in government."

He felt honored, as a former Democratic governor, to be offered a place in the GOP administration. But when the President-elect asked if he would be interested in some other sort of appointment, he had to reply "nothing"—just as he had done to overtures from two preceding presidents.

Paradoxical as it might seem—since he had helped in the campaigns of all three—it was really quite in character for this Pied Piper of Texas politics, a precedent-breaker who dragged state government, screaming and kicking, into the 20th Century, and who more than doubled state spending while acquiring a "conservative" label.

Shivers was the first lieutenant-governor to succeed to the top Texas office on the death of the incumbent. Then he won re-election to three terms, breaking the no-third-term precedent in the process, and served longer as governor of Texas than anyone had. He broke just about every record in the book for Texas governors and undoubtedly set a national record by passing up three cabinet offers.

Shivers did accept two minor positions: a place on Eisenhower's Commission on Intergovernmental Relations, which he thought might help his goal of keeping government as local as possible; and, under Nixon, two terms as chairman of the Export-Import Bank's advisory board of directors.

Ultimately, he got one favor from the Eisenhower administration. Shivers received a letter from a lady in Shivers, Mississippi, the small community named for his forebears, some of whom came to Texas in the 1840s.

"They're going to close the post office at Shivers," she wrote the Texas governor. "Can't you save it?" Shivers promptly wrote Postmaster General Arthur Summerfield, and the decision to close the Shivers post office was reversed. Shivers laughs about it, describing it as the only time he used his political influence in Washington.

As senator, lieutenant-governor, governor, and now elder statesman, Shivers has had the same goal he sought as president of the Chamber of Commerce of the United States. That is to convince businessmen they have a responsibility to engage actively in politics. Businessmen made up much of the Shivers political organization which never lost an election until, in 1960, it failed narrowly to carry Texas for the Nixon ticket.

Shivers' ties with Nixon went back to a 1952 meeting of nine men hurriedly called to New York by Eisenhower, upon the revelation that California businessmen had created a fund to help pay Nixon's political expenses between campaigns. The conference felt that Eisenhower should keep Nixon on the ticket. This resulted in the famous "Checkers" speech in which Nixon insisted that he was "as clean as a hound's tooth"; the Nixon dog, "Checkers," was the star and Mrs. Nixon's cloth coat was "Exhibit A."

After the 1960 loss, Shivers again gave Nixon important political advice. There were indications of fraud in several places, but Shivers cautioned Nixon against contesting the election in several states, including Texas. It's an old political axiom in Texas that people don't like a poor loser. Nixon agreed with Shivers' advice, saying he would not like to try to tell the American people that the presidency can be bought.

Shivers had an advantage in talking with business leaders that many politicians lack. His personal wealth made it possible for him to speak the language of the businessmen he influenced, and at the same time to avoid the fiscal pressures which come to many low-paid public officers.

He was a governor with strong personal beliefs and an ability to convince others. And yet his personality and career are full of paradoxes. He was a conservative who advocated what then were great advances in public spending He was a preacher of states' rights, yet as senator sponsored two of the largest of the New Deal programs—old-age assistance and unemployment compensation.

He was a Baptist who supported pari-mutuel betting on horse races. He was a strong law-and-order man, yet he took on J. Edgar Hoover in a series of bitter exchanges. He acquired the greatest power a Texas governor ever had, yet he never was able to convince the Legislature that there should be a real strengthening of the governor's power and responsibility.

Shivers has been a Democrat all his life, yet he was the only Democrat ever to be the Republican Party's nominee for governor, to advocate the election of a Republican for president, and to survive it politically.

He was certainly the only Texas governor to make the cover of both *Time* and *Newsweek* the same week (Sept. 29, 1952). Governor James V. Allred made *Time*'s cover in 1936 as he rode a horse into a New York hotel lobby to publicize the Texas Centennial. But Shivers' cover stories were on his issue which would affect the nation—the bold bolt from the Democratic ticket being led by the 44-year-old Texas governor.

No one was neutral on Shivers, but some of his alliances were as strange as some of his enmities. He was the first governor of Texas to pay union dues, and was backed by labor in his early races, yet organized labor became one of his most implacable foes. He was a friend of Lyndon B. Johnson, yet they engaged in the bitterest convention campaign ever in 1956. (Both said later they should not have had that fight.)

Still another anomaly was his constant fight against strong government—while he was becoming the strongest lieutenant governor and governor in Texas history by learning and using the powers of the office. But in spite of his strong convictions and hard fighting, his wife says he "never brought his office problems home with him."

He was one businessman who dealt with Houston financier Frank Sharp without losing his shirt—or his reputation.

He was a college drop-out before the term was invented, yet he went back to college to attain scholastic success. He could have become a United States senator, but didn't want to go to Washington. He could have become a big-city bank president, but didn't want to move to Houston.

He was the first governor to select proteges and help elect them to high state offices in the days when "he held Texas in the palm of his hand."

In short, he was an enigmatic but almost completely predictable public man who rode boldly across the pages of Texas history in the 1930s, 1940s and 1950s and left his size 13 tracks on both the lawbooks and the backs of his enemies.

This, then, is the "Pied Piper of Texas Politics," who proved that if the national Democratic fathers wouldn't pay what he considered their bill, he could pipe another tune and lead their Texas children into another party.

Chapter 2

It Was a Barefooted Kind of Life

Lufkin boasts a historical marker attesting that it was the birthplace of Allan Shivers on October 5, 1907. But Woodville, to which his family returned when he was 10 months old, has the best claim as the home town of its most famous son, whose personality and philosophy still bear a heavy East Texas imprint.

It was a barefooted kind of life for young Shivers, growing up in Woodville. Hunting, fishing the year around, skinny-dipping in the creeks in summer, and, of course, going to school. His father, Robert Andrew Shivers, was a lawyer, involved in politics as county judge. Politics was the talk around the supper table at home, and the young Robert Shivers (he began to use the middle name of Allan when he got to The University of Texas a few years later) assimilated it quite naturally. Since the Shivers family lived just across the street from the courthouse, there were times when his Dad's talk of a trial aroused more interest than the fishing or swimming. So he would go across to listen to the trial of the week, absorbing the drama of the courtroom, and renewing his feeling that he wanted to be a lawyer, just like Dad.

Judge Shivers' service as county judge sent the political adrenalin coursing through young Allan's veins, and it still courses when time comes for the debating and the voting.

The first state candidate he ever saw was Pat Neff, running for governor the first time in 1920. Neff came to Woodville, where Judge Shivers was his county campaign manager. At the "speaking" on the courthouse square, twelve-year-old Allan was there to join in the cheers when Pat Neff "laid it on" Joseph Weldon Bailey. And when Neff beat Bailey in the Democratic runoff primary by nearly 80,000 votes, it was a time for celebrating at the Shivers home.

Judge Shivers had the problem of getting the votes for Neff from Doucette, Town Bluff, Colmesneil, Hicksbaugh and even out at Fred, in addition to the county's metropolis, Woodville. In the first primary, Bailey led Neff, 523 to 444, in Tyler County. But Judge

Shivers pitched in for the run-off, and got out the Neff votes plus some from the eliminated candidates. Bailey's voters expected victory, and did not bother to vote. So Neff led in Tyler County, 518 to 321, and the reversal contributed to Neff's statewide victory. That accomplishment was made possible by the factors that not only was Neff a Baptist, but also that Bailey had been connected with Standard Oil. And in the Piney Woods of East Texas, exoneration of Bailey by both the U.S. Senate and a House Committee didn't matter when he was running against a good dry Baptist like Pat Neff.

Law practice in Woodville wasn't very lucrative, and neither was being county judge. So, Judge Shivers' son Allan went to work as soon as he could. Some later summers he worked in the sawmill, but the summer he was nine he worked in the *Tyler County Messenger* office, trying to learn to set type by hand.

"I pied more type than I set," he jokes. "But I was a big, strong boy, so they had me turning the old hand press once the type was set."

When Allan got tall enough to reach the syrup pumps and to dip into the ice cream tubs, he got jobs at Minter's Drug Store and later at Dr. J.B. Cruse's Drug Store, jerking soda. He worked after school and on Saturdays and Sunday afternoons. (Of course the stores were closed Sunday morning for Sunday School, so there were no soda jerkers' jobs available until after Sunday dinner was over.)

Mrs. Shivers, his mother, was always a devout Baptist. She grew up on a sandy hill farm near Kennard in Houston County. Her name was Easter Creasy until the young school teacher, Robert Shivers, married her and took her to the family farm, Magnolia Hills, where they set up housekeeping. The farm had been in the family since 1846, when Allan's great-grandmother came out from Mississippi, a widow with her son and three daughters. Her son, Robert McGee Shivers, Allan's grandfather, went back to Mississippi to join a company for the Civil War, then returned to Magnolia Hills, the 605 acres of sandy pine land near Woodville.

It was there that Robert Shivers and his bride, Easter, lived while he taught in the public schools and studied law on the side. He owned Magnolia Hills for a time but sold it to an uncle when he moved into Woodville to practice law. Marialice and Allan bought it back in 1939 and built the log cabin house which grew steadily over the years as their family grew.

"When we did that," he says, "I said I was one politician who wasn't born in a log cabin, so we built one."

Throughout his political career, Woodville was "home" to

Shivers. In later years when he had a problem to solve or a tough decision to make, he would tell aides he was "going to Woodville for a few days." When he returned, he always seemed to have the answer.

Allan's mother was a great cook, and they invariably had hot biscuits for breakfast. The big Sunday dinners were memorable, and Allan often turned the freezer to make home-made ice cream, a regular item on the Sunday menu.

One winter, snow came to Woodville. Allan and Maurine, his sister four years younger than he, went out to gather pans of snow, to which Mrs. Shivers added sugar, vanilla extract and cream freshly skimmed from milk supplied by the family cow, to make snow ice cream, a special treat for the kids.

That freeze was hog-killing weather, of course, and young Allan helped his father butcher a hog in the back yard of their home. They made sausage and smoked bacon in the old smoke house, like those which graced the yards of most Woodville homes.

"Mother was pretty tough when I was growing up, but not nearly as tough as my Dad was," he recalls. "I'll never forget one Sunday morning; after Sunday School I had slipped off without going to church, to watch the train going by. That was part of the excitement in Woodville when I was a kid growing up. Everybody went down every Sunday afternoon, to watch the train going by, but there wasn't much of a crowd Sunday morning. So I sneaked away.

"We found out that right near the depot a fellow was going to try to ride a wild mule, after the train passed through. So, of course, I was late getting home for dinner. It was dinner—not lunch—in those days. Dad met me about 200 yards from the house with a whole handful of switches."

The barefooted and barelegged boy caught it all the way to the house. He wasn't late for dinner any more, and he didn't slip off from church to watch the train go through.

Both of Allan's parents were quite religious, and for a number of years Judge Shivers was superintendent of Sunday School at the Baptist Church a block and a half from the Shivers home on the Woodville courthouse square. One of young Allan's duties during this time was to go to the church early on frosty winter mornings and build fires in the wood stoves to have it warm by Sunday School time at 9:30 a.m. Then he would ring the bell, pulling on the manila rope to call the faithful to the white frame church.

After the Shivers family moved to Port Arthur, Judge Shivers taught a Bible class in the church there. Allan was to continue in that tradition, and from 1950 to 1970, he taught a men's Bible class at the First Baptist Church in Austin. He and his wife, a Roman Catholic, never let their religious beliefs affect their marriage.

It was while Judge Shivers was teaching his Bible class in Port Arthur that church and state got crossed up. An evangelist came to the First Baptist Church during the presidential campaign between Herbert Hoover and Al Smith. The evangelist had bad things to say about Smith, the Catholic, which riled Judge Shivers, a lifelong Democrat. He was equally critical of the evangelist, and the congregation divided somewhat on the issue.

Judge Shivers was "churched," the Baptist term for a hearing to decide whether or not to throw him out of the church. But Judge Shivers and the Democrats had the majority vote, and he remained in the church.

Mrs. R.A. Shivers, at 91 in 1973, was still driving herself to the First Baptist Church in Port Arthur every Sunday. But she became tempered with the times. Allan can recall when his mother wouldn't allow a deck of cards in the house. In her later years, she took up bridge, whist and other games, and became an expert bridge player.

The move to Port Arthur came after Allan and his sister, later to become Mrs. James L. Wilson of Dallas, had moved up through the Woodville schools. But those schools were not fully accredited, so in 1923 the Shivers family moved to where Allan could be graduated from an accredited school system and not have to take entrance examinations to enter college.

Those were the "old days," so he took four years of Latin, the last one at Port Arthur, where he saw his first football game. (Woodville, with a population of about 900, couldn't stir up enough players for football, but they played basketball and baseball the year around.) Young Shivers was graduated from Port Arthur High School in 1924, and that fall entered The University of Texas in Austin. Since his father was having trouble getting a law practice started in the city, after one year Allan became a college drop-out. He went back home to Port Arthur and got a job at the Texaco refinery in June, 1925. He had worked there the summer before as a laborer and a roustabout in the "barrel house," where oil barrels were repaired. When he returned, it was as a laborer in the railroad car repair shop, and by the summer of 1928, at 19, he had worked his way up to office manager, making $165 a month.

"It was one of the hardest decisions I ever had to make," Shivers relates, "to quit that good job and go back to the University."

But he had that idea that he wanted to be a lawyer, and he also had the political bug. His father had become city attorney, and was participating in every political campaign, as was his young son. Allan had grown up in politics, and the law seemed to be the way toward a political career.

A funny thing happened on the way to that law license. Allan had applied to Congressman John C. Box of Jacksonville for an appointment to Annapolis or West Point. Just after he got back to Austin, ready for college with the money he had saved while living at home and working, he got a telegram that the boy appointed by Box to West Point had resigned, and Robert A. Shivers was being nominated.

"My Dad sent an old friend of ours, who had been in the Army in World War I, down to Austin to persuade me not to go to West Point—not to become a professional soldier. I often wonder what would have happened . . . ."

Instead, he got a job selling shoes Saturdays at J.C. Penney's on Sixth Street in Austin. Forty-three years later, while chairman of the board of the Austin National Bank, Shivers was presiding at a luncheon for Penney executives as they opened a huge new store at the Highland Mall in Austin. He said he probably worked for the chain store company before any of them, and recalled that in those days the clerks weren't allowed to take off for supper on Saturday nights. Instead, the store manager sent out for a half pint of milk and a thin cheese sandwich for each of them.

"They are still doing that," one of the executives quipped.

Shivers continued to work his way through the University, with a job at the State Treasury, and as bouncer and later auditor at the "Germans," the University dances on Saturday nights.

And it was at the University that he took that first step as a first-hand politician. He ran for the Honor Council in 1931, to start a series of ballot victories which was never broken. He got his B.A. degree in 1931, and that spring had won election as president of the Student Association. The barefoot boy from Woodville had become the "Big Man on Campus" at the biggest university in Texas.

His campaign for student president was a lulu. They still talk about it on the UT campus. A drifter who called himself Simon Legree came to town and ran a ticket for student offices. He accused the Shivers group of kidnapping his candidate for sweetheart. He and Shivers got into a bit of fisticuffs over it, and this incident was later a turning point in his first race for public office.

Legree turned out to be John Patric, who became a well-known writer. Patric authored several books and a successful play, "Teahouse of the August Moon," a satire on military government (which, incidentally, Shivers entered during World War II).

In those days, it was possible to take the State Bar examination without going to law school. Shivers took the examinations in 1931, after he had taken some law courses and had his B.A. degree, and passed them. During the summer he practiced law with his father, who was ill and needed a hand at his law office. He went back to the University that fall to serve as student president and complete law school.

"I didn't know whether I would be able to finish my law education, because my father was sick at the time, so I thought it best to try the Bar exams early," he said.

Allan survived the rigors of the School of Law and the student presidency, and when he got his law degree in 1933, he returned to Port Arthur, looking for law clients, and looking also for a political opening.

He had made speeches for the $20,000,000 "bread bonds" amendment advocated by Governor Miriam A. Ferguson in 1932, and had begun to make himself known in the political life of Port Arthur. Then came the move—the first of the long steps up the political ladder.

"In politics there is really more to timing than there is in a track meet," he explained. "There's generally a time when the best man who offers for a position couldn't be elected—either because of the lack of interest, or apathy of the voters, or because he really doesn't have the opportunity to present his views. On the other hand, for exactly the same reasons with a few variations, there's a time when almost anyone can defeat an incumbent."

So Allan Shivers, at 26 a late law school graduate, got busy in civic clubs, meeting people, looking for his chance. After several suggested that he run for the Legislature, he asked his father whether he should run against the incumbent, Senator W.R. Cousins, completing his third term, or whether he should run for a seat in the House.

"I'd rather get beat for the Senate than win a seat in the House," Judge Shivers advised.

About then, Allan won his first workmen's compensation lawsuit, and got a $700 fee. He felt that was enough to launch a Senate campaign. So the handsome bachelor decided to tackle the Beaumont senator, after touring the district—Jefferson, Hardin, Liberty and Orange counties—and getting encouragement from his and his father's friends.

Senator Cousins had been in office a long time, and looked unbeatable. But he had neglected to keep up on the issues—old-age pensions, labor legislation, unemployment and others. It was a time of unrest. Organized labor's leaders were ready to help young Shivers oust the old senator. And, as it turned out, so were the majority of the voters.

Cousins tried to low-rate Shivers by saying, "Well, he's a good boy, but he's just a boy." But the "boy" made all the rallies held in all the population centers in those days before TV abolished the campaign rally. He got out and "saw the folks," and besides, he got a break.

One night at a rally in Port Arthur, Shivers had word from Byron Simmons, the Democratic county chairman of Orange County, that there would be a rally in Vidor that same night. At the Port Arthur rally, he asked Cousins if he was going to Vidor, and Cousins said that he didn't know, he might and he might not. Shivers rushed over to Vidor, but Simmons wouldn't put him on the program because Cousins was not there.

Finally, at the end of the rally, Simmons let Shivers speak, on condition he say nothing against Cousins. So Shivers merely told the story of his conversation with Cousins that night, leaving the impression, of course, that Cousins didn't take much interest in Vidor folks. Cousins' son, Roy, Jr., then demanded the right to speak, and charged that Shivers was a "jail bird." What young Cousins was talking about was a fine Shivers had paid after that fist fight with John Patric over campus politics at Austin.

"It hit the headlines the next morning," Shivers later recalled. "We were speaking in Beaumont the next night. We used to draw to see which one would speak first, and everybody liked to speak last. That was a vantage point. I told the master of ceremonies that I had something important to say and I wanted to speak first. Senator Cousins agreed.

"Everybody there knew about this incident. So I told them the whole story: that I did not go to jail, but that I did pay a $10 fine, and I had a fight for what I thought was right, and I would fight for what I thought was right when I went to the Senate.

"Then I said that I wanted to say to Senator Cousins that the next time he wanted to charge that I had been in jail, or make any other accusations about my character, my reputation or anything else, I wanted him to have guts enough to do it himself, and not send a half-baked kid over to make the accusations for him. That crowd just ate it up, and that kind of thing was what helped me in the election."

Shivers was for old-age pensions, and had campaigned for the bread bonds issue to show his concern for human welfare. Those were important issues in the Jefferson County area in 1934. But he also had shown the natural political ability to turn an opponent's mistake into a big fat plus mark for himself. He was to exploit that talent through a long career, like a quarterback calling an audible when he sees a defensive linebacker out of position.

He carried all four counties in the district over the entrenched incumbent, won the Democratic nomination in the July primary, and won the election that November to become the youngest state senator in Texas history. That was back when winning the Democratic nomination was called "tantamount to election"; before Shivers himself, nearly two decades later, was to tilt Texas toward two-party statism with his cry that "It's the man, not the party."

Chapter 3

The Boy Senator

Governor Miriam A. Ferguson called two special sessions of the Legislature in the fall of 1934, and Shivers, anxious to learn about this new job as senator, went to Austin to observe. Senator Cousins magnanimously agreed to a resolution giving his successor-to-be the "privileges of the floor." So Shivers attended all committee meetings, listened to discussion and debate, and studied the senators with whom he would serve.

During one of those sessions, former Governor James E. Ferguson sent for young Shivers to visit with him in the governor's private office, then located on the first floor of the Capitol. Although "Ma" was governor, "Jim" held sway in her official office. The aging man who, with his wife, had dominated Texas politics for two decades, talked of many things, but near the end of the conversation came a piece of advice Shivers was to remember throughout his life, and to follow closely:

"Well, I'm winding up a political career of a great many years, and you're just beginning one that may or may not last many years. But I want to give you one bit of advice. Don't let yourself get to hating so many people that you don't have time to *like* anyone."

Shivers took that advice to heart, and tried to follow it. "Today I don't know of anyone I've taken time to hate," he said in his senior years. "I don't mean to say that there are not a great number of people, or *were* not, during my years of political activity, that I just didn't have time for, but I don't think I ever put myself in the position of hating people. I don't think it is worthwhile. I have always been known as a man of strong likes and dislikes, and I certainly agree with that appraisal, but hating, or disliking, or not having time for, is something else."

His time for on-the-job advanced study ended, Shivers took his first oath of office in January, 1935, and joined a fascinating club—the 31 Texas senators. He immediately began trying to learn all he could from them.

At the head of the roll call was Dr. J.E.H. Beck, a physician from DeKalb. He resigned a short time later and was replaced by Harold Beck of Texarkana (no relation), who, with Shivers, made up the more exclusive club of the only two senator-bachelors. Shivers was later to appoint Beck to the Board of Control. E.J. Blackert of Victoria carried a gold-headed cane and dozed when the debate became tiresome. Wilbourne Collie of Eastland and Clay Cotten of Palestine were tall, smooth lawyers, persuasive in argument, Shivers recalled.

Eph Davis of Brownwood, a former prosecutor and judge, continued to prosecute as a senator. Then there was Tom DeBerry of Bogata, almost blind from a Fourth of July fireworks accident, vicious in debate, willing to make any sort of accusation or charge when his beloved "Splivins Boys," symbolizing the common man, were threatened by the import of a pending piece of legislation.

Arthur Duggan of Lubbock, with whose son, Arthur, Jr., Shivers had attended law school, was an imposing, distinguished senator, soon to die and be replaced by G.H. Nelson of Tahoka, who pushed unavailingly for a unicameral Legislature like Nebraska's.

Then there were the incomparable oratorical duelers—Joe L. Hill of Henderson and Thomas Jefferson Holbrook of Galveston. Holbrook opened the Senate sessions every morning by making a speech against something—generally Franklin D. Roosevelt. Hill rebutted him, waving his short stubby arms and shaking his rotund body as he defended the New Deal in all its phases. Hill represented the East Texas oil field but wanted to tax oil. He was to become Governor James V. Allred's Senate leader, and later to harass Governor W. Lee O'Daniel.

"Holbrook was astoundingly outspoken," Shivers remembered. "When a delegation of people from his district, school people and county commissioners, came to ask him to support this bill or that, he was just as apt to tell them that he not only would not, but he would do all he could to see that it did not pass. Then he would take the Senate floor to denounce his constituents for having the temerity to ask him to vote for such an outrageous bill."

There was Welly Hopkins of Gonzales who left the Senate to become an attorney for John L. Lewis and the United Mine Workers. Hopkins was probably the most conservative member of the Senate, yet became a confidant and dear friend of the mighty John L.

Down the roll was Austin's senator, John Hornsby, whose "You're mighty welcome to your capital city" greeted all visitors to the Capitol. Will Martin, whose son Crawford was to follow him to the Senate and then become attorney general, represented Hill County, a political bastion all its own.

Next was Weaver Moore of Houston, a stormy petrel all his political life. Shivers and other old friends helped bury him in 1971, and Wardlow Lane felt it was quite fitting that there was a thunderstorm underway, because "Weaver was in a storm all his life."

Once when Moore was raising rules questions with Senator Jim Neal, a Webb County rancher, Neal spit his cud of tobacco into the desk drawer that he kept filled with sand for that purpose, and threatened to pull off a boot and "beat hell" out of Moore and his rules.

Frank Rawlings of Fort Worth, a shrewd lawyer who later specialized in insurance law, John Redditt of Lufkin, salty with his East Texas twang, and Clint Small of Amarillo, cool and calculating in debate, but with a twinkle in his eye, were others of Shivers' first Senate.

These were but a few of the senators with whom Shivers was to serve during his 12 years as a senator and three years as lieutenant governor. But during his first term, Shivers seldom joined in the ringing debate which could be heard across the rotunda. They needed no public address system for the Senate in 1935. The 31 had won their seats by speaking to noisy crowds on courthouse squares and at country picnics, cemetery workings and rodeos. The "boy senator's" view that term was simple: "Freshmen should be seen but not heard."

However, Lieutenant Governor Walter Woodul gave Shivers some good committee assignments, including Game and Fish, which was important to a Piney Woods senator from the country where a squirrel or deer season bill could make the difference in re-election. In those depression days, hunting deer and squirrel and fishing weren't sports. They were the way to feed a family, and woe be to the lawmaker who trifled with those God-given rights to hunt and fish.

There is still a running battle in part of Shivers' senatorial district, Hardin and Liberty counties, over the use of dogs for hunting deer. It's the way the Kentucky and Tennessee mountain men hunted deer when they came to Texas, and by cracky, no do-gooder game warden is going to tell them different by law.

Two of that year's senators, Roy Sanderford of Belton and Clint

Small of Amarillo, had aspirations to be governor, but neither made it. Shivers, the "boy senator" of 1935, was the first senator of this century to become governor.

Albert Stone of Brenham; L.J. Sulak, the Czech newspaper publisher from LaGrange; Olan Van Zandt of Tioga, a blind man; and Claude Westerfeld of Dallas also were in the 1935 Senate. Mrs. Westerfeld once said that her husband had run for justice of the peace, county judge, county clerk and county commissioner.

"I told him 'Claude, if you keep running for all those offices, some morning you're going to wake up and find you've been elected'," she said. "Sure enough, here he is in the state Senate."

Allred had just taken office as governor, and Shivers got along with him well enough until, as Shivers put it, "Allred got the idea that he was entitled to cast my vote in the Senate because he had appointed my father district judge."

The highlight of their break came when Shivers insisted on voting to retain pari-mutuel betting on horse races, and Allred went to Shivers' district to make a Fourth of July speech.

"He didn't wave that flag," Shivers says. "He waved mine. He was really rough on me."

Allred did not raise the question of pari-mutuel repeal in the 1935 session, as Shivers remembers. The betting had been legalized by a last-minute rider on the Department of Agriculture appropriations bill in 1931, and then had been validated by proper legislation in 1933. Supervision was put under the State Tax Commission, and Allred had appointed R.B. (Bob) Anderson to regulate it. Three big tracks had been built as Alamo Downs, San Antonio; Epsom Downs, Houston; and Arlington Downs, Arlington, and there were licenses for some smaller tracks as well.

Not until the race track owners felt they no longer needed Elbert Hooper (who had been Allred's first assistant attorney general) as their general counsel did Allred join the plea of retail merchants in Dallas, Houston and San Antonio that the tracks were taking the money which poor people needed to pay their bills.

This started a bitter fight, and Allred called two special sessions of the Legislature to repeal the betting law. Senator Neal of Mirando City, a rancher, had been voting to keep the race betting, but surprisingly switched and made the difference of one vote in the Senate to give Allred a victory. A threat by Allred that he would veto a building appropriation for Texas College of Arts and Industries unless Neal voted "right" seemed to have been the final "persuader."

(Shivers remembered that technique and used it when he got into the job of persuading senators to vote for his programs as governor.)

Those were depression days, and a great deal of what would now be called liberal legislation was passed. Following the lead of the Roosevelt program in Washington, Texas set up old-age assistance, and unemployment compensation was created, both in special sessions in 1935, with Shivers' support.

These radical innovations drew fierce opposition from Senate conservatives like Holbrook, but the mood of the times to worry about the old and poor and unemployed prevailed, and so the state government of Texas took its first tentative steps into fields which would lift the cost and expense of state government like a skyrocket.

When Shivers came to the Senate, the state budget, adopted by the session in 1933, totalled $111,001,067 for the year ended August 31, 1935. By 1949, it had doubled twice, while he had a direct hand in budget-making for the expanding new programs in education, welfare, highways, and care of the mentally ill and retarded. By the time he left the governorship in 1957, the state budget had almost doubled again. And 15 years later, the State was spending $4.8 billion a year.

Young Senator Shivers did not take a big hand in the actual spending, preferring to serve on Jurisprudence and other committees rather than on Finance, which handles the appropriation bills. But he was making a name for himself as one of the quiet men who work out acceptable compromises in the privacy of the conference committee meetings where five senators and five representatives settle the "differences between the two Houses." In fact, conference committees often went far beyond the differences, and injected new material into the final version of bills, which then went back to both houses to be accepted or rejected without amendment and, usually, with little debate or explanation.

Lieutenant Governor Woodul recognized Shivers' ability quickly, and named him to most of the conference committees on important bills, except Appropriations, during that 1935 session.

One of the big issues was what to do now that Prohibition had been repealed nationally. From about 1910 on, Prohibition first, and then Repeal, had been issues in every governor's race and many legislative races. Now Texas went gingerly into wetness. In 1933, 3.2 percent beer was legalized by constitutional amendment. And in 1935, the voters approved another amendment allowing local-option sale of hard liquor. Shivers worked on the tailoring of that proposal, and on the Liquor Control Act which followed it.

In the regular session of 1935, Shivers served on seven conference committees, including the one which proposed the constitutional amendment to allow the sale of hard liquor. When the voters approved it, and the constitutional authority for an old-age pension program, Allred quickly called a special session to act on the enabling legislation for these two important items, and to levy the taxes to support the welfare program.

Woodul named Shivers as chairman of the conference committee on House Bill 14, the first effort to work out a compromise on how liquor and beer sales were to be regulated and taxed. This effort failed because the committee's product was defeated by the Senate on the last night of the special session.

Allred brought the legislators back for another 30-day session the next day. This time, Shivers was on the conference committee on the old-age assistance program, but did not sign the report, because he disagreed with portions of it. He voted against it, but then changed his vote to "aye" to help give it the two-thirds majority needed to make the revenue and pension plan effective immediately. That session he also helped write the final version of the first driver license law in Texas, and the Liquor Control Act.

Just a mere vote of the people didn't change many of the lifelong "drys" in the Legislature. They wanted to make liquor as hard to get as possible. Strong wets wanted it in corner saloons. And they were all representing their constituents, because even by 1973 Texas still remained, in general, dry across the north half of the state and wet across the south half.

The language in the proposed constitutional amendment was hard to write, but to get the needed 21 votes in the Senate and 100 in the House, it had to prohibit the "open saloon." A crafty compromise bit of language allowed the Legislature to define the term. There were efforts to use this as a means of legalizing liquor by the drink through legislation alone, in later years, by defining an "open saloon" as one which sells mixed drinks between 2 a.m. and 7 a.m.

One big fight in the conference committee on the regulatory act was over the size of liquor containers. The compromise was that nothing less than six ounces of liquor could be sold, for fear that a two-ounce bottle might be used to sell it by the drink. Another compromise was to set up two types of beer sale places—one for on-premise consumption and another for take-home sales.

Looking back over the years since that plan of enforcement was worked out, under an appointive board of three citizens with a full-time administrator, Shivers recalled the thinking of 1935:

"It is difficult to adequately regulate the liquor, wine and beer business without a lot of objections on one extreme by the people who are in the business, and on the other by the people who don't want anybody in the business," he said. "The administrative system we set up in the Liquor Control Act, in my opinion, has contributed largely to its general acceptance during this period of 35 years of regulation."

Shivers could look back and see how this compromise, hammered out on the hot anvil of pro and anti views in the Legislature, was indeed tempered well enough to stand the test of time. Only one brief period of misuse of powers under the law came during those years, and until liquor-by-the-drink was authorized in 1970, no major change was made in the law which the young senator helped write in his first year in the Legislature.

It is perhaps ironic that Shivers, who later was to fight the encroachment of the federal government into state and local affairs, had a hand in the first two big invasions—welfare and unemployment compensation. On the latter, Congress had passed a law taxing employers 1 percent of their payrolls to set up a fund from which unemployed workers were to get a living allowance when they were out of work. But Congress said that if the states would set up their own compensation systems and levy a tax, they could administer the program and lower the tax rate below 1 percent on those employers having few lay-offs.

The legislation came down from Washington, and Shivers was asked to be the sponsor in the Senate. It was tough, complicated, confusing legislation; the Texas Unemployment Compensation Act remains one of the most complicated in the Texas statutes. Allred named Shivers and others to a committee to study the federal law, and put such a law on the agenda for the Third Called Session, which began September 28, 1936.

Shivers dug in to study the bill as he had studied to take the State Bar exams before he finished law school. It passed the Senate by a vote of 23 to 6, and several senators conceded privately to Shivers that they didn't understand the bill, but were going along with him because they believed he did. This law has paid hundreds of millions of dollars to unemployed workers, and tax rates of Texas employers have been held to a minimum.

It took a constitutional amendment to bring the old-age assistance program into being, because the Texas Constitution prohibits making a gift of public money to anyone. Also approved by the voters that year were the first program for a retirement system for public school and college teachers and employees, and the amendment dividing the pardon and parole powers between the governor and a three-member board. This was an Allred dig at the liberal parole policies of the Ferguson years. It said simply that the governor could grant clemency only when it was first recommended by the three-member board, which had one man appointed by the chief justice of the Supreme Court, one by the presiding judge of the Court of Criminal Appeals, and one by the governor.

Shivers was on the conference committee which worked out details of this major change in state policy, melding the views of the Ferguson-haters and the Ferguson-lovers in the Legislature into a workable compromise.

Shivers also had a hand in the launching of Allred's program for the first old-age assistance plan. When the first payments were made in July, 1936, they went to only 59,999 persons and averaged $15.82 each. The rolls were to rise steadily and double in two years, causing a cut in checks and providing the big issue for the 1938 elections.

Allred's special session in September, 1936, was a tax session. Shivers was on the conference committee on that subject, but was on the losing side and one of eight senators voting against the bill which resulted.

Shivers learned in that special session how a governor, by the opening of special sessions to local and special bills, can get legislators and others obligated to him. Allred let him introduce a bill to permit the hunting of wounded deer with one dog in Liberty and Hardin counties. He also got approval of a bill giving his home town of Port Arthur some state land. Such local bills are the heart of a legislator's program, often more important to the folks back home than the broad-gauged social and tax bills which legislators spend most of their time worrying about.

When the Legislature came back in regular session in 1937, Shivers was well established as a senator. (That was the year that A.M. Aikin, Jr., of Paris reached the Senate as a freshman. He eventually became its dean.) Shivers was well-enough established that the Senate *Journal* index spelled his given name correctly. It had been "Allen" instead of "Allan" the previous session, but it was spelled properly in the 1937 *Journal* and thereafter.

That session, Shivers served on 18 conference committees, more than did any other senator and twice as many as most. He moved up to the chairmanship of the Labor Committee, sponsored three pure food laws for the Health Department, a bill for pay raises for chief deputies in county offices, a life insurance bill, and a county officer's bonding law.

This was also the session where the young senator learned about incurring the wrath of the chief executive. Governor Allred wanted pari-mutuel betting at race tracks ended. Because of his appointment of Shivers' father, R.A. Shivers, as a district judge, the governor demanded a vote to repeal race track betting in return.

Shivers said he thought those who had made investments in tracks were entitled to a little longer trial in the state, and voted against the repeal. That vote, he figured later, was perhaps responsible for getting him an opponent for governor in 1952. Ralph W. Yarborough—later to become United States Senator—was thinking about running for attorney general in 1952, but, Shivers believed, changed to the governor's race because Allred and J.R. Parten, a Houston oilman, promised to help with campaign expenses.

That Legislature finally repealed horse-race betting, but it failed to provide revenues for old-age assistance, and the session ended in acrimony.

The boy senator then turned to a very important matter—romance.

Photo Courtesy of the Shivers Museum Collection

The wedding at Sharyland, Oct. 5, 1937.

Chapter 4

The Boy Senator
Takes a Wife

Going back to the lawbooks after his first session as a lawmaker
in 1935, Shivers had returned to Port Arthur, scratching for clients
with fellow hard-pressed young lawyers like Gilbert Adams, Nola
White and others of those Depression days.

Tall, thin, handsomely brunet and now 27, he was quite naturally
the subject of speculations. But he avoided "entangling alliances"
with the girls around Port Arthur, keeping busy with law practice
and politicking. The $5-a-day expense allowance for legislators,
with no salary, didn't leave much money for anything else for one
who was trying to make a living after losing four months to a legislative session.

Then that fall he got a call from Virginia Abshire. She wanted
him to come to a yachting party in honor of a friend of hers,
Marialice Shary of Sharyland. The Abshires had invited their old
friends, the Shary family, to visit them. The two men went off duck
hunting in Louisiana, and Virginia thought that a party on her
father's yacht was just the thing to get Marialice acquainted with
some young men of the town, including Senator Shivers.

Marialice had been graduated from Our Lady of the Lake College
in San Antonio in 1932. Although her foster parents guarded her
jealously, she had met many young men, but not the one she
wanted for a husband. But that fall night in 1935, with a harvest
moon over the Gulf of Mexico and the yacht as an added fillip to the
romantic background, the tall, brown-eyed brunette from Sharyland met the tall, brown-eyed brunet from Port Arthur, and "it continued from there."

Marialice had grown up in the 24-room house that John Shary
built before World War I. He had been one of the original land
developers of the Lower Rio Grande Valley, and had built a
clubhouse beside the lake to entertain prospective land-buyers he

brought down from the Midwest in special trains. The mansion, with 15 acres of landscaped grounds, giant palm trees and a huge artificial lake in front of it, was and is perhaps one of the finest homes in Texas. Once Shary invited the entire Texas Legislature to Sharyland, and there was room for all of them to be seated in the 60- by 70-foot living room.

Shary was born in Nebraska of Austrian immigrant parents, worked his way through Doane College, got a pharmacist's license and operated two drug stores. Most young men would have been satisfied with one, but he was a man who thought big. He became a salesman for a California firm and was assigned to Texas, where he saw the possibility of converting the rich but dry and brushy South Texas area into irrigated farming for year-around production. He and some associates bought a 30,000-acre ranch and sold it in tracts for a $100,000 profit, and he was off to a fortune. He developed irrigated land in the Corpus Christi area, then moved to the Valley. Over 40 years, he sold $55,000,000 worth of real estate. He was the first developer of commercial citrus groves. He organized irrigation, shipping and marketing companies to handle the flood of production that irrigation had brought to the Valley.

He entertained William Jennings Bryan and many other notables at Sharyland, and after his death in 1945, Governor and Mrs. Shivers had President Eisenhower as a guest in 1953 when he came down to dedicate Falcon Dam, the structure which protected the Valley from both floods and drought.

Mr. and Mrs. Shary had no children, but they adopted Marialice, daughter of Mrs. Shary's sister, and brought her up in this palatial home. So, when an obviously talented but also obviously poor Southeast Texas lawyer started courting Marialice, Shary was somewhat suspicious.

But after the yachting party in 1935, Allan and Marialice began to find ways of seeing each other. She would visit a college friend in Houston or Austin and somehow the senator would hear of it, and the courtship would continue.

"If Mr. Shary was so strict," Mrs. Shivers was asked years later, "how did he let you go to Port Arthur that time in 1935?"

"He was there," she laughed, "but Mr. Abshire took him hunting in Louisiana. He didn't know anything about the party."

However, Mrs. Shary began to get the message. In 1936, Shary and Shivers were both delegates to the national Democratic convention in Philadelphia. Marialice was visiting her grandmother in Nebraska, where she had another beau, and she used the opportunity to see him while her parents were at the convention. One day the phone rang. It was Mrs. Shary.

"Marialice, we ran into Allan at Philadelphia and your Daddy asked him to stop by the Ozarks place and go fishing. He has a young man with him, Alf Roark, and I wish you'd come down and help me entertain them."

This was a summer place, Sharyview, owned by the Sharys, on Lake Taneycomo near Brantley, Missouri. It was one of Mr. Shary's favorite retreats, with good fishing in the White River and the good climate which prevails in the summer in the Ozarks.

So Marialice went to Missouri, and when the party from Philadelphia arrived on the Fourth of July, it turned out that it was Roark who went fishing with Shary. One day Roark almost "blew the works." They were ready to go fishing and Shary asked, "Where's Allan?"

"Oh, I think he has some courting to do, Mr. Shary," said Roark.

Marialice overheard the conversation, and always thereafter would giggle as she remembered her fear that Alf Roark had given away their secret.

But while Shary and Roark fished, Marialice and Allan talked, and romance deepened. Through the rest of 1936 and on into 1937 and the regular session of the Legislature, the two found opportunities to visit. Marialice came to Austin for the Senate Ladies Club dinner the night before the session opened, and Allan had a ring for her.

All the while, Mrs. Shary was helping in the "campaign," bringing her husband around to the idea that his daughter was getting serious about the young senator. The message was coming through to him so loud and clear that, every time Allan would go to Sharyland at Mrs. Shary's invitation, Shary would find an excuse to leave. One time he scheduled a hurry-up fishing trip to Port Isabel, and the young couple called to say they would just come down there to see him.

"But he said, 'Oh, I'll be coming home before long,' and put us off like that, because he knew what was coming," Marialice recalled.

Those were, of course, the days when a suitor asked the father for the daughter's hand in marriage. Mr. Shary was taking evasive action to put off the inevitable. But two strong wills had met, and, when Allan finally caught him, Mrs. Shary and Marialice quietly disappeared, going up the stately stairway to await the decision.

"We didn't hear anything for the longest time, and I said, 'Mumsy, we'd better go down and see if they are both still alive.' But they heard us coming."

Shary said to Shivers, "Let's have some fun with the Kid" (the pet name he always used for Marialice). "You go tell her I said nothing doing—not until I'm stretched out under those ebony trees over there."

(The ebony trees were a clump across the road from the house. When they were clearing the land, Shary had ordered those trees left alone, because he wanted to be buried there. He was, and Mrs. Shary built a chapel nearby. She also is buried there.)

Allan called Marialice aside and gave her that message, which she believed for a moment, until she noticed that his eyes were laughing. Then she looked at her dad and saw a matching twinkle in his eyes.

As far as Marialice was concerned, the long campaign she, her mother and Allan had waged was over—a campaign more important to her than any they were to win later in the political arena.

They decided to have the wedding at Sharyland, and chose his birthday, October 5th, for the date. "That makes it certain he'll remember our anniversary," she told her friends.

Virtually the entire Legislature went to Sharyland for the wedding, filling a train for the occasion. Politics shortened the honeymoon, as Governor Allred called a special session of the Legislature for that fall; so, after a brief stay in Monterrey, Mexico, Allan and Marialice dashed back to Austin to get on with the lawmaking at the thirty-day special session.

An interesting footnote on the wedding is the fact that in 1962, on their twenty-fifth anniversary, the Shiverses invited the twelve men and women who had been in their wedding party to a silver anniversary celebration. It began in Austin, then moved to Sharyland and then to Monterrey. All twelve were still alive, all attended, and all were still married to their original partners. This may be a course record in these times of frequent divorce.

The Shiverses' first home was an apartment at Enfield and West Lynn in Austin, just a few blocks from their later permanent home. After the special session adjourned, they went back to Port Arthur, where Mrs. R.A. Shivers had rented a house on Fifth Street for the bride and groom. Allan's mother had written that it "faced the lake." They moved in at night, and when Marialice woke up the next morning and looked out, all she could see was a row of houses across the street. She had been expecting a lake like the one in front of Sharyland.

"Where's the lake?" she asked her new husband.

"Oh, that's an expression we have in Port Arthur for houses that face to the south," he explained gently.

Soon they bought a home at 4600 Twin City Highway, where they were to live until Shivers went off to World War II in 1943. It was there, soon after their first son was born June 1, 1940, that Governor W. Lee O'Daniel came one day, on a tour of the state, visiting legislators in their homes to convince them of the need for his tax plan which had failed in 1939.

"Where's the baby?" the Governor asked.

"In his crib," he was told.

O'Daniel rushed to the back bedroom, gathered up tiny John Shary Shivers, and brought him back to the living room, where the Governor's photographer snapped his picture with the Shivers baby.

It was also in this home that the Shiverses grieved when their second child, a daughter, died after just one day of life in January, 1942.

And, of course, as their first real home where they started their family, it was the one they remembered fondly even though they were to have three much grander homes than the one on Twin City Highway where they lived as newlyweds.

Elect For a Second Term

ALLAN SHIVERS
State Senator
Hardin, Orange, Liberty and Jefferson Counties

FRANK R. CHANCE CO.   PORT ARTHUR, TEXAS

Courtesy of the Shivers Museum Collection

1938 Campaign placard

Chapter 5

Sally Rand and
W. Lee O'Daniel

Sally Rand and W. Lee O'Daniel caused some problems for Senator Shivers in 1938, when he ran for his second four-year term.

Representative Harry McKee of Port Arthur decided to run against Shivers. Both were strong for higher old-age pensions, because the growth of the pension rolls and the lack of money had cut the average pension down to $13.76 a month. O'Daniel was running for governor on that issue, among others. Both Shivers and McKee had support from organized labor, and Shivers had been chairman of the Senate labor committee, so there was no great issue between him and McKee, until Sally Rand became one.

Texas had had its big Centennial celebration in 1936, and one of the main attractions was Sally Rand, the fan dancer, at Casa Manana at Fort Worth. At one of the campaign rallies in Jefferson County, McKee charged that Shivers (who had been single in 1936, but now in 1938 was a married man) had given a party in Dallas entertaining Sally Rand.

"If you ever saw a confused candidate, I was the one," Shivers reminisced. "I was standing out in the crowd listening to his speech when he told this story. I wondered, 'Well, what kind of an answer do you give that?' It wasn't true. And I said to myself, 'Well, if I get up there and deny it, everybody will say 'He's not telling the truth. He did it and now he's denying it. He's not telling the truth.'

"And if I admitted it when it wasn't true and somebody found out about that, everybody would be mad at me, and all of the moralists and so forth would say, 'Well, what's this young fellow doing up there entertaining that fan dancer?' So I finally decided that the one way I could rebut him was neither to admit nor deny, but just say that he was jealous because he wasn't invited. And that went on . . . we debated Sally Rand for about half of that campaign for re-election."

Shivers learned about the power of Pappy O'Daniel when he crawled through a fence to campaign with a man plowing a field. He gave the farmer his card, and told how he was for old-age pensions and such. The man said, "Well, young man, I believe I'll vote for you. You sound about like what Pappy says."

That word began to get around more and more, and Shivers asked his father about O'Daniel, thinking, as did most Austin-centered people, that the race was between Attorney General William McCraw and Railroad Commissioner Ernest O. Thompson.

"If you don't know it, O'Daniel is going to be the next governor of Texas," Judge Shivers told Senator Shivers.

He was right. The senator went back to Austin in January, 1939, with a new four-year term and entered the oddest sort of legislative situation Texas had ever seen. O'Daniel had the people on his side in huge numbers, but he was getting his advice on state government and politics from the most conservative of the business lobbyists, mainly oil, gas and sulphur people who had been tapped a bit lightly for welfare money during the 1937 session of the Legislature in the first "omnibus tax bill" which Shivers helped put together.

So O'Daniel proposed a "transaction tax," which was a multi-decked sales tax, and wanted it put into the Constitution with a provision freezing the severance taxes on oil, gas and sulphur at rates just above then current levels.

Shivers was opposed to the sales tax, and, fortunately for him perhaps, he did not have to run again in 1940 when O'Daniel took to the radio to stump for a second term for himself and no new term for the senators and representatives who had blocked his constitutional amendment. O'Daniel purged so many of them that it looked as if he would have the majority in 1941. But 56 House members, called by the press the "Immortal 56," prevented passage of the constitutional amendment, and forced adoption of another "omnibus tax bill" to finance state government.

Lieutenant Governor Coke Stevenson had named Shivers as chairman of the Senate Committee on Governor's Nominations in 1939. Tradition had it that a governor "cleared" appointments with the home senator of the appointee, because the Senate simply would not approve an appointee who was objectionable to his own senator. But O'Daniel was not following this custom.

As a result, O'Daniel's appointees were being turned down by the Senate in droves. Shivers got Senator Jesse Martin of Fort Worth, O'Daniel's Senate leader, to set up an appointment with O'Daniel for him, wanting to be helpful. Shivers explained to

O'Daniel the long-standing custom, and offered to help Martin check to see what the home senators thought about his appointees in advance.

"He sat there in his chair and looked right straight at me for what seemed an interminable length of time," Shivers said. "I didn't think he was going to say anything. Finally, he just kept looking right straight at me and said, 'Senator, I read in the Constitution where the Governor nominates and the Senate confirms, and I'm going to nominate and the Senate can do what it pleases about it.' And that's what he did the balance of his term." And the Senate kept turning them down, jealous of the prerogatives which the newcomer-to-politics governor wouldn't recognize.

But Shivers analyzed O'Daniel's voter appeal, and filed away some ideas he would use later as he moved up the political ladder.

"His appeal was not to their personal desires and their personal emotions, but to the love of their own family and their religion," Shivers says of O'Daniel's political success at mowing down fourteen other candidates, some of them well-known, in his first race for governor.

"It's the emotion of the day; it's the psychological approach to almost everyone's desire for love of mother, home and country. O'Daniel was a master strategist in that. When it was shown that he hadn't paid his poll tax and wasn't qualified to vote, he immediately came up with the answer that he didn't believe in the poll tax and that was the reason he didn't pay it.

"He was, in his public announcements, always for the under-privileged, the underdog, the old-age pensioner, for example. A lot of politicians have made great capital of that in the past, but history will record that O'Daniel's supporters—the people who persuaded him to enter the governor's race in the first place—were among the most wealthy people in Texas, some of the people connected with the largest corporations in the state. Some of the things he did after he became governor were more in their interests than anyone else's."

But a decision by O'Daniel really amounted to "downfield blocking" for Shivers' next political move, which was to be delayed until the end of World War II.

O'Daniel won a special election for the U.S. Senate in 1941, moving Lieutenant Governor Coke Stevenson up to the governorship, which he was to hold until 1947. John Lee Smith was elected lieutenant governor in 1942 and 1944, and a dispute between the O'Daniel-Stevenson regents of The University of Texas and Dr.

Homer P. Rainey, president of the University, led to a real cat-and-dog fight in the 1946 gubernatorial race. Smith decided to get into that one against Dr. Rainey, Railroad Commissioner Beauford Jester, Attorney General Grover Sellers and others, leaving a wide-open situation for lieutenant governor.

Shivers had been re-elected with comparative ease in 1942 over former Senator W.R. Cousins, Sr., trying for a comeback. But Shivers spent only a short time at the 1943 legislative session. A few weeks after it convened, he got word of approval of an application he had made for an Army commission.

Chapter 6

Instant War

Like the apocryphal Texan who charged Hell with a pail of water, Captain Robert A. Shivers went ashore on the beachhead at Salerno armed only with a .45 automatic.

It wasn't entirely according to plan—certainly not his—but there he was, a military government occupation officer on ground the 36th Division wasn't at all sure it could hold. And there wasn't much of it.

Shivers was part of a cadre of what must have been the least-trained men the United States sent overseas during World War II. It was a group of military government officers who were poorly armed, even worse acquainted with how to handle their weapons, and who got to the beachhead partly by mistake and far, far ahead of any need for occupation forces. The Texas 36th Division had a small bit of sandy beach and considerable doubt about their ability to keep it.

But Shivers had one advantage over some of his 27 American companion officers. He knew how to shoot and re-load his pistol—a carry-over from elementary training in East Texas hunting. Many of the others did not. They had been in service—and in uniform—slightly less than eight weeks, and most of that time had been spent at the University of Virginia on the "book" side of the military.

Yet once ashore, the basic protective tactic came by instinct, and all knew how to drop to the sand and dig in when the German shells came their way. It didn't take much training to make them stay behind the slowly advancing 36th and under the protective umbrella of shells being fired by the British Navy to cover them. By the time they finally got to Salerno, they knew enough to run for the still-standing city hall when the Germans lobbed mortar shells over the hills and into the city.

Shivers always remained hazy about the reasoning behind his hurry-up and roundabout trip to Europe. He had been commissioned in the military government force and sent to Charlottesville, Virginia, for a three-month training course. His wife and three-year-old son accompanied him for the period.

At the end of six weeks, 28 of the trainees were given secret orders to be prepared to leave immediately—without even telling their families. They were flown to New York, then to Florida, then to Brazil, across Africa and finally sent by boat to Italy—to a different part than they had expected. It was a quite different pace, too, from that by which most of them had gotten into the Army.

Shivers, not knowing how short a war it might be, had wanted to get re-elected in 1942, and did so with comparative ease. With a four-year guarantee on his office, he started out to see how he could fit into the military. And, finding that the Army wanted military government officers to supervise captured territory, he applied for a commission. But it was no swift affair. He had begun the legislative session in 1943 before he got word to go to Virginia, and left when it was a few weeks old. The trail was to lead to Africa, Italy, France and Germany before his return.

It was a strange lot of men he encountered when he got to Virginia for the training course. They knew no more about the Army than he; not even enough to discount rumors when they came. There were times when Shivers let his mind wander to thoughts of how different his situation might have been if he had accepted that appointment to West Point a decade earlier.

But the group studied their lessons, figuring they'd have it all down at the end of their three months. Then came the word for 28, and those who were married told their wives good-by and left for Europe. For Mrs. Shivers that meant a return to the Rio Grande Valley and volunteer work with wives of the men teaching and taking pilot training at Mission.

Shivers' rookie officer companions, who knew more about military government and law than about taking a salute, made their circuitous trip to Africa without incident. There, they met reality. They were greeted by some English officers who had been trained to serve with them—and apparently knew more about their work.

And all got to sleep on the floor of a nearly destroyed building in which rats disturbed some by running across their bodies all night. They also encountered their first rumor, without which no Army can operate. It said, on the usual good authority, that the Italians were about to surrender to the Allies, and that military government officers and men were to move into Rome and run things.

The first part proved to be correct, and soon, bolstered by

enlisted men they had picked up from both armies, the American and British officers took off from Bizerte in landing ships for the trip across the Mediterranean and eventually to Rome.

But the Germans had also heard of the rumor, and started defensive action which the military government detail decided was too offensive to oppose. So, because of the Navy protection available, the unit was diverted to Salerno. There was lots more help there. And lots more opposition.

Ultimately the American infantry moved inland and the military government began its steady push toward Rome, and then Shivers went on to Naples. It was there that he made his historic acquaintance with General Dwight D. Eisenhower that led to the strong personal and political friendship which changed Texas' political history and gave Shivers a place in that history.

Shivers returned in the middle of the 1945 legislative session to find himself dean of the Senate in seniority, and that a search was on for someone the senators could support as their presiding officer. He was an Army major, in the middle of his third four-year term, and there was lots of talk that the "senator from Jefferson" might be the man for lieutenant governor.

Not sure what had happened in his absence, Shivers did nothing to encourage the movement. But it had an appeal, and he did nothing to discourage it, either.

Chapter 7

How to Use Power

On a warm spring day in April, 1945, Senator H.L. (Heinie) Winfield of Fort Stockton, chairman of the Committee on Nominations, called for an executive session at 4:45 p.m. Sergeant-at-Arms A.W. Holt and his assistants scurried across the green carpet of the Senate chamber, hustling the pages and other Senate employees out. In the gallery, other assistants told tourists that they must leave. The lobbyists were already moving out.

A couple of senators walked briskly across the floor to make last-minute checks on votes needed to confirm. Henry Reese III, Gonzales publisher, was up for a vote as a director of Texas A&M, and the votes were all lined up. Other nominations to be confirmed were routine—branch pilots and public weighers.

Mrs. Martha Turner, the calendar clerk, locked away her books in the green filing cabinet behind her desk, and hurried out. So did Journal Clerk Noel Brown.

Doorkeeper A.W. Childers shooed the last 12-year-old page out the tall front door of the Senate, then went outside himself to make sure that the outer foyer and the reception room were clear. Then he stood outside the outer door, to make certain that no one could hear what the senators were saying in the huge, two-story chamber. Only the pigeons, strutting on the granite ledge outside the open windows, could hear as Winfield got quick approval of the short list of nominations by Governor Coke Stevenson. Then Lieutenant Governor John Lee Smith called on Senator R.A. Weinert from Seguin for "other business."

"It's time for the Senate to decide whom we want for lieutenant governor," Weinert declared. "Governor Smith isn't going to run again, and the Senate ought to pick the lieutenant governor. I think that our dean, the senator from Jefferson, is the man who ought to run, and we ought to get behind him."

Shivers had that same idea, but he knew it's good politics to be just a little bit reluctant.

Senator James E. Taylor of Kerens told it this way:

"Shivers would say that he didn't want to run. Weinert would say he had to run, that he was an ideal candidate. Then someone else insisted that Shivers run, and finally, all the other senators agreed to support Shivers. And then he agreed to run."

The executive session ended. Capitol newsmen scurried in to get the list of the nominees who had been confirmed that day, wondering why so little took so long, not knowing that an even more important decision had been made that day.

Boyce House, the newspaperman, raconteur, humorist and historian, and State Representative Joe Ed Winfree, a veteran Houston lawyer, turned out to be Shivers' main Democratic primary opponents.

"Shivers hit the ground running, with a built-in campaign organization of senators," a man who worked on the opposing side recalled. "You could not budge those senators, and it was really noticeable the way he got votes everywhere.

"And he used that radio. I remember his early-morning talks on the Texas State Network, aimed at farmers. He sounded good on radio with that voice of his—I guess he and Franklin D. Roosevelt were the best ever at using radio. They both really came through on it.

"Shivers drove around the state a lot by himself. We would see him as we drove along, and he'd wave and smile at us in our campaign car," said the opposition worker.

Winfree was an old-time legislator. He had served fourteen years in the House of Representatives, and was later to serve two more terms. He had been one of the anti-sales-taxers whom O'Daniel could not purge, but he had most of his strength in the Houston area.

"We spent more dollars than we got votes in places like Waco," his son Harris Winfree, years later the Gulf Oil lobbyist in Austin, said.

House had more of a statewide following. His books were widely read, and his "Eastland Court House Horned Frog" story had made him a household word. Many newspaper editors endorsed him as an old friend, so he got lots of free publicity.

Shivers pushed his theme of experience in the Senate and his knowledge of state government against House's general popularity.

In contrast with that year's race for governor, which was bitter, the Shivers-House-Winfree race was gentlemanly. There was no acrimony, no personal vendetta, just old-fashioned campaigning, handshaking, seeing the folks as much as possible. Since none of the three had made a statewide race, there was no built-in advantage from that standpoint.

The 29 other senators made up an important part of the campaign organization (one did not support Shivers). Each of them sent out letters or postcards to all the voters in his district, urging them to support Shivers. "If you want me to be an effective senator, then help me elect my friend as lieutenant governor," one of the postcards said.

At times, Garland A. (Chink) Smith traveled with Shivers, and the home senators usually traveled with them in their respective districts.

"It was a hot July day, and we stopped at Oakwood to campaign," former Senator Jim Taylor recalled. "That day Shivers made up his mind to run for governor some day. We had stopped, and were out shaking hands and handing out cards. Shivers had his coat over his arm, and it was really hot. We talked to everybody in Oakwood, and as we got back in the car, Shivers said: 'I've just made up my mind. I'm going to run for governor. I like this business.' "

Taylor had been elected to the Senate at a special election in November, 1944, while he was with the 36th Division in Southern France. He didn't even know that he was a candidate until he got word that he had been elected. He and Shivers started home together for the legislative session of 1945. Taylor managed to wangle an air flight, but Shivers got stranded in London and came home by slow boat. So Taylor arrived for the session early, while Shivers was late. The two were firm friends, and Taylor's active campaign for Shivers was to bring Taylor the important Senate Finance Committee chairmanship. They campaigned together across Taylor's district, and it brought in the results.

It was then that Shivers began to campaign for a reform which has not yet been sold to the voters of Texas—annual sessions of the Legislature. He advocated 60-day sessions for budgetary purposes and emergency matters in the even-number years. (He later came around to the view that every-year sessions are not needed.) Shivers, fresh from Senate discussions of a unicameral Legislature, proposed a compromise there—to reduce the size of the House of Representatives from 150 to 93, three for each Senate district.

On another subject, Shivers said, "I am the kind of Texan who believes colored people do not want to attend school with the

Photo courtesy of the Shivers Museum Collection
Shivers enjoyed his first statewide campaigns (1946 and 1948) so much that he kept the pace at the American Legion convention in Miami in 1948. Here he is shown getting flowers from girl welcomers before riding in the mammoth parade.

whites." He subsequently did not recall this as the issue of integration which was to come along later, but as a part of a discussion of
the need for improving Negro schools. Carrying out the "separate
but equal" doctrine was neglected "by those of us in a position of
responsibility," Shivers said, 28 years later, adding: "It was
neglected—there's no question about that—and today I think it's
reaped the whirlwind."

A battle between Dr. Homer P. Rainey, president of The University of Texas, and the board of regents had become the big issue in
the governor's race. Dr. Rainey was running for governor, and
Railroad Commissioner Beauford Jester, a former regent, was the
leading defender of the regents' right to fire faculty members
whose views differed from those of the regents. Jester and Rainey
were in the run-off, and they got most of the attention from the
voters that year. Shivers stayed out of that discussion.

"The issues were so definitely drawn that there wasn't any room
for a mere member of the Senate to be mixed up in it," he said.

He and House were generally kind to each other in the run-off.
Again Shivers used his wit in handling the question of qualification. He complimented House as an author, after-dinner speaker
and joke-teller but insisted that his own experience as a senator for
eleven years was a more important qualification for a lieutenant
governor.

Shivers still had much support from organized labor, but one incident in his home town on first primary election night got him a lot
of publicity. He went to the Democratic precinct convention, and
was elected a delegate to the county convention, along with others.
A second convention was held, and its leader, a CIO official, announced that Shivers would not be allowed to attend the county
convention. Shivers retorted that he would like to see anybody try
to keep him out. It made headlines for a few days; Shivers got into
the convention and also got publicity, the lifeblood of a political
candidate.

He led the first primary, and then won the run-off in August with
575,674 votes to 446,463. Of course, he also won in November, to
become lieutenant governor, and more importantly, president of
the Senate.

At his inauguration January 19, 1947, Shivers laid out what was to
become the thesis of his career in state government. Many who
were there that winter day thought he sounded stronger and more
positive than his Democratic running mate and chieftain, Beauford
Jester.

Shivers had been in a process of change which he considered quite normal for people in political life. Then, too, times were changing, and so was his constituency. No longer was he representing the strongest organized labor area in Texas, but the whole state which had been talking a lot during the war about the need for strikes, the minimum wage, and the 40-hour week. O'Daniel had campaigned extensively against organized labor, and had succeeded in passing some anti-union legislation in 1941.

In addition, John H. Shary, Shivers' father-in-law, had died, November 6, 1945, and this had shifted to his shoulders the active management of the vast Shary estate, including the very real fact of heavy inheritance taxes to be paid on the estate. He and Mrs. Shivers had moved solidly into lives of wealth, and this brought more awareness of the federal government's "breathing down your neck."

So Shivers, who had sponsored such laws as unemployment and welfare, was to become more a supporter of states' rights than he had been as a young lawyer in Port Arthur, happy when a federal court awarded his injured client a big enough judgment that his fee of $700 allowed him to run for the Texas Senate.

But Shivers did not become an anti-everything-federal man. Instead, he became one who felt deeply that the federal government had become so big and so costly because the state and local governments had failed to do the jobs they were supposed to do. The United States Congress had simply been more responsive to the needs of the people than had the legislatures and city councils and commissioners courts.

So, his first inaugural as lieutenant governor had the theme of "state responsibilities" to do the jobs which needed to be done at its level, without running to Washington for handouts and without usurping the powers and duties of local governments.

He also called for reforms in state government to make it more responsive and responsible, including four-year terms for executive officers and constitutional revision to make more offices appointive so the governor could have some responsibility for the operation of state government. But it was 25 years later, in 1972, before the voters agreed on four-year terms and made a start toward constitutional revision through a constitutional convention.

Years later, he still believed this way, although many reforms he sought were denied to him and to the legislatures which tried to carry them out. He attributed much of this to the public's failure to understand the existing system. He pointed to the fact that Bascom

Giles, elected to nine terms as land commissioner, eventually went to the penitentiary for malfeasance in office. Shivers was governor at that time, and he had a thousand letters asking him in different ways why he had ever "appointed a sorry man like that in the first place."

"For anything that happens here, the governor gets credit or blame, so why not give him the authority and let him accept the responsibility?" Shivers asked.

It was a clear, cool day on Jan. 21, 1947, and Bill McGill, who was handling the inaugural details, had a real problem. Beauford Jester had invited all the governors of Mexican states to the ceremony, as well as the President of Mexico. The morning of inaugural day, the chieftain of the 80-piece band of the Mexican Navy called McGill from the edge of Austin.

"Where do my men stay?" he asked McGill, who then had to scurry around for dormitory space for the band, which had not earlier advised him of its intention to come to the ceremony and march in the parade.

General Jonathan Wainwright was among the distinguished guests there to hear the new Lieutenant Governor Shivers say:

"Even as muscle tissues strengthen with exercise and weaken and wither from disuse, the powers of state government live on action and decay and die from dormant sleep. Inertia invites infringement. Action is the path to preservation. The energetic exercise of its powers by a revitalized state government is destiny's call to us today. Action is the watchword. The place is here. The time is now."

The new lieutenant governor, given the oath of office by Commissioner Lloyd Davidson of the Court of Criminal Appeals, then laid out some subjects he considered to be the challenge of the day—higher pay for school teachers; veterans' housing, protection and instruction; a university for Negroes; protection against lawlessness; investigation of the pardons and paroles system; legislation to protect the public against strikes in important public and private industries; and an adequate public health program.

With twelve years in the Senate as a voting member ended, the big, confident lieutenant governor took up the gavel and began to apply what he had learned.

He had made out his list of committees ahead of time, and outgoing Lieutenant Governor John Lee Smith appointed them for him, so they could get to work before inauguration. He chose his committees carefully to carry out his program. The Finance Committee, headed by Senator Taylor, was agreed with Shivers on improving education. The State Affairs Committee, headed by Senator George (Cotton) Moffett of Chillicothe, was ready to approve the bill to create the Texas State University for Negroes. The Labor Committee, headed by Senator Roger Knight of Madisonville, was ready to give quick approval to the list of nine anti-union bills, most of them by Senator Ben Ramsey of San Augustine and Representative Marshall O. Bell of San Antonio.

The regular session of the 50th Legislature was a busy and productive one. The state's budget was increased to $403,000,000 a year, since a wartime surplus made it possible to spend that much without new taxes. School teachers were put on a pay schedule starting at $2,000 a year for those with a bachelor's degree. Aid to rural schools for equalization purposes was raised to $18,000,000. More importantly, this session created the Gilmer-Aikin Committee to study the needs of public schools. Its report, enacted by the Legislature in 1949, was to give the State a greater role in financing public schools. And, through its successor studies, it was to precipitate major fiscal crises in state government for decades.

J.B. Golden and others active in the Texas State Teachers Association gave Shivers credit for the idea of creating the study group which became the Gilmer-Aikin Committee. As the presiding officer of the Senate, Shivers helped push through the study plan which was to lead to the greatest reform of public education in Texas history.

As lieutenant governor, Shivers began to use the power inherent in the Chair of the Senate, but barely used by his predecessors. The "president of the Senate" not only appoints the committees but also decides which committee shall consider each bill. Thus, a bill he likes will go to a friendly committee; one he dislikes will go to a committee of its enemies, never to be heard of again.

But the Senate's antiquated calendar rule provides that bills go onto the calendar in the order in which they are received from committees. Because a few controversial ones, with authors who want no action, get to the top of the calendar and stay there all session, the calendar system is meaningless. This means that if a bill is to be brought up, it must be by a motion to suspend the regular order of business, which requires a two-third majority of the senators present and voting. It also means that the sponsor of the bill must be recognized by the Chair to make his motion during the brief session time each day. And, to get that recognition, the senator must quite often agree to vote for this bill or that which the Chair wants passed.

So, in actual practice, the real "Senate Calendar" is the list the Chair prepares each day—the senators who are to be recognized to make their motions. Shivers kept the list on a note pad on his desk.

The system also gives eleven senators veto power over any bill, a strong method of minority control, because it takes 21 of the 31 to make up that vital two-thirds majority.

Shivers polished this tool with careful use. It came in handy the next-to-last day of the session, when he needed the 21 votes to pass a bill to create Lamar State College of Technology at Beaumont, a project which was Number One in the hearts of his homefolks in Jefferson County.

W.R. Cousins, Jr., the youngster who had attacked candidate Shivers at the rally in Vidor in 1934 when Shivers was running against his father, had been elected to replace Shivers in the Senate. They were never very friendly, especially since many people in the district still looked to Shivers to get things done for them. But the Jefferson County House delegation had succeeded in getting House approval of the Lamar College bill, and it was up to Cousins and Shivers to get it through the more conservative Senate.

Taylor and the Finance Committee sat on the bill until June 4, two days before the session was to adjourn. There were guesses that Shivers had to trade a lot of "recognitions" to get the bill out, or perhaps Taylor felt he had delayed it fatally. Cousins' motion to suspend the rules failed, 17-11, and again 19-10. But Shivers had a word with Senator Charles Jones of Bonham, and Senators Bob Proffer of Denton and Alton York of Brenham came back to the Senate chamber. There was a quick agreement to cut the appropriation by a third to pick up another vote, and presto, the rules were suspended, 23-8, and the bill passed second reading.

But it takes a four-fifths majority to suspend the rules to pass a bill finally on the same day it passes second reading, and the balky Senate just would not go along. The vote was 19-10. By June 5, Shivers had done some more "recognizing" of desperate senators who had their pet bills to pass. So his own favorite bill was taken up by a vote of 23-5, and was finally passed.

However, it ran afoul of the "pay-as-you-go" amendment to the Constitution and Comptroller George Sheppard had to "veto" it by declaring that there was not enough money in sight to finance it and the new medical school at San Antonio. This meant that in 1949 Shivers had to go through the whole process again, and in even tougher fashion, leaving many hard feelings in the Senate against the iron-gaveled Chair. The school was to become Lamar University, a respected part of the higher education system in Texas. Its creation was the prime demonstration of how the new lieutenant governor had learned to use power, when persuasiveness wouldn't do the job.

The Senate took something of a hand in the University of Texas fight by refusing confirmation in 1947 to two regents Governor Coke Stevenson had named—Orville S. Bullington, a long-time Republican leader of Wichita Falls, and Dr. Walter H. Sherer of Houston, two of the anti-Rainey regents. The only other appointees rejected were also Stevenson's: D.S. Buchanan of Buda and H.J. Brees of San Antonio to the Texas A&M Board. All of Beauford Jester's nominees were confirmed, demonstrating that the Senate was back in its proper place after the O'Daniel years.

That session was the beginning of the long fight to tax natural gas pipelines. The House passed the gas-gathering tax, but the Senate killed it, only to have it pop up again and again during the next several sessions. The Board of Pardons and Paroles was investigated by a Senate committee, which found that "clemency-seekers" had undue influence, and recommended that the clemency power be given back to the governor, and that district courts be given the power to grant probation. The latter became law, but the switch back to executive clemency failed to pass.

Shivers had, after all, been dean of the Senate, and knew most of the members well enough that he could use them to their best abilities. Senator Wardlow Lane of Center, with his rough-and-ready wit, was used to needle sponsors of bills Shivers didn't want passed. One of Lane's masterpieces came when Senator Dorsey Hardeman of San Angelo voted for the gas-gathering tax. Gas was a major commodity in Lane's district, just as sheep were in Hardeman's. So Lane sent up an amendment to levy a "tax on wool-gathering," and debated it seriously for a long time before it was tabled.

Senator R.A. Weinert of Seguin handled many bills for Shivers. Although he was more conservative than Shivers, he felt some responsibility for the young lieutenant governor, so he often did what he was asked to.

"I don't have to explain my bills," Weinert said one day when he was questioned about a proposal, "because I don't handle any bad bills."

Senator Weaver Moore of Houston was a good bill analyst. He read all the bills and reported on them to Shivers, giving him reason for passing or killing them. Later, when Shivers became governor, Moore taught young John Osorio how to analyze bills, and helped him check them for Shivers when they arrived for veto or signature.

As Finance Chairman, holding hearings on appropriations bills, Taylor reported every afternoon to Shivers on what the committee had done. That way, when the phone calls came in objecting to what the committee had said or done, Shivers would have the facts to handle the irate agency head, board member or regent.

Shivers also knew about senators' pet projects. Weinert had been trying for years to get money for a historical marker at the Alamo, and Shivers got Taylor to put it in the appropriations bill.

"Shivers picked out a Finance Committee of 21 members who agreed to stick together," Taylor reminisced. "In his two terms, there was never a floor amendment to the appropriations bills," he said. "Shivers would really raise hell with you if you promised him something and then didn't deliver. We learned in a hurry."

Taylor also recalled an incident when Shivers had referred a bill to State Affairs, headed by the late Senator George Moffett of Chillicothe. Shivers wanted the bill killed, but Moffett was going to set the bill for public hearing.

"Shivers got it re-referred to the Finance Committee, and told me to stick it in that roll-top desk in the Finance office and forget about it," Taylor laughed. "And I sure did."

"Shivers was the beginning of the making of the lieutenant governor as a powerhouse," Taylor went on. "When John Lee Smith was lieutenant governor the Senate ran the Senate. But Shivers began to take things over, and soon was running the Senate, with the Senate's consent."

When the session adjourned at midnight June 6, everything on Shivers' agenda for the session, as outlined in his inaugural address, had been passed. The spending he said was necessary for a state to live up to its responsibility had begun, with the total operating budget going up by more than $200 million from fiscal 1946 to fiscal 1949. The budget was now almost four times the size it was the year Shivers reached the Senate as a freshman.

John Lee Smith had been living most of the time in the lieutenant governor's apartment in the Capitol. The Shiverses had redecorated it, but their growing family (John, born in 1940, Bud, in 1946, and Cissie, in 1947) preferred life at the Shary estate in the Valley, or at the family farm near Woodville. Mrs. Shary lived much of the time at Mission, and Mrs. Shivers, the lieutenant governor's mother, was still in Port Arthur, where he maintained his voting address until he left politics.

At the close of the 1947 session, Shivers began his plans for a race for a second term in 1948, and, right up to the filing deadline, it appeared that he would have no opponent. At the last hour, Turner Walker of Houston filed. Walker made no campaign, neither did Shivers.

That was the year political interest was involved in the U.S. Senate race between Coke Stevenson and Lyndon B. Johnson. There was also in Texas the usual sort of "protest" vote against incumbents, but it centered on Governor Jester, who had said that a veterans' bonus would be "un-Texan." Jester had seven opponents, and between them they came close to matching his vote. He got 642,025 out of 1,205,257 cast. The protest vote against Shivers was the lowest of any of the state incumbents who had opponents. He beat Walker by more than three to one, and in November trounced Taylor Cole, the Republican candidate by a seven to one vote, and won a second term. He voted the Democratic ticket that year, from Harry Truman on down, and was sent to Truman's inauguration as the State's official representative.

Before Shivers went to Washington, he struck boldly with proposals for reform and strengthening of the Legislature, because of the growing complexity of lawmaking. He called for a full-time Legislature, with annual sessions, annual salaries and annual state budgets instead of biennial budgets. He called for a Legislative Budget Board to work on budgets between sessions of the Legislature, and for a Legislative Council to do research for the Legislature. And, to cut down on the drain of campaigning on the public officials, he called for four-year terms for elective and appointive state officials. Shivers also asked for more money for public welfare, teacher salaries, college and universities, prisons, state hospitals and special schools (still called eleemosynary institutions in those days), and for a farm-to-market road program and soil and water conservation programs.

Jester had all those things in his program for the 51st Legislature that January, 1949, plus many more, including an anti-lynching law, higher unemployment compensation benefits and a study of the poll tax problem. The State Democratic Party's platform had called for a constitutional amendment to repeal the poll tax as a requirement for voting. Jester supported such an amendment successfully in the Legislature. Jan. 12th, the date of Jester's speech, was the governor's birthday and a congratulatory resolution was adopted by the joint session, an unusual legislative procedure.

Thus was launched a historic session of the Legislature, one in which the "Third House," the lobby, lost control of the House of

Photo courtesy of Shivers Museum Collection

The leadership lineup for the 1949 legislative session—House Speaker Durwood Manford (left) with Lieutenant Governor Allan Shivers (center) and the late Governor Beauford Jester (right).

Representatives on many issues, particularly on that of holding spending to the amount of money available during the biennium.

The Shivers family moved into an enlarged apartment in the Capitol for the session. During the interim, the Board of Control had spent $15,000 adding two bedrooms, a bath, kitchen and dining room. There were also nine new senators, most of them World War II veterans, and across the rotunda were 58 new House members, a great many of them GI students at The University of Texas. There was about $100 million surplus left in the General Revenue Fund, but ideas on how to spend it were rampant. Taylor resigned as public relations director for the Texas Manufacturers Association, and Shivers re-appointed him chairman of the Finance Committee. Cousins was made chairman of the Labor Committee. The Texas Rural Roads Association prepared a proposal for a natural gas tax to finance a road program on a permanent basis. The Texas Water Conservation Association began pushing for a $200 million revenue bond program to finance water projects, but it was to be later in the seven-year drought of the 1950s before it finally would be passed by the Legislature and approved by the voters. Senator Rogers Kelley of Edinburg introduced a constitutional amendment to repeal the poll tax. A package of bills completely reorganizing the public school system was introduced on recommendation of the Gilmer-Aikin Committee.

When Senator Kilmer Corbin of Lubbock introduced a resolution praising Franklin D. Roosevelt, denouncing the Republicans and memorializing Congress to make FDR's birthday a national holiday, static broke out from some conservatives. In the Chair, Shivers proposed a compromise, which was adopted: "Just take out everything except the part praising Roosevelt and memorializing Congress," he suggested.

It was going to be a tough session, and Shivers didn't want it to start by fighting too early over side issues. It was to be the longest session in Texas history, lasting until midnight July 6, when it went out under a filibuster by Senator Hill Hudson of Pecos, who blocked passage of a constitutional amendment to remove the $35 million annual ceiling on public welfare spending. It is likely to retain that record, since the Constitution now limits sessions to 140 days. In those days, members got $10 a day for the first 120 days of a session, and $5 thereafter, but there was no automatic date for adjournment.

Jester was planning to retire after the then-traditional second term. Shivers was running for governor in 1950. Caso March, who had run against Jester in 1948, had announced in November of that year that he would run again in 1950, and he began campaign travel immediately. Attorney General Price Daniel, Land Commissioner Bascom Giles and Railroad Commissioner Olin Culberson were also potential candidates for 1950.

So Shivers, the only one of the five on the firing line, was being watched closely during that session. The tidelands issue, badly misnamed because it only dealt with the open Gulf of Mexico, and not the land affected by tides, had begun to appear. Tom Clark, a Texan and President Truman's attorney general, had filed a suit in the U.S. Supreme Court against Texas and Louisiana, claiming the Gulf of Mexico beyond three miles out for the federal government, and that had become Price Daniel's "White Horse." The Legislature quickly provided $100,000 for Daniel's use in fighting the federal case. Giles was busy lobbying in Washington for a compromise bill.

So with all the issues liberally salted with gubernatorial politics, the 51st Legislature had a wide-open session that year.

The Gilmer-Aikin bills, to abolish the elective state superintendent of schools, L.A. Wood, and to substitute a "commissioner" to be chosen by an elective State Board of Education, divided school people and brought as many as 3,000 to Austin for committee hearings, one of which lasted all night. The rural roads financing issue also drew 3,000 farmers and small-town businessmen to a House Revenue and Taxation Committee hearing, and this show of power brought the bill out of committee by a single vote. But the natural gas lobby had enough strength, under the leadership of Andrew Howsley of the Texas Midcontinent Oil and Gas Association, operating from his 14th floor command post at the Stephen F. Austin Hotel, to deny passage to the gas-tax-for-rural-roads bill by Representative Charles McLellan of Eagle Lake.

Heavy cuts in oil production decreed by the Railroad Commission forced Comptroller Robert S. Calvert to revise his revenue estimates downward by $22,000,000 and thus put Governor Jester's budget $80,000,000 in the red. Passage of single-shot spending bills, such as for the construction funds of Prisons Director O.B. Ellis, further threatened taxation. The Gilmer-Aikin Minimum Foundation Program plan of automatic allocations to the school districts, without legislative action, with a teacher pay scale of $2,400 to $4,032 a year, took almost all of the $100 million surplus which had been on hand. And the surprising thing was that a conservative like Taylor was a sponsor of some of the Gilmer-Aikin bills which were

to more than double the state's spending for public schools over-
night.

There were filibusters in the Senate and "chubbing" (as it was
called) in the House against the bills, but Shivers and Speaker Durwood Manford held the House and Senate in session until they
were finally passed.

Democrats had a Jefferson-Jackson Day dinner at $25 a plate, to
hear Speaker Sam Rayburn blister the Republicans. Austin Mayor
Tom Miller, the dinner chairman, denied a *Dallas Morning News*
item that the dinner would be segregated.

"Since no Negroes are being invited, how could there be segregation?" Miller asked blandly.

Shivers bought a $25 ticket for each of the senators, and con-
tributed toward the $70,000 raised in Texas that year for the Demo-
cratic National Committee, which had a Texas problem before it at
every meeting—the fact that the Texas Democratic convention in
September, 1948, had named Byron Skelton of Temple to replace
Wright Morrow of Houston, who had bolted the party to support the
States' Rights ticket against Truman and Barkley in 1948. Miller had
both national committeemen sit at the head table, and avoided the
question by introducing everyone at the head table without titles.

Back at the Capitol the next Monday, the Legislature went after
the issues hammer and tongs. Cousins had that Lamar College bill
again. The *Beaumont Journal* had endorsed Shivers for governor in
1950, expressing confidence that he would pass the Lamar College
bill this time, and make it stand up, unlike the "ghost bill" of 1947
which passed but had to be vetoed by the Comptroller because
there was no money to finance it. In May the lieutenant governor
was able to get Senator Bill Moore (always to remain an unshaken
foe of new colleges) and Wardlow Lane to switch, and to catch
Senators R.A. Weinert and W.A. Shofner out of the Senate chamber. Then he quickly recognized Cousins, got the two-thirds majority and passed the bill on second reading. Two weeks later, after
several efforts had failed to produce the two-thirds, Shivers went to
work in earnest. He did some "recognizing" on his personal Senate
calendar. And he promised some committee appointments,
perhaps, or called in some "due bills" for past favors.

At any rate, the bill passed, and as it was ahead of major appropriations bills, it became law.

One of the colorful incidents of that session came when Senator
Fred (Red) Harris of Dallas, pushing a bill Attorney General Daniel
badly wanted, drew a figurative line down the center carpet of the

Senate, as Travis did at the Alamo, declaring: "All of you who are for Humble Oil & Refining Company and the King Ranch get on that side. All of you who are for the school children of Texas, get on my side."

The school children lost, 15 to 14. So the bill to transfer a lawsuit to Travis County from Kenedy County, where most prospective jurors work for the King Ranch, was not brought up for consideration. It involved title to 32,000 acres of land in Laguna Madre claimed by both the King Ranch and the State Permanent School Fund. The state finally won the case, anyway.

The fight over welfare was a hot one. The House wanted to remove the $35,000,000 ceiling on welfare spending. The Senate was willing, but it wanted the State to take a lien on the homestead the old-age pensioner might have, and collect back what had been paid when the oldster died. Shivers kept appointing Senate conferees favoring the lien. Speaker Manford kept appointing conference committees dead set against it.

Once, when Shivers was out of town, Senator Kyle Vick of Waco was presiding over the Senate. He named a conference committee stacked 4-1 against the lien. Taylor moved to reconsider the vote by which the House request for a new conference committee was granted, and to "spread it on the *Journal*."

The less-expert senators did not know they could have forced an immediate vote; when Shivers got the gavel back, the motion to reconsider carried by one vote, and Shivers named the committee. He was criticized strongly when Senator Rogers Kelley resigned from the conference committee, saying he was committed against the lien. Shivers named Cousins, a pro-lien man, and that blocked things again.

Finally, on the last night of the session, a new compromise was reached by three members of each side of the conference table. It included a lien and removed the welfare ceiling. But it was too late, and Hudson's filibuster during the closing minutes of the session ended hope. Shivers, like most recent speakers and lieutenant governors, had refused to allow business to be conducted after the midnight hour for adjournment by stopping the clock.

There was a 32-hour filibuster against the basic science bill proposed by the medical doctors as a swipe at the doctors of chiropractic, and that issue had to be wound up with a compromise by which the M.Ds got the basic science examination law and the D.C.s got a chiropractic examining board.

Senator Jimmy Phillips filibustered vainly against a bill to decontrol rents. There was even a filibuster against a bill to set up a state citrus commission.

And in between, there was the continuing argument over taxes versus cutting back on the spending proposals for the mentally ill, the colleges and the state agencies.

Jester finally came out for new taxes, and Shivers proposed several solutions, one of them the adoption of a one-year budget, with a return for a special session in 1950. He also proposed financing Jester's program for state hospital construction with a bond issue. The Senate passed the Shivers plan, but the House refused to give it the needed 100 votes. With legislative expenses (there was then no salary for legislators) down to $5 a day, there were no more than 110 to 125 House members present, and with a few anti-spenders and a few anti-going-in-debtors, the 100 votes just couldn't be found. A second proposal for a State Building Commission with authority to issue $20,000,000 worth of bonds for hospitals and other state buildings produced the final showdown of the session.

It passed the Senate, and went to the House, where the vote for it was 89-48, even after Jester and the anti-tax lobby had rounded up as many members as they could. The heat then really went on the 48 nay-voters, because this was a solution which would avoid new taxes. The effort failed when the vote was 94-37. It was then amended to give a new Building Commission a $3,000,000 unneeded surplus in the Confederate Pension Fund, and sent back to the Senate. But it never did pass.

The session wound up with some hits, some runs and some errors. Jester, Shivers and Manford all agreed that there would have to be some sort of tax bill at the special session. Going into the red was averted when Jester vetoed the eleemosynary appropriations bill for the second year of the biennium, thus forcing the calling of a special session in 1950.

Shivers' own platform of four planks, laid out in his inaugural address, was three-fourths completed. A Legislative Budget Board, which would before many years make a mockery of the governor's budget, was created. A Legislative Council, to do research for the Legislature, was formed. And the four-year terms for state officials was defeated. The voters were to say "no" to Shivers' annual-sessions-annual-salaries proposal that fall.

Jester had the legislators over to the governor's reception room for a buffet supper the final night of the session. He had been tired, but warm and friendly as the long battle drew near an end.

The Shivers family packed up quickly and drove to Woodville to relax at the farm from the hard and wearing session, and to begin to think about the campaign for governor.

Once again, Shivers extended for two more years that promise to Marialice Shivers that he would, as she often expressed it, "Run for nothing but home."

This time, he could point out to Marialice the accomplishments of the past two years:

Creation of the Board for State Hospitals and Special Schools, taking the mental hospitals and the schools for the retarded away from the Board of Control thus eliminating a way of rewarding old faithful friends of the governor;

Adoption of the Gilmer-Aikin school program, compromised a bit, of course, by the George Nokes amendment in the House, but still a vital advance in bringing public schools into the 20th Century;

Constitutional amendments for annual sessions and salaries for the Legislature, badly needed (but to be rejected by the voters in November because the Third House would oppose them so violently);

Repeal of the poll tax as a requirement for voting, although the Senate had insisted on putting on a county fee (and the voters would turn it down in November, despite the support of Lyndon Johnson, Sam Rayburn, Lloyd Bentsen, Jr., the AFL and CIO, the REA co-ops, and many others, because it, like annual sessions and salaries, was a bit ahead of its time);

A session in which Austin Report said that all the big issues but three were faced and settled, and many of the niggling things, like basic science, chiropractor licensing, voluntary unitization of oil and gas leases, gas measurement and real estate licensing, were disposed of;

An end to political selections of school textbooks on the basis of who contributed to whose campaign; a system which had become so flagrant that a radio newsman on KVET was able to predict 15 out of 16 selections the day before the Board of Education hearings on the textbooks was opened;

A law against lynching, 20 years ahead of some of the Southern states;

Creation of a citizens' Youth Development Council, to take over Gatesville and other youth facilities, later to provide a youth probation system;

Provision of $5,000,000 for soil conservation work; creation of a water laws study group which was to begin the real state program for water planning;

Decent pay for state employees; retirement for judges and teachers and county employees;

Expansion of higher education, with more money for existing colleges, creation of Lamar College of Technology and a new medical school in Dallas;

Creation of study committees on water laws, criminal code revision, and election laws.

So when Allan and Marialice talked of those accomplishments, and dreamed in Woodville of the other possible improvements, she said "yes" to two more years, and Shivers decided to try to become Governor Shivers.

Fate was to take a hand quickly.

Photo made by Mac's Studio, Jasper, for the Shivers' Collection.

Governor and Mrs. Shivers, their mothers and the children they had at that time were pleased at the first inauguration at Magnolia Hills, near Woodville. From left are Mrs. John H. Shary, mother of Mrs. Shivers, the governor's wife and at his left, Mrs. R.A. Shivers, his mother. In front are R.A. (Bud) Shivers, Jr., John Shary Shivers and Marialice Sue (Cissie).

Chapter 8

"We're Fixin' To Inaugurate a Governor"

The rural party-line phone at Magnolia Hills, in the "cabin" on the Shivers farm near Woodville, rang about 8:15 a.m. the morning of July 11, 1949. It was Vernon Smylie, a reporter for the *Houston Press*, calling.

"Governor Jester died this morning," Smylie told the lieutenant governor.

"You're kidding," Shivers replied. "It's too early in the morning for pranks."

"No, it's true," Smylie insisted. "Governor Jester was found dead in a Pullman berth on the Southern Pacific when it got here this morning from Austin."

In those days, passenger trains were popular in Texas, and people often took the one leaving Austin about midnight, to enable them to wake up in Houston the next morning. Jester had chosen that route, but when the Pullman porter tried to arouse him it was discovered that a heart attack had ended his ebullient, country-gentleman sort of life.

Shivers had seen Jester just three days before, and he had been jovial and in good health. Shivers told Smylie it just couldn't be true. But Smylie insisted. He was getting a good story. Besides, the longer he tied up the phone, the longer it would be before the *Houston Chronicle* could get Shivers on the phone.

City Editor Gordon Hanna, listening to one end of the conversation as he sat at the battered semicircular desk at *The Press*, reached for the phone. Hanna had known Shivers when the former was the Austin correspondent for the Scripps-Howard papers and also when he worked for the *Port Arthur News*.

"Governor Shivers, this is Gordon Hanna," he opened. "It's true. Governor Jester is dead. How does it feel to be governor?"

That typical *Houston Press* kind of question made Shivers realize that it was indeed true. He sought details, which were skimpy, because Ben Kaplan had just called in the bare facts from the Southern Pacific depot, and was interviewing the Pullman porter who had discovered that Jester did not respond when he tried to awaken him.

"I couldn't believe it, of course," Shivers said of the momentous occasion. "I had seen him just three nights before, at a buffet in the governor's office the last night of the session. He appeared tired, as we all were, but was looking as well as usual."

Marialice Shivers, getting breakfast ready for her husband and three children, heard the distress in Allan's voice, and came to the phone. They got the few details then available, and it all added up to the fact that Allan Shivers was now governor of Texas.

He had been to Breckenridge for a rodeo the Saturday before, then had flown back to Dallas and then driven to Woodville Sunday. The five of them, Cissie, 2, Bud, 3, and John 8, and Marialice and Allan, were getting started on a vacation after the grueling legislative session, when the bolt hit.

The folks on the same party line got precious few calls of their own that day in July. Vernon Smylie's call was followed by many others as the radio and then the afternoon newspapers spread the word.

One of those quick decisions was made—to have Shivers' swearing-in at the farm, down a four-mile, one-lane sandy road from the highway. That would launch his career as governor as a rural man, rather than a city lawyer from Port Arthur.

District Judge Clyde E. Smith, who had studied law in the offices of Judge Shivers, came out to administer the oath of office. The Alabama-Coushatta Indians came from their nearby Polk County reservation. The ladies from Woodville brought out a picnic lunch, because the invitation had been public and open to all who would come.

Highway patrolmen and Boy Scouts helped direct traffic, and one man from Louisiana, thinking they were sending him on a detour, came down the sandy lane and into the crowd gathering under the pines and hardwoods around the lake in front of the farmhouse.

"What's all this?" he asked.

"We're fixin' to inaugurate a governor," he was told.

"Hell, I don't want to be here. I want to get home to Louisiana," the traveler growled as he backed his car around and started trying to get out against the stream of dust-churning traffic.

About 2,500 people got there for the ceremony, and for the picnic on the shore of the lake which followed. Capitol newsmen came, and Dave Cheavens of the Associated Press set up shop with his portable typewriter on a nail keg, with a hand-written sign reading, "AP Woodville Bureau."

"Informal as an old-time camp meeting" was the way one writer, Aaron Jefferson, of the *Houston Informer and Texas Freeman* described it. He got a picture of Shivers shaking hands with Mack Hannah, a Port Arthur Negro, saying, "I am the governor of all citizens of Texas. Glad to have "y'all" here today. I wish your father and my father were here today." Shivers was later to appoint Hannah, a long-time friend, to the board of directors of Texas State University of Negroes.

Judge James E. Wheat was master of ceremonies at the inauguration. The Rev. John E. White of the First Baptist Church of Port Arthur, the home church of the family, gave the invocation. Honor guards came from American Legion, Veterans of Foreign Wars and National Guard units, but there were no bands, no parade, no inaugural balls, and only a brief inaugural speech:

"As I accept the governorship of the great State of Texas, I do so humbly and with a deep and abiding sense of responsibility to every citizen. I do so while asking for divine guidance and for your counsel and your prayers. For my part, I pledge that all my energy and ability will be devoted to your service."

Shivers, tall, thin, black-haired and 41, really was not known to a great many Texans, who tend to ignore their lieutenant governors. He was, after all, the first in Texas history to become governor upon the death of a governor.

Next day, the Shivers family headed back for Austin, and Texans groped in their memories, asking, as did one headline on an editorial: "What Kind of Man Is Our New Governor?"

One newsman, attempting to explain it, wrote that Shivers had shifted from a position of power to a position of persuasion, and that much would depend on his relations with the Legislature. Since taxes were needed in the coming special session of the Legislature to finance the hospital and special schools budget Jester had vetoed, plus a building program, Shivers' stand on taxes was important. *Austin Report* editors, noting that the tax to support programs passed on Jester's urging had yet to be passed, wrote:

"That brings up the question of Shivers' attitude on taxes. As a senator from Jefferson County for 12 years, he was recorded by the AFL as voting favorably for labor 19 times and against labor 8 times. Among the 8, most of which came late in his Senate career, were votes for both the O'Daniel and the Manford labor laws and for the 1939 movement for a sales tax. He voted to exempt food sales from it. In 1949, when the omnibus tax law was passed, Shivers voted for it on final passage after voting with the conservatives on many of the amendments offered. Among his votes was one against the income tax, which lacked just one vote of being adopted in the Senate.

"Thus Shivers is on record for the sales tax, against an income tax, and for as mild as possible a version of the omnibus tax bill which includes taxes on oil, gas, sulphur, and sales tax on automobile sales, radios, cosmetics and playing cards. In recent interviews, Shivers reversed his stand on the sales tax which he said he opposed and doesn't think would pass, but maintained his stand against the state's levying an income tax. He would favor, he said, as broad a tax as possible along the lines of the 1941 omnibus tax. But he also said the state would have to look for new sources of revenue.

"Shivers is not likely to make many mistakes as governor. He must play his cards right if he is to follow Coke Stevenson's example of winning a second term with only token opposition. Shivers has a rough legislative session ahead, but, like Stevenson, he has a long legislative background and knows how to get along pretty well with the lawmakers. He has, of course, lost the axe he wielded as presiding officer of the Senate. He will have to develop a smoother approach based on persuasion rather than power to get his ideas turned into law. Where Jester said what he thought, even when it was unpopular like the "un-Texan" remark, Shivers is more cautious in his comments. His first move as governor demonstrated his ability to give the right answers. He would keep Jester's staff (William L. McGill, Weldon Hart, and L.D. "Sadie" Ransom), he would make the appointments on which Jester was already committed, he would not veto the second-year appropriations although he personally favored one-year appropriations. Even his swearing-in was politically wise. As a city lawyer, Shivers might not be popular with rural voters. But as the Baptist boy from Woodville, in deep East Texas, he put some rough edges on his smooth background by having the ceremony at his farm on a sandy country road."

Shivers quickly welded up a crack in his armor by closing ranks with Attorney General Price Daniel and Land Commissioner Bascom Giles on tidelands, as will be shown later. He cemented many of Jester's friends to his administration by making every appointment Jester had decided upon, except two, and one was to cost him the only county in Texas he lost in his 1950 race for "a term of my own."

In an effort to get Senator Rogers Kelley of Edinburg to approve Paul Brown for fire insurance commissioner, Jester had promised to name Judge Harry Carroll of Corpus Christi to the Fourth Court of Civil Appeals, and to appoint Luther Jones of Corpus Christi as district judge, replacing Carroll. It turned out that George Parr, the "boss" of Duval County with influence in other counties in the area, wanted those appointments, and no second choices. Carroll withdrew when it came into controversy, and Shivers named two judges closer to Parr than Carroll and Jones, geographically at least—District Judge Lorenz Broeter of Alice to the Fourth Court, and Sam Reams of Alice as district judge. Kelley agreed to these two, but Parr was not mollified. In his typical hot-headed fashion, he pledged support to Caso March for governor, and Duval County came through in the primary the next July, 4,239 for March and 108 for Shivers. Shivers later was to battle Parr again and again.

One of Jester's promises gave Shivers a bit of trouble. Jester had agreed to appoint Neville Penrose, Fort Worth leader in the Dixiecrat movement, to the Good Neighbor Commission, replacing R.E. (Bob) Smith of Houston. Lloyd Bentsen, Sr., an old friend of Shivers, said he would not accept reappointment if Smith were replaced. The new governor went to Sharyland in July, met with Bentsen and cleared it up, then went ahead and named Penrose.

Moving carefully, Shivers went to the right places and did the right things to smooth potential rough spots. When he made Jester's appointments to the first board of regents of Lamar State College of Technology, he dropped off one in order to name Ernest Winstel, a member of the AFL Boilermakers Union and a schoolboy friend, in order to have a union member on the board of this new technical college in a strong union area. Caso March was out campaigning the union halls, and Shivers wanted to hold as much labor strength as he could.

He moved to take a position of influence with the State Democratic Executive Committee by selecting Judge James E. Wheat, a lifelong friend, as secretary of the committee, where there was a vacancy. The Committee was strongly Loyalist as opposed to the Texas Regular-Dixiecrat element in the party, and accepted Wheat after it had been assured that the Texas Regulars had made a mistake in 1944 by leaving Wheat on their list of presidential electors whom they had attempted to instruct to vote against Franklin D.

Roosevelt even if he carried the state.

It was August, four weeks after he became governor, before Shivers made a major speech. It hewed to the Jester line: he would call a special session of the Legislature in January to act on the eleemosynary building program, and a tax program to finance those building and eleemosynary operations, and no more. He was careful on taxes, saying he favored some additional taxes on natural resources which "are already producing a considerable portion of our revenue," but no state sales or income tax. He favored higher old-age assistance, but the removal of the $35 million ceiling could not be done in a special session, and would be possible in 1950 only if the voters approved the annual sessions amendment. He knew March was campaigning on an increase in pensions from $35 to $50, and that W. Lee O'Daniel was making noises as if he might run for governor again. And he wanted oldsters to forget that he had appointed Senate conferees who had held out for the lien amendment.

In August he started building his organization of bright, knowledgeable men. He had John Ben Shepperd of Gladewater in for a talk, and put him on the election laws study committee. Later he was to name Shepperd briefly to the State Board of Education, to fend off a push for textbook contracts before the new elective State Board of Education could be elected in November. Shepperd was also given an assignment to become informed on economy in government, because Olin Culberson was talking along that line, and Shivers had an idea for a citizens committee to work in that field. The next spring, he was to name Shepperd secretary of state when Ben Ramsey resigned to run for lieutenant governor.

Looking back at the summer and fall of 1949, one can sense that the new governor made up a list of things to do, and carefully went about the state winning friends and influencing people. He attended a barbecue at the Amarillo Bull Barn honoring Railroad Commissioner Ernest O. Thompson of Amarillo, wooing the oilmen and the Panhandle people. He went to the Interstate Oil Compact Commission meeting in Estes Park, Colorado, and made a strong impact which was to lead to his election as chairman of that group in 1951.

"He was called on to preside at one session when the chairman was not available," one oil company lobbyist recalled. "The night before, he asked me for a briefing on the participants, and I told him a little about each of them.

"There he was presiding, saying exactly the right thing, falling into the spirit of the meeting as if he had been attending them for years. He was a big hit, and he was responsible for reviving the commission. When he became chairman, he was able to get most of the other governors to participate, instead of sending aides.

"And by golly, he turned it into a working, effective organization and restored its prestige among the states and nationally. I never saw a man do as good a job, walking into a meeting cold."

In September, Shivers moved Garland (Chink) Smith, who had managed his campaign for lieutenant governor and had become secretary of the Senate, into his office as administrative assistant. Sadie Ransom, who had been Jester's assistant, was moved into the secretary of state's office.

That same month, Shivers went to Mexico City on a friendship trip worked up by the Good Neighbor Commission. It also gave Senator G.C. Morris, the president pro tempore of the Senate, a chance to be governor for a day. Shivers was greeted by President Miguel Aleman, and praised Mexico's cooperation on the Aftosa program for control of the hoof-and-mouth disease in cattle.

Mexican newsmen, asking questions through an interpreter, got a reply which they translated as saying that he would run for governor in 1950. He later told Capitol newsmen in Austin that it came out as, "Yes, God willing and the people favoring," when asked if he expected to be governor after the next election. He let that stand as an informal announcement, leading Culberson to growl:

"If and when I decide to run, I'll make the announcement here at home in Texas, and not in a foreign country." Shivers laughed 22 years later when Governor Preston Smith made the same premature announcement of his intention in Mexico City, again with the benefit of inaccurate translations.

Jesse Jones gave an off-the-record dinner for Shivers, to give the Houston Establishment a chance to look him over, and sound him out on issues. Garbled reports from the meeting got into some papers, saying Shivers had told them that new taxes could be avoided. That this wasn't correct was evidenced by an open speech he made to the Texas Manufacturers Association in October. He served them an after-dinner course of "cold turkey." He defended the growth of state government, saying it had grown just as had the population and the economy and the cost of living.

"State government will continue to grow as long as the Texas Legislature and the state administration are responsive to the requests of the people for more and better state services . . ." he said.

He promised that there would be more spending for the mental hospitals and schools for the retarded, and reminded the manufacturers that O'Daniel had in 1939 vetoed appropriations for new buildings for the hospital system in the name of economy. Since then building costs had risen, and now they would cost more.

And, Shivers told the TMA,"If the State doesn't do the things the people want done, the federal government will." That was a favorite selling pitch to conservatives. With it, he was to lead the Legislature into doubling state spending during his administration.

Surveys were being made at the time of the needs of the hospital system by U.S. and state health experts and by private agencies working for the new Board for State Hospitals and Special Schools. That board was headed by Claud Gilmer, the former speaker who later became a telephone company lobbyist. Shivers was keeping in touch with those programs, as he cast about for an acceptable tax plan which the Legislature would buy easily.

He traveled a lot. One weekend he went to a Young Democrats meeting, then went to the Texas-SMU football game with Henry Luce, the publisher of *Time* and *Life*. In October, he spoke to the Austin Professional Chapter of Sigma Delta Chi, the professional journalism society, on the needs of the hospital system. The chapter included most of the members of the Capitol Press Corps, and they voted to undertake a public information campaign on hospital conditions. An inspection tour was made, and series of articles appeared in most Texas daily newspapers as a result.

Traxel Stevens, one of the newsmen who made the tour, summed up his findings in this way:

"A bad dream was what newsmen saw this week when they went inside several of the State's dilapidated institutions recently taken over by the Board for State Hospitals and Special Schools. Reporters were shocked by the crowding of patients into dangerous fire traps. At Terrell Hospital, for example, 77 Negro women live in a building condemned several years ago as unsafe from construction and fire hazard standpoints. Hundreds of patients lined the dark, dank halls in the San Antonio hospital for lack of any other place to go. All recreation and lounging space was taken up by beds. In the Abilene State Hospital for epileptics, the worst visited, 316 patients live in six ancient buildings, four of which have no fire escapes. The other two have fire escapes which probably are as dangerous as fire itself. After viewing these and other shameful conditions, reporters weren't sure who is better off—the white patients at Abilene or Negro epileptics who have no such refuge, however doubtful, in Texas. At Rusk State Hospital for the mentally ill there is a waiting list of 30 Negro women for admission. Half of those are waiting in jails.

"Personnel shortages existed in all institutions seen. Not enough doctors, nurses and ward attendants anywhere. Terrell has no registered nurses for 2,000 patients. Superintendents can't get enough doctors at the present starting scale of $325 for general practitioners and $425 for psychiatrists. Top salary is $500, but no doctor is getting it because the State Board hasn't authorized it. At Rusk, an attendant in charge of a ward has just been raised to $220 a month, plus board and room, after 30 years' service. Salary, deplorable living conditions and unattractiveness of the work caused a personnel turnover of almost 100% at Abilene in the last year."

Weldon Hart wrote a series which went to all weekly papers under Shivers' byline, to complete the press coverage of the horrible hospital system.

Culberson had been making strong speeches in support of rural electric co-operatives, then having fierce fights with private or investor-owned companies both in the Legislature and in Washington. Shivers went to El Paso for a convention of the co-ops, endorsed their programs warmly, reminded the members that he, too belonged to an REA co-op, and opposed the then current proposal to levy a state tax on co-ops. Culberson was working the same crowd which on that day elected John B. Connally as general counsel of the Texas Power Reserve Electric Co-operative.

Connally and U.S. Senator Lyndon B. Johnson flew back in the plane Shivers had borrowed from Ralph Rush of Trinity Drilling Company. It was not until Connally became governor—13 years later—that the State bought its governor a plane so he would not have to wheedle private planes for his trips around the state and elsewhere.

Shivers had a hand in the selection of Coke Stevenson, Jr., as administrator of the Liquor Control Board, and he began to make some appointments of his own, in each case making a careful choice, because the best way for a governor to make friends is by appointing men to desirable positions. Conversely, former friends can be made enemies by his making ill-advised appointments. Bob McKinley, the employees' member of the Employment Commission, died. Shivers called in Paul Sparks and Jeff Hickman, executive secretaries of AFL and CIO, for advice. He appointed Dean Maxwell, Sparks's assistant, to replace McKinley, thus carefully honoring labor's view that the employee member should come from their ranks. Then he named Tom Slick, San Antonio millionaire, to the Good Neighbor Commission.

Ten constitutional amendments were coming to a vote Nov. 8. Shivers had advocated annual sessions and annual salaries for legislators in his inaugural speech the previous January, but he stayed out of this campaign. Business lobbyists fought the amendment hard, thinking that salaries for legislators would make them less amenable to the blandishments of the Third House.

Phil Fox, the Dallas master publicist who had handled W. Lee O'Daniel's first campaign in 1938, put on the campaign against legislative pay. He centered his campaign on business groups, and it worked. Johnson, Speaker Rayburn and others campaigned for repeal of the poll tax, but Shivers stayed away from that one, too. He spoke up for the amendment for waiver of jury trials in lunacy cases. It was defeated, along with jury service for women and all but two of the ten amendments submitted. Only two relatively minor ones were approved in the light, off-year turn-out. But the annual-session, annual-salary amendment was defeated by the largest vote of all, nearly three to one. Again, Shivers and the Legislature were ahead of the times.

In November, Shivers went to his first Southern Governors' Conference in Biloxi, Miss., in which Negro education was the major topic, as well it might have been. Attorney General Price Daniel had just filed his brief on the appeal to the U.S. Supreme Court by Thurgood Marshall in the Heman Marion Sweatt case, where a black was seeking admission to the University of Texas School of Law. The Legislature had created the Texas State University for Negroes because of Sweatt, and had set up a temporary "law school" in an old home just north of the Capitol to provide law classes for Henry Doyle of Houston until TSUN could get its law school going. Doyle took the State Bar exams, after only two years in the TSUN school, and was on the list passing the Bar exams issued the week the Sweatt case reached the highest court.

Shivers got the Southern Governors' Conference to set up a tidelands committee; he was named its chairman, his first interstate office.

When he got back to Austin, he resumed his speaking engagements, and when the Dallas Citizens Council gave a dinner for him, hoping for much more money for the soon-to-be created University of Texas Southwestern Medical School, they got some "cold turkey," too.

"Let me warn the Southwestern Medical Foundation that there
are other needs in the state, too," he said.

"There was no Citizens Council to speak to the Legislature for
those who involuntarily inhabit our eleemosynary institutions.
They have not had a lobby, a chamber of commerce or a Citizens
Council to lobby for them. There are war orphans, seniles and
epileptics who need money for buildings and care." He also told the
medical men that they must devise a way of sending doctors to rural
areas, where medical care was badly needed.

Shivers was establishing himself as a strong, outspoken governor
for he knew it was very important that the special session of the
Legislature pass the program and the taxes quickly. This would
proclaim him as a governor who could get along with the Legislature and "get things done."

So he was shelling the woods, both publicly and privately, to get
all the ducks in a row by Jan. 31st, when the Legislature would con-
vene. It was suggested that Shivers made some warm friends by
delaying the session until that date, because so many House members (and some senators) were in college and wanted to finish out a
semester. Among these were two in powerful positions who didn't
appreciate that date. They were Representatives Joe Fleming and
Ray Kirkpatrick, the former, chairman of the House Committee on
Revenue and Taxation, and the latter, of the Appropriations Committee, both Baylor law students. They were on a quarterly
semester system, and it was tough for them to come to Austin.

Repeated cuts in oil allowables because of imports had created a
potential deficit in the General Fund. The allocations for the
Gilmer-Aikin school program were taking more than had been expected, and Comptroller Calvert was expected to say so in his official revenue forecasts. So a tax plan had to be worked out carefully;
if the appropriations for other state activities were left alone,
Shivers explained, the General Fund deficit would not hamper the
special session.

On New Year's Day, 1950, Marialice Shivers served the traditional black-eyed peas for good luck during the year. Her husband
needed it, with the Legislature coming to town, with Culberson,
Daniel, and W. Lee O'Daniel all talking about running against him,
and March already running!

Shivers spent the first week of the new year working on the platform for his campaign, and on the membership of the Texas Economy Commission he was planning to create. He wanted to have it
ready to trump Olin Culberson's ace when Culberson played it.

Photo Courtesy of the Shivers Museum Collection

Allan Shivers' first inauguration, coming on the death of Beauford Jester, was simple and subdued. Here he is shown taking the oath of office from the late District Judge Clyde Smith of Woodville, who studied law in the office of Shivers' father. At the governor's left is James E. Wheat, another long-time family friend. The ceremony was on the front steps of Magnolia Hills, the Shivers family farm home.

Chapter 9

"A Term of My Own"

The thirty men sitting on the ornate antique chairs and sofas, or on chairs brought in from other rooms, knew what was coming, but they didn't know the details. This was something new for lobbyists such as Ed Burris, Homer Leonard, Hubbard Caven and Charles Neville.

Here they were in the Governor's Mansion, after a few drinks and a good dinner, and now the governor was going to tell them something about what he had in mind in the way of taxes to support the mental hospitals and schools for the mentally retarded.

"You have seen the news stories about the terrible conditions in the hospitals," Shivers began. "We must do something about it. I have already met with the House Revenue and Taxation Committee, and they have agreed on a plan for everybody to pay just a little."

The plan was really fairly simple. Representative Joe Fleming, chairman of the taxing committee, called it "just a little bitty bill." It would be a "temporary" increase on the 25 businesses and commodities taxed in the 1941 omnibus tax law—between 10 and 14 percent more, depending on the comptroller's revenue estimate. The increase would expire Aug. 31, 1951, when the operational emergency would be over. A raise in the cigarette sales tax from three to four cents a package, to be in effect for seven years, would raise the money for a long-range hospital-building program that had been worked out by Claud Gilmer's board.

Gilmer explained the needs of the hospital system, and then Shivers called on one of the lobbyists he already had lined up to agree to the tax.

"If it's fair like you say, and temporary, we'll go along," the bellwether lobbyist announced.

"If you don't help me handle it this way, some of those wild taxers in the House are going to put it to one or two of you mighty heavy," Shivers responded as he called the next name on his list.

And so it went. The thirty men left the Mansion that night, pledged to ask their bosses in Houston and Dallas if they would go along.

Shivers had a chance to talk with some of the bosses himself. Gus Wortham came to the governor's office with a delegation of Houston business leaders. They wanted $7,475,696 from the special session for buildings at Houston's state institutions. That gave Shivers a chance to do some selling to the Houston big-wigs, and to get them to work on the Houston delegation in the Legislature.

Shivers had called in the lobby for probably the first time in history, because he saw that as the way to assure compliance. He already had Speaker Durwood Manford's approval and that of acting Lieutenant Governor G.C. Morris and other senators. But Shivers was worried about the House, with its no-taxers, its heavy taxers and its small body of middle-roaders. He didn't want the Third House stirring up the anti-taxers at a time like this.

Railroad Commission Chairman Ernest O. Thompson helped out, too. At a statewide oil proration hearing, Thompson hazed the spokesman for Texaco, one of the larger importers of crude oil. The chairman asked whether the company "loves those Arabs better than Texans." Texaco took the hint, and announced the next day that it was cutting its imports by 14,000 barrels a day. This and other brightening oil prospects put some rose in Comptroller Calvert's spectacles; he was able to freshen up his revenue estimates and thus reduce the size of the necessary tax bill.

Finally, the agreement was ready to be released to the public. Gilmer floated the cigarette tax increase as a trial balloon. Shivers was asked about it at a press conference, and had the figures showing it would produce in seven and one-half years the $41,133,000 needed for hospital building. He did not recommend it. Nobody did. It just appeared out of the blue.

The Fort Worth Chamber of Commerce came out with an "economy" plan very similar to the one the Texas Manufacturers Association had been proposing. It suggested cutting all appropriations for other state agencies, to trim the new school program somewhat, to kill the new farm-to-market road program and finance the hospital program that way. The plan was debunked in a *Fort Worth Star-Telegram* article, and Shivers rushed to Fort Worth that weekend to explain some fiscal facts to Fort Worth business leaders.

"If other appropriations are opened up, you would have to cut out $26,000,000 before you could start cutting the other state agencies and schools," he warned them.

He explained that because of the pay-as-you-go amendment to the Constitution, all spending would have to come within the comptroller's estimate of money in sight—or get a four-fifths majority vote in the House and Senate. He reminded them that the original appropriations were final as they stood, and had better be left alone.

When the session opened with its color and fanfare, Representative Jim Heflin of Houston resigned from the revenue and taxation panel with a blast at Shivers for "cracking the whip." Representative Jack Ridgeway of San Antonio tried to sponsor a resolution calling on Shivers to submit other appropriations so the Legislature could economize—but his effort was buried in a committee by vote of 66-60.

There was no question that Shivers was cracking the whip. He ignored the advice of old friends when he asked for total rehabilitation of the state hospital system—not just operating funds. It was against the background of no-new-tax sentiment that Shivers talked with Weldon Hart about this message to the Legislature. It was their first, and a good one was needed. After conference, Hart wrote the first draft. Shivers worked it over, and finally trimmed it down from 30 to 12 minutes. Many consider it one of his very best speeches, and he always referred to it as his "goat speech."

"None of us likes special sessions, nor do we like to talk of treasury deficits and tax measures," he began. "But when the only alternative is to close our state hospitals and turn out the helpless insane, the needy seniles, the epileptics and the feeble-minded to fend for themselves—then no choice exists.

"The laws of both God and man require us to meet this problem courageously and solve it adequately and quickly."

He then outlined and endorsed the operating-fund requests of the Board for State Hospitals and Special Schools, calling them sound and reasonable. Next he laid out some examples of what he had seen on the tour of the institutions:

"I have seen epileptics eating in bathrooms for lack of dining space. I saw 77 aged and mentally ill women locked up in a condemned building. I saw 400 mentally defective children and 800 seniles housed in prisoner-of-war shacks constructed mostly of plywood and tar paper. I saw dilapidated, non-fireproof buildings without fire escapes, with hundreds of mentally ill persons locked in them, and I shuddered when I picked up a newspaper and saw the headlines: '40 Mental Patients Die in Hospital Fire.'

"That happened in Iowa. It can happen here."

"To us has fallen the duty—it might indeed be called a privilege—of making a start toward better treatment and greater hope for our unfortunate insane, the senile, the epileptic, the blind, the deaf, the mentally deficient and the victims of tuberculosis."

Shivers then spelled out in cold dollar terms the fiscal crisis facing the state, with a deficit which he said "must be overcome before the hospital appropriating can even begin." He slapped down arguments that "economy" in other fields could produce the money.

Then he laid out his tax program, and promised the submission of special subjects when the hospital program was complete. He urged fast action within the 30-day period allowed the session, and concluded:

"To fail to do so would mean turning our backs on those less fortunate citizens in crowded mental hospitals, on children who are physically and mentally handicapped and need a helping hand, on thousands of fellow Texans who are dying of tuberculosis.

"Texas, the proud Lone Star State—first in oil—48th in mental hospitals.

"First in cotton—worst in tuberculosis.

"First in raising goats—last in caring for its state wards.

"These things are unthinkable. Texas can do this job."

His effective speech was to win him his primary objective.

Shivers watched the session like a young mother hen. He met constantly with legislators and lobbyists. He made many trades on the one thing a governor has to offer lawmakers during a special session—the opening of the session to consideration of the local or special bills which are a political must to a senator or representative.

When the House Revenue and Taxation Committee held its hearing on the tax bill, it was a scene unlike anything in previous legislative history.

Charles Neville of Lone Star Gas, Robert B. Anderson of Texas Midcontinent Oil and Gas Association, Hubbard Caven of Texas Gulf Sulphur and others marched to the microphone to say that if the tax was fair, their companies would not object to "paying their share for those who can't speak for themselves—the mental patients."

Only one lobbyist, a life insurance company spokesman, voiced opposition to the across-the-board raise in existing taxes.

After both Senate and House had passed the hospital and special school appropriations bill, the tax bill was reported favorably by the House committee. And, perhaps just to remind the gas lobby to stay in line, the committee also gave a favorable report to the gas-gathering tax bill sponsored by Representative Jimmy Horany of Archer City. The omnibus tax bill contained increases of 10 percent of the rates in the 1941 tax law, but it was pointed out that unless there were two-thirds majority votes in both Houses, the tax-rate increases would have to be 14 percent. This was because it takes two thirds to make a new law effective immediately. Otherwise it is not effective until 90 days after adjournment of the session. The House gave it a 107-32 vote, and also passed the boost in cigarette taxes to finance the hospital building program.

The Senate quickly agreed, and the whole package was quickly wrapped up by February 22, a Thursday. Shivers then carried out his promises on opening the session to other subjects.

How many of the votes he got by trading with members will never be tallied. You don't keep score on this kind of political activity. But after the main business of the session was completed, 45 special bills were passed, and others which Shivers had permitted to be introduced fell by the wayside. The big Houston delegation got its reward. One of the bills which passed provided $1,350,000 for construction at M.D. Anderson Hospital. Shivers thus had a hand in the first state appropriation for cancer research, to which he remained devoted ever since. He made the dedication speech at the hospital. In 1972, he was chairman of a group which set out to raise $34,500,000 from private sources for capital improvements at M.D. Anderson, which was to become one of the world's greatest centers for cancer research and treatment.

Among the special bills was one to allow rural electric co-operatives to set up telephone systems. C.S. Slatton, a former Supreme Court justice, headed the opposition for Southwestern Bell. John B. Connally, attorney for the co-ops, was the only witness to testify for the bill, when the whole House, sitting as a committee of the whole, considered the bill. It led to a session which lasted all of Saturday night, as telephone lobbyists got their friends to leave the House to try to break the quorum. But Sunday morning, the bill was passed.

That same weekend, Governor and Mrs. Shivers entertained the State Democratic Executive Committee at the big house at Sharyland. It was also the week that Olin Culberson wrote to a list of oil men, saying he would run for governor. That week, the Texas Supreme Court held that the action of the 1948 Democratic convention, requiring party loyalty oaths of party officers and participants in its conventions, had been valid. The executive committee enforced that oath on its precinct and county chairman, and thus posed an issue which was not important to Shivers at the moment—but was to be the key issue in the 1952 party parleys.

Shivers returned to Austin to make a public service report to the people on all three statewide radio networks. He reviewed the overall accomplishments of the regular and special sessions on education, rural roads, juvenile control and mental hospitals. The governor took advantage of his unusually large audience to announce that he would set up a Texas Economy Commission to review the executive branch of state government and suggest ways to make it more efficient and economical. But he pointed out that 90 percent of the state budget went for schools, highways and welfare, and the citizenship, through their representatives in the Legislature, had said they wanted those programs continued.

When Shivers signed the rural phone bill, Representative W.O. Reed of Dallas was there with the large crowd of "country boys" grouped around the big reception-room oval table. And Representative Dolph Briscoe, Jr. of Uvalde—later to become governor—had a comment on the help from Reed, who was going to run for lieutenant governor.

"More of those big-city members ought to run for statewide office," Briscoe quipped. "It broadens their viewpoint."

Early in March Culberson made his formal announcement for governor, and hired Phil Fox, W. Lee O'Daniel's 1938 publicist, as his press agent. Claud Wild, an Austin attorney who had been campaign manager for Lyndon Johnson's 1948 campaign, was named Culberson's campaign manager. Shivers signed up Booth Mooney, who had been Coke Stevenson's publicist in 1948, and J.J. (Jake) Pickle, who had been a campaign organizer for Johnson in 1948. However, Shivers declined to announce his selections even after they leaked into the press, nor would he admit that he had hired John Van Cronkhite of McAllen. He actually had in a sort of unusual way. When in the Valley for the Democratic meeting in February, he had seen Van Cronkhite at a barbecue and had said, "I hope you'll help me this year."

Shivers didn't know that Van Cronkhite's public relations firm in the Valley was a bit shaky, but he learned it a few days later when the unflappable Van Cronkhite showed up at the governor's office, asking "Where's my desk?"

Culberson's announcement stressed heavily his intention to economize in government, and Shivers was ready for that. He announced the names of 537 citizen members who would serve on his Texas Economy Commission. The press called it "The Shivers

Club." It had been worked up by the new secretary of state, John Ben Shepperd. And Shivers opened his campaign for governor by taking a ten-day vacation and business trip with Mrs. Shivers to Chicago and New York, leaving Senator Wardlow Lane of Center, his old Senate crony, as acting governor.

But in early April a second heart attack within a year gave Shivers a break. Culberson had the attack, and his doctor prescribed withdrawal from the race for governor. He made his withdrawal statement from an oxygen tent, leaving Shivers with no major opponent for a full term of his own.

When Shivers added Wick Fowler to his staff for the campaign, *Austin Report* noted that Fowler played the accordion and the move was insurance "in case W. Lee gets in the race and the campaign takes on a musical note."

Caso March still was running, and was due to get the AFL and CIO endorsements. The Railroad Brotherhoods would have been for Culberson but were up in the air. And W. Lee O'Daniel was sending out "I may run" messages. But they turned out, on the night before the filing deadline, to be publicity for an insurance company he was organizing to have its home office in an apartment house he had bought. The firm's operation there would keep federal income taxes on his apartment rentals at the minimum level.

In April, Shivers started a series of weekly radio talks on prime time (7:15 p.m.) on the Texas State Network. March was in the Capitol Press Room the day Weldon Hart announced the series, and immediately called Gene Cagle, manager of the network, to demand equal time. Shivers called a quick press conference to announce that the talks would be non-political. They were, except that they kept his name and voice before the voters at no cost to his campaign committee.

Shivers had succeeded in drawing some varied support. He introduced Vice-President Alben Barkley at the Jefferson-Jackson Day dinner in Austin in May. And *The Southern Conservative*, Ida Muse's paper in Fort Worth, said the only black mark against Shivers was that he attended President Truman's inauguration in 1949.

Shivers was wrestling briskly with the economy issue, sometimes with pretty straight talk, such as:

"There can be no cut in spending as long as organizations like the East Texas Chamber of Commerce demand economy while urging more spending on particular programs," he told a meeting of the chamber in Tyler.

"I am not hopeful of reforming human nature and Chamber of Commerce psychology to the extent that such paradoxical practices will cease. I am afraid a lot of people will continue to be for economy generally and for spending specifically."

When the filing deadline arrived, there were seven candidates—Shivers, March and five others. Shivers did little campaigning because the next week the Supreme Court held that Texas didn't own the tidelands and that Heman Marion Sweatt should be admitted to The University of Texas because the $10,000,000 spent on Texas State University for Negroes and its law school had not created "separate but equal" law education for him.

The tidelands decision called up the money and leadership and the Sweatt case the manpower for the revival of the 1948 Dixiecrat movement, which was to turn into the "Democrats for Eisenhower" movement in 1952. Shivers called a meeting of the tidelands committee of the Southern Governors Conference, and got a go-ahead to work with its blessings on congressional legislation to overturn the court's decision.

Shivers was also working on organization of the Democratic precinct conventions, assigning Pickle to that chore and giving him help from some members of the state committee. The party pledge, ordered by the 1948 convention, was to be an issue in the 1950 conventions, but not of the significance it would reach in 1952. The issue was dramatized when the State Democratic Executive Committee voted to refuse Agriculture Commissioner J.E. McDonald a place on the primary ballot because he had repeatedly supported Republican candidates for president in prior elections.

The committee, made up of strong party loyalists, knew its action might not be legal, but it wanted to advertise McDonald's party infidelity at primary time. And the Supreme Court did put him back on the ballot by vote of 9-0, but he was defeated in the run-off in August by John C. White, a 25-year-old agriculture teacher at Midwestern University. That small-college faculty later turned out another giant-killer when Assistant Professor John G. Tower won a seat in the U.S. Senate.

Texas leaders of the 1948 States Rights Party announced they would try to win the Democratic conventions, so they would have control of the party machinery in 1952. But Shivers was determined that he, rather than the Dixiecrats or the Loyalist-Liberals, would control that machinery. And he had the help to do it.

On July 22, Shivers beat his six opponents by the largest peacetime majority in a primary (next to that of Coke Stevenson in

1944). He got 829,730 to 195,997 for March, the next-highest contender, who received only 10,000 more than he had against Jester in 1948.

In November, Shivers defeated Ralph W. Currie, the Republican nominee, by 335,010 to 39,737 and became a beneficiary of the "tantamount to election" virtue of the Democratic nomination.

And so it was that Shivers won "a term of my own" with the greatest of ease in 1950. The folks at Woodville had indeed inaugurated themselves a governor.

Photo Courtesy of the Shivers Museum Collection

Here is the Mexico City press conference at which Shivers, through
a mixup in translations, was quoted by Mexican newspapers as an-
nouncing for re-election in the 1950 elections. At far right is Barry
Bishop, now of Austin, who then was Mexico City correspondent
for *The Dallas Morning News.*

Chapter 10

Land: It's What Texas
Is Made Up Of

Land is why Texans came to Texas in the first place, be they Indians, Spaniards, Tennesseeans, Mexicans or Germans. It was there; there was a lot of it, and generally it was free, or almost so.

Texas has been profligate with its public lands. The Republic of Texas gave away much of it—41,570,733 acres to people, and 72,292,000 acres big chunks of what is now New Mexico, Kansas, Colorado and Wyoming, to the United States as a part of the price of admission to the Union. The State of Texas gave away or sold at low prices 44,457,370 acres, either as grants to railroads, or to individuals. It traded 3,050,000 acres in the Panhandle for construction of the State Capitol which is still in use in restored magnificence. The State assigned part of its public land to the public schools and the University as endowments, but most of it was later given to individuals. In some cases, the Permanent School Fund retained the mineral rights, which the Carpetbag Constitution of 1866 had given to the surface owners.

Texans' love for the land was to provide three important issues to Governor Shivers during his three and three-fourths terms as governor. Land was used both "fur" and "agin" him on the political hustings.

Far the most important were the so-called "tidelands," the malapropism which stuck. They were the submerged lands off the Gulf Coast which were given, along with the riverbeds, bays, inlets and coastal lakes which in the 19th Century nobody else wanted, to the Permanent School Fund.

Texas had generally claimed the Gulf of Mexico out to the three marine league mark (10.5 miles) as its seaward boundary, but nobody bothered very much about it until it began to appear that there might be oil and gas under the water on the relatively shallow Continental Shelf. There had been some production in the Caplen Field near High Island, Galveston County, a short way offshore, before World War II, on School Land Board leases. But it was not until 1937 that Secretary of the Interior Harold L. Ickes triggered the great tidelands controversy by claiming that the federal government, not the states, owned the minerals under the oceans off the coasts.

Senator Gerald Nye of North Dakota introduced a bill in 1937 to take the marginal land into public domain, but there still was not much interest. Texas and Louisiana had no offshore oil production, but California had substantial production, and since there was no proration by the State, supporters could argue that its uncontrolled production was breaking the price of oil. But Texans weren't worried. With remarkable foresight, Dallas Countians had re-elected Hatton Sumners so many times that he was now chairman of the U.S. House Judiciary Committee, and he would see that Texas came to no harm. Inland states may have outnumbered coastal states, but Texas outnumbered the United States in its number of House Judiciary chairmen.

It was in that same year of 1937 that Shivers passed a resolution declaring the state should claim not 10.5 but 75 miles out from the shore. It was based upon the original concept of the Treaty of Guadalupe Hidalgo, which set the 10.5-mile limit as the distance the areas could be protected by cannon. The resolution said cannon fire by 1937 could protect up to 75 miles and that should be the offshore claim basis.

Interest in the subject lagged during the war. German submarines rather than drilling rigs were operating in the disputed Gulf waters. But with peace the movement was revived to obtain federal title or control of the offshore minerals.

Texas and other coastal states took the offensive, and Sumners started hearings on a bill to quitclaim to the coastal states the land out to their historic boundaries. In 1946, the bill passed Congress, but President Truman vetoed it Aug. 2, 1946. He was flying in the face of an unusual array of state officials. Attorneys general of 46 of the 48 states supported the bill. And in the course of the Congressional debate, Truman had nominated Edwin Pauley, a California oilman, as undersecretary of the Navy. Secretary of the Interior Ickes charged that Pauley had told him he could get $300,000 in campaign funds for the Democratic Party if he would drop the federal claims to offshore lands. Ickes opposed Pauley's confirmation, and resigned from the Cabinet when Truman would not back down on the appointment.

Also while the bill was under debate, the United States had filed suit in the U.S. Supreme Court against California. On June 23, 1947, that court held that the United States had paramount rights over the marginal seas, and as an incident to those rights, had control of the minerals under the sea.

Texas made two moves in 1947 to strengthen its claim to the offshore lands. The Legislature passed SB 338, by Senator Rogers Kelley of Edinburg, extending the boundaries of the coastal counties out to the Continental Shelf, the edge of which lies from 50 to 130 miles off the coast, with the widest part off the lower Gulf Coast region which Kelley represented. Then the School Land Board, made up of Land Commissioner Giles, Attorney General Daniel and Governor Jester, took bids and awarded leases on enough Gulf of Mexico land to collect almost $8 million in cash bonuses and one-eighth royalty. In all, Texas laid claim to nearly 18 million acres of the Gulf, of which about one-sixth lay within the three-league (10.5-mile) line.

An impasse developed when U.S. Attorney General Tom Clark advised the Interior Department that it did not have authority under the existing mineral leasing law to award leases on the California lands. Such legislation could not get through, just as quit-claim legislation could not override a Truman veto. So there was a "Mexican stand-off" in Washington.

Arguments raged, and, to some extent, real concern developed in state capitols about this invasion of states' rights. It was fueled when the State Rights Party was formed in 1948, with Governor Strom Thurmond as its candidate for president. It became hot enough that when President Truman crossed Texas on a campaign train in September, he heeded the warnings of Speaker Rayburn and Mayor Tom Miller of Austin. In his Austin speech at Third and Congress Avenue, Truman said that Texas was in a class by itself because it once was a sovereign nation. This smoothed some ruffled breasts, and Truman carried Texas by an overwhelming margin.

But in December, 1948, Attorney General Clark filed suits in the U.S. Supreme Court seeking to apply the rule of the California case to Texas and Louisiana.

It was at this stage that the powerful Texans in Washington began talking compromise. Speaker Rayburn, using estimates from the U.S. Geological Survey that most of the oil and gas in the Gulf of Mexico would be found outside the 10.5 mile line, proposed that the coastal states and the federal government share the oil and gas revenue from the entire offshore area.

Daniel was determined that the battle be fought in the court on the historic Texas claim, and would consider no compromise. His colleagues on the School Land Board, Jester and Giles, agreed with him. It was perhaps for this reason that Rayburn called Shivers and asked him to come to Washington.

Shivers let it be known that he was going on personal business that May 16, 1949. This drew some criticism from legislators, because appropriations conference committees had not been named by the lieutenant governor.

Shivers met with Rayburn, Senator Lyndon B. Johnson, Secretary of the Interior Julius Krug, Attorney General Clark and others. He became convinced that it would be practical to work out a compromise, and said so in a statement issued from Washington. "After reviewing it considerably, I thought they were right about it," he said.

So Shivers came out for a compromise which would involve extension of the State's police and tax authority to the edge of the Continental Shelf, and a division of the oil and gas proceeds for the entire Shelf area.

Both Daniel and Giles issued statements back home attacking him. After all, they were the state officials entrusted by the voters with defending the school children's lands. Why was Shivers getting into it?

Shivers guessed later that because Jester, Giles and Daniel had taken such firm stands on "three leagues or fight," the Texans in Washington wanted someone in the state administration to consider the compromise, and he was the highest ranking one they could get.

When he came home, he defended himself in a May 23rd statement:

"By the continued loss of the legal maneuvers in connection with the dispute between Texas and the United States over control of the oil deposits in the tidelands, we are faced with the proposition of losing all or trying to out-trade the federal government in a controversy in which very few lawyers feel Texas can prevail. All agree that she should. The time has come to stop a lot of name-calling and try to save the most possible for the school children of Texas. This is certainly more important to Texas than the course which has been followed for the past two years. It should no longer be continued as a political football and name-calling contest."

Shivers went on to argue that chances of winning in the U.S. Supreme Court were doubtful, as well as chances of passing a quit-claim bill over Truman's veto. He pointed out that no oil had been produced in the 10.5 mile strip, and that geologists believed that the really great deposits were in the part of the Continental Shelf beyond the portion Texas was claiming.

"Supposing the geologists are right, we would not only gain more in minerals under either plan of settlement than we could get by winning the 10.5 mile strip, but would also derive additional millions in tax revenue," he wrote.

"I have not committed myself to any specific plan of settlement, but I feel very deeply that our representatives in Washington should be encouraged in their efforts to obtain a settlement which actually will mean more to the people of this state and particularly to the school children, than either the winning of the lawsuit or the enactment of an quit-claim bill."

He concluded by proposing that the Texas Legislature be asked to pass on any compromise, warning that the lawsuit might be decided while Texans talked against a better solution.

One interesting bit of newspaper speculation arose out of Shivers' trip to Washington. Jester had recently visited President Miguel Aleman in Mexico, and had a very pleasant reception. Jester had also come out for new taxes to finance his hospital building program, while Shivers was contending that economy could handle the financing job.

Texas newsmen coupled these with the fact that Shivers was planning to run for governor in 1950, and with speculative reports that Shivers was in Washington trying to get Jester appointed ambassador to Mexico, so Shivers could run for governor in 1950 as the incumbent, which would give him an edge over Daniel and Giles and Culberson. It was checked out carefully in Washington and Mexico City, but seemed to be just a "good guess."

Shivers and Daniel swapped blows over the compromise proposal. Daniel refused to compromise, and Jester backed him up in refusing to consider the Rayburn proposal.

In later years, Rayburn and Shivers would say "I told you so," with facts to back them up. "I saw nothing wrong with it then, and do not now," Shivers said two decades later. "We were not able to do that [effect a compromise] because immediately Daniel and some members of the Legislature began to accuse me of trying to give away Texas' claim, and that this was a patriotic thing and they didn't care whether we never got a nickel out of it. As a matter of record, of course, everything that was discussed in that conference in Washington about Texas and where the mineral resources were and about the federal government prevailing in the courts, came true."

A few months before Rayburn's death, one of these authors wrote an article saying that Shivers and Rayburn had been correct, and that the school children of Texas would have been better off in money and property if their compromise had been accepted.

Rayburn wrote the author, saying he had had the article put into the *Congressional Record*, and added: "This is just about the only truthful thing about the tidelands that has been published."

Figures gathered by State Auditor C.H. McNiel show that oil and gas royalties from the Gulf of Mexico lands had reached only just under $25 million, by Aug.31, 1972; more than half of that came from wells inside the three-mile limit. Oil companies had paid Texas $156 million in cash bonuses for leases and more than $19 million in annual rentals. So by that time they had not yet come close to recovering that amount from their 7/8 or 5/6 of the oil and gas produced. Louisiana also found that the federal lands beyond that state's three-mile limit were far more productive than the state lands they won after the compromise was rejected.

But fate cut off the compromise plan. Six weeks after Shivers and Daniel were blasting each other in press conferences, Jester died, so Shivers became governor and a member of the School Land Board.

"Feeling that there should not be a conflict in the Texas position or an open conflict between the Texas officials, I, as governor, went down to Attorney General Daniel's office, and told him that I wanted him to know that he had my full support and that I would not openly make any conflicting statements against his claim as long as he had any claim."

Newsmen at the time had a hard time figuring out what was going on, because the terms of the "Rayburn bill" compromising the situation were still known only to people pledged to secrecy.

When the School Land Board met July 18, 1949, with Shivers as a new member, they laid out their objections to the Rayburn bill in a statement written by Daniel, and adopted unanimously by Shivers, Giles and Daniel. They agreed not to oppose the Rayburn bill as it affected other states, but wanted special provisions for Texas. Surprisingly, the Board agreed to enter into talks about the compromise, under these terms: It would be changed into an interstate compact, subject to ratification by the Legislature; the State would manage the lands within state boundaries, where the U.S. wanted full federal management. The federal people wanted a maximum of one-eighth royalty, while the State Board held out for a flat one-eighth, then the policy on state leases, to be revised some years later to one-sixth. They also wanted state control of seismographic exploration of the area, at the state's charge of $50 a day, where the federal law allowed free seismographing everywhere.

The big pusher of the compromise was Bill Kittrell, lobbyist for Mel-Ben Oil Company, a firm formed to take over the Texas offshore leases bid in by five companies owned by Mike Benedum of Dallas, the "king of the wildcatters." H.L. Hunt's firm had obtained more Texas offshore leases than anyone else, and at low prices, by bidding the minimum cash bonus and getting leases when no one else bid. But Benedum had sizeable holdings among the state leases.

Attorney General Clark had said that when he won the U.S. Supreme Court case, he would recognize the state leases, and this took away the concern of many holders of the State of Texas leases. It was during this month that Clark was elevated to the Supreme Court, to become one of the abstainers on the 4-3 decision in 1950 giving the federal government "paramount rights" to revenues from the offshore lands.

Rayburn went along with most of the School Land Board's demands, giving Texas title to 10.5 miles against other states' three miles, and giving the states 62 per cent of the revenues inside their limits and 50 per cent of the revenues beyond the state line. The one-eighth flat royalty, annual rentals of $1 an acre and state forms for seismographic operations were accepted in the final draft. But left open for later fighting was the question of state or federal management. And it was to be fatal, because President Truman would not accept the Rayburn compromise in full. Another quit-claim bill was passed in 1952, and again vetoed by President Truman.

From a Texas political outlook, the unanimous agreement of Shivers, Daniel and Giles meant that they would rise or fall together on the tidelands issue. And it eliminated a big issue Daniel and Giles might have used in a race for governor in 1950.

But tidelands was to become a still bigger issue, on which Shivers would lead Texas out of the Democratic Party in 1952 because General Dwight D. Eisenhower agreed to sign a quit-claim bill overruling the U.S. Supreme Court's 1950 decision, while Democrat Adlai Stevenson said he would not sign such a bill. Eisenhower signed it in 1953, and the issue was settled.

It was not until a decade later that Texas quit talking and writing about the "oil-rich Texas tidelands." They had turned out to be poorly productive in the fought-over area between 3 and 10.5 miles.

While Daniel was to ride his tidelands "white horse" to the U.S. Senate in 1952, and Shivers was to become a nationally known political leader on the same issue that same year, the third party to the School Land Board was to find another land issue—land plus money—irresistible. And he was to put Shivers and Daniel in a highly uncomfortable position, since they were members with Giles of the Veterans Land Board, which was buying up tracts of land for resale to World War II veterans on 40-year, three percent interest loans.

Shivers and Daniel generally sent aides to sit in for them at board meetings, and it was not very long after the program got started that the "block deal" was invented. Friends of Giles would buy a ranch, cut it into small tracts, kite the price, and find veterans to buy the tracts from the Veterans Land Board. They sold the tracts to the state for cash, so they were pocketing huge and quick profits.

After a time, it seemed like too much trouble to find veterans who really wanted the land. They were out paying veterans $50 to sign some papers, and the GIs would never know that they owed the State $7,000 or so until the payments came due.

This scandal, discussed more fully in Chapter 19, came to light in 1954, after Shivers' third and last race for governor, so it did not become an issue in any of his campaigns. It may have contributed to the decision by Attorney General John Ben Shepperd not to seek a third term in 1956, since he had been a member of the Veterans Land Board from 1953 on. It certainly did create some problem for Price Daniel in his 1956 race for governor, since he had been on the board when some of the deals were made.

The other Shivers experience with land was the famous "Hidalgo County Land Deal" which came to light during the 1954 campaign for governor. Federal Judge T.M. Kennerly opened some sealed depositions made by Shivers and others in an eight-year-old private suit brought by a Nebraska couple against Lloyd Bentsen, Sr., of McAllen and associates over some land sold to the Midwesterners.

Shivers' deposition, made in 1952 in the case to which he was not a party, had been that on May 31, 1946, while he was a candidate for lieutenant governor, he had bought from Bentsen for $25,000 an option to buy 13,569.69 acres of land in Hidalgo County for $75 an acre. He sold the option that December for $450,000 to Texan Realty Company, a company set up by Bentsen and then sold to eight men who were salesmen for Bentsen.

The release of the deposition made news, of course, and Shivers, asked for comment in Big Spring, where he was campaigning for governor against Ralph Yarborough, replied: "All that deposition shows is that in 1946 I made some money on a land deal. There is nothing wrong with that."

Opponents implied that Hidalgo County Water Control and Improvement District No. 16, formed to include the land covered by the option in 1946, got a permit Aug. 3, 1949, from the State Board of Water Engineers, for use of "surplus water" from the Rio Grande to irrigate the land. This was three weeks after Shivers became governor, and before he had appointed any member of the Board of Water Engineers. But it was a little hard to conclude that his $425,-000 profit in 1946 was related to the granting of a water permit in 1949. This was particularly hard to sell in view of the fact that the State Board of Water Engineers on Feb. 1, 1954, had entered an official order declaring the water rights of District 16 to be worthless. And this was after Shivers had been governor nearly five years and had appointed members of the Board of Water Engineers.

Then there was a matter of juxtaposition of land deals. In March, 1946, the Shary Estate of which Shivers was an executor had sold 20,000 acres of land to Rio Development Company, a Bentsen company, for $1,800,000. This was the money needed to pay inheritance taxes on the Shary Estate.

But other things were being talked about, and the "Valley Land Deal" was just a passing charge in the night.

Shivers' administrative staff varied as various members took leaves or resigned to help on campaigns. But here is most of it at Christmas time 1954. Left to right are C. Read Granberry, Jimmy Banks, Jack Dillard and Maurice Acers.

Chapter 11

Shivers' Lieutenants

Nearly every office has some form of a STUN FILE or a FILE 13. Some use other captions, and some substitute waste baskets for STUN files.

Shivers' office had both, and while he was governor the STUN file got its greatest accumulation because his assistants were more careful than most about saving the often useless material. STUN spells "NUTS" backward, and that is why it got its share of mail. Margaret (Mrs. Richard) Craig started it under W. Lee O'Daniel, first of the four governors she served as secretary. (She continued with Coke Stevenson, Beauford Jester and Shivers, then went with Shivers for five years after he left the governor's office and entered the pipeline construction business.)

Most days, Mrs. Craig sorted the mail and assigned batches to various assistants according to the nature of the inquiry, demand or request. They made lists of the mail by subject matter and assistant to whom referred. These were put into one report which showed the governor and other assistants who had what business to handle. Shivers could look over the report and get the import of as many as 400 letters a day.

He set up a companion system by which assistants gave brief reports—emphasizing the brevity. They would state the problem, a bit of background, a recommendation and usually offer a choice of "yes" or "no" on action. If he disagreed or needed more information, he would make a note to "C 21." That was his telephone branch, and all inter-office correspondence was to or from the inter-com numbers of the various assistants.

Mrs. Craig held out the STUN matters, showing only an occasional one to Shivers when he needed a laugh or when he needed reminding of the problem of allocating the mail.

The assistants handled the correspondence, often writing replies for the governor's signature or recommending action he should take. Mostly he signed the letters or took the advice, but sometimes he suggested a different approach or language. At any rate, the mail got prompt action—except for the crank letters. Sometimes Mrs. Craig got back some of her original assignments to assistants, with the recommendation that the subject matter go into the STUN File.

As she explained them, the STUN items consisted largely of communications which obviously were from neurotics or borderline mental cases, or from folks with problems for which there were no solutions in the governor's office, or for which the writers apparently wanted none.

Overall, Shivers had a competent staff, partially inherited and partially rounded up.

The totally unexpected death of Jester, a fun-loving executive who had been swimming with his staff the day before his body was found in a Pullman berth at Houston, did two things for Shivers: it projected him into the governorship at a time when the lieutenant governor was just one of four state officials planning to run for the post; and it gave him a legacy that included Weldon Hart. The events had lasting benefits for both men.

They came to have a relationship much closer than merely employer-employee, with Hart becoming the governor's speech writer (although he was the first to admit Shivers was a master phrase-maker himself) and political advisor ("although I learned most of what I know from him").

Hart directed the 1952 campaigns that made political history by putting Texas Democrats behind the Republican presidential nominee by formal party action. To do that, he had to leave the governor's office; later he was appointed chairman of the Texas Employment Commission. But he returned to help Shivers again officially and then unofficially in the second round of Texans for Eisenhower in 1956.

Between and along with those activities, Hart served as secretary of the Shivers-led delegation to the Democratic National Convention in 1952 and filled a vacancy as secretary of the State Democratic Executive Committee. Their ties remained close long after Shivers left public office.

Hart had been unofficial press secretary to Jester—there never had been such a designation in the appropriations bills—and he recalled the details of his continuing in the position.

Shivers, with his customary verbosity, said, "You can stay on if you want to, and I'd like you to." Equally conservative with words, Hart told him he'd like to.

The men had known each other since University of Texas days,

19 years earlier, when they were on opposite sides in campus politics. Later Hart, as Capitol Bureau chief for the *Austin American-Statesman*, had covered Shivers during a part of his service as senator from Port Arthur and much of his time as lieutenant governor. He was one of several Jester assistants kept on by Shivers—some until they found other places, some for his entire administration.

Jester's top man had been William L. McGill, a lifelong friend from the governor's home town of Corsicana and a bachelor who worked day and night. His duties were trimmed and divided among other employees but he stayed with Shivers until transferred to the job as head of Civil Defense. Also kept was L.D. (Sadie) Ransom, another Corsicana man, who continued until employed by the Texas Real Estate Commission.

Miss Caroline Roget, Jester's private secretary, was kept on the payroll until she found another place, as were Robert B. Baldwin and Nelson Brown, who were technically on the Board of Control payroll as budget planners but whose function had been transferred to the governor's office in 1949. Baldwin remained nearly three years, leaving to enter business for himself, and Brown stayed until employed by the Commission on Alcoholism.

Shivers brought in Garland A. Smith, who had been secretary of the Senate while Shivers was presiding there; Maurice Acers and John Van Cronkhite, who had been associated with Shivers interests in the Lower Rio Grande Valley, and Wick Fowler, Austin newsman, war correspondent and congressional committee investigator.

Later Shivers was to hire for relatively short terms William H. Gardner of the *Houston Post*'s Austin Bureau; Ed Felder, Austin photographer; Jimmy Banks, former *Dallas News* writer in Austin who later was with the Texas State Teachers Association and became an author, editor and political publicist; Ed Reichelt, a lawyer-newspaperman from Beaumont, later of Fort Worth; and Earl Braly of Austin, who worked in the public relations firm set up by Hart and Van Cronkhite.

Also added to the Shivers staff were Jack Dillard of Waco, former Baylor University ex-student director who later served as U.S. Senator William A. Blakley's aide; and C. Read Granberry, University of Texas professor who headed the Legislative Council and served as parliamentarian of the House while on leave from the University. Dillard, a former Federal Bureau of Investigation agent, managed the 1952 Shivers race and in 1954 joined the staff, where he remained until the end of the administration.

Another addition to the staff was John Osorio, a young law school graduate who worked in Shivers' office and for a while in the secretary of state's office. Later, when the insurance scandals broke and corrective laws were passed, Shivers appointed Osorio to the Board of Insurance Commissioners to straighten things out.

Osorio stayed on after Shivers' administration ended, until the agency was reorganized in 1957. When Shivers bought the National Bankers Life Insurance Company, Osorio was made its president. It was out of this role that Osorio became involved several years later in another insurance scandal—involving alleged manipulation of stock in the insurance company, which by that time Shivers had sold to Frank Sharp, Houston financier. As a result of investigation into charges that some state officials were allowed to make quick profits on NBL stock—bought with loans from Sharp's bank—Osorio was indicted for filing a false statement with the state regulatory agency. He also was named as one of numerous defendants in a civil suit alleging use of stock and other company assets to influence market quotations. He was convicted on a federal charge of misusing pension funds.

Most of Shivers' staff resigned at intervals—or took leaves of absence—to help on campaigns. These separations were in order to avoid involving the governor in charges of using state employees in politics. Acers probably had the longest uninterrupted service. Also a former Federal Bureau of Investigation agent and a lawyer, Acers handled the clemency routine for the governor, as well as numerous other administrative matters. After about four years, Shivers appointed him as the employer member of the Texas Employment Commission. (Hart had been the chairman and public representative on the commission, which includes spokesmen for employees, employers and the public.)

But Hart was the main character in the transition after Jester's death since he had most of the information that Shivers needed. One of Hart's chores with Jester had been maintenance of the book on appointments to the many state boards and agencies. He kept track of vacancies as they occurred, kept files on prospective appointees and the usual letters urging or opposing re-appointments.

The 1949 legislative session had adjourned only a week before Jester's death, and many appointments were up in the air. He had talked with senators in whose districts the potential appointees lived and had made commitments on some 100 of them. Hart knew, the senators knew, and, in many cases, the appointees knew.

Shivers honored nearly all of them—out of regard for Jester and for the senators who might have made announcements prematurely.

There were enough holdover employees to show the new ones the ropes in Austin; and enough new ones to implement Shivers' innovations.

Garland Smith, who had formerly been chief clerk for the State Treasurer, Jesse James, had managed Shivers' 1946 and 1948 campaigns for lieutenant governor. He moved to the governor's office and became the "hello man" in the front office until his ill-starred appointment as casualty insurance commissioner. Fowler took over the front office job when Smith left, traveled with Shivers during the campaign years, and had the dubious privilege of persuading the candidate to get out of Cadillacs and into ordinary cars. After auto airconditioning began to come into vogue, Fowler also had to convince Shivers that most voters at that time didn't have that luxury and probably resented those who did.

Fowler was broad-minded, though. He figured that voters wouldn't mind if press secretaries rode in air-conditioned luxury during those burning July and August days—they'd just not want candidates so comfortable.

Fowler had a good way of getting rid of callers he knew the governor didn't want to see. "I haven't seen him myself for two weeks," he would confide, sorrowfully.

He sometimes turned the governor aside, too.

Shivers always called his staff together at the start of a legislative session and reminded them that during a session each member of the Legislature thought he was the "most important SOB in the state" and sometimes was. For that reason he wanted all staff members to be courteous to lawmakers and to get them into his office in a hurry if they asked it.

But one day after the close of an unusually long session, the governor walked into his outer office and found several legislators sitting there, with Fowler paying them no mind.

Shivers asked if any of them wanted to see him, and Fowler said he had no idea— that the governor had said to be nice to them when the Legislature was in session but now that it had adjourned he felt no requirement to be nice or courteous to them.

Van Cronkhite stayed on the staff for a time, then was moved to the 1950 campaign staff. Later he was appointed secretary of the Good Neighbor Commission, where he tried to work out the near stalemate in it when there was a showdown between R.E. (Bob) Smith of Houston and Neville Penrose of Fort Worth. Van

Cronkhite resolved it by having Shivers create a Human Relations Commission, made up of those who were concerned with the problems of Mexican Americans in Texas (they called them Latin Americans then), while the Good Neighbor Commission was concerned with relations with Mexico.

In 1951, Van Cronkhite and Hart resigned their state jobs to form a public relations firm to handle the big political year of 1952—first the battle to control precinct, county and state Democratic conventions; then the fight at the national convention over delegate seating, and finally the campaign to carry Texas for Eisenhower.

When that year-long contest was over, Hart went back to the governor's office for six months, then was appointed to the Employment Commission. After nearly three years there he got an offer of a place with a business lobby, but Shivers asked him to come back to his office if he was going to leave the commission. Hart agreed—except that he left before that term was over so he could help in Shivers' challenge of House Speaker Rayburn and Senate Majority Leader Johnson over control of the Texas delegation to the Democratic National Convention of 1956.

Bill Gardner took Hart's place after his first resignation, but only on a one-year contract because his publisher did not want to grant a longer leave of absence. Two decades later, after his retirement, Gardner handled public relations in Dolph Briscoe's race for nomination as governor. Earl Braly was Shivers' press secretary for a time.

Next was Jimmy Banks, in the first of two tours of duty he served with Shivers. Banks left the Texas State Teachers Association to join Shivers in February, 1954. He resigned in 1955 to set up his own public relations firm, in the expectation of handling the campaign of Senator Jimmy Phillips for governor in 1956. When Phillips did not make the race, Banks went back as Shivers' press secretary in early 1956, replacing Garland Farmer of Henderson.

It was while Banks was at the teachers' association that he and Hart began negotiations which ended with settlement of Shivers' fight with the teachers over a pay raise. It was an unlikely setting—the press box at The University of Texas' Memorial Stadium—where they met and decided (in the spring of 1953) that something should be done and that getting the two principals together was not the answer.

The two "negotiators without portfolio" decided a committee of outsiders probably could determine how big a raise should be granted and how it should be financed—the two points on which

Shivers and the teacher lobby disagreed. The governor set up such a committee and called a special session early in 1954 to consider its suggestions.

Banks was, incidentally, the first to set up a statewide political telecast. Until then, broadcasters had thought programs could only move to the south, and most started in Dallas. He persuaded them they could go east and west as well. Reichelt, Braly and Farmer filled out the game of musical chairs that was played in the press secretary's office. Braly had the post during most of the fight with the Rayburn-Johnson coalition. Banks was on duty at the close of Shivers' term, and was kept on by Price Daniel for three months as the only staff member retained for the change-over. Braly returned to the public relations firm operated by Van Cronkhite.

Hart had the job of maintaining public confidence in the Shivers administration in spite of the insurance and veterans' land program scandals. Shivers made a ringing defense on statewide television, declaring that the veterans' land program actually would not lose any money, that Land Commissioner Giles had gone to prison for bribery, and pointing to the relatively few insurance failures.

Hart had a personal involvement in the insurance matters. He was due to be on the Travis County grand jury—already had been selected—when he heard that investigations were to be made of Insurance Board Members Smith and J. Byron Saunders, two Shivers appointees. He hesitated to call a judge at home at night, but hated worse to explain his situation in open court. So he called Judge Jack Roberts, later a federal district judge, and got permission to withdraw from the panel.

Smith and Saunders were two of the "disappointments" Shivers confessed to having had among some 2,500 appointees. What must have worried a lot of others is that he said those two "and one I won't name" were the only ones in the group he put in that category.

Hart never sought election to State Democratic Executive Committee office, but he served as secretary during the closing part of the 1951-52 term. Judd Stuart, who was elected in 1950, resigned after a bank embezzlement case in which he was involved, and Hart was named to succeed him. In that capacity he had many of the problems of party work during the hectic 1952 year.

George Sandlin, Austin realtor and a cousin of Hart, was elected to succeed him as secretary, and later was elected chairman of the committee to succeed Wallace Savage of Dallas. (Savage and his law partner, Alvin Lane, simultaneously headed both the Democratic and Republican committees in 1952.)

All of Shivers' former employees would agree it never was any trouble to get his views on a subject. He was plain without being blunt, they'd say. And he would talk with the highest and lowest of constituents if they had something to talk about; but he hated to waste time.

He had no compunction about saying "no" but had a way of doing it without offense. To use Hart's words, he was "diplomatic and fair but firm." And he seldom reprimanded subordinates—"he just showed disappointment over failure or delay, and that frequently was worse than reprimand."

Banks and Hart agreed that Shivers had an uncanny knack for timing. He had "intuition, natural rhythm and the feel of politics." According to them, he could have handled any job in his administrative set-up as well as, or better than, the man he had in the post.

Hart brought some know-how to the Shivers administration and took some out when it closed. He had handled the campaign for Pat Neff, Jr., when he lost for attorney general against Price Daniel in 1946, and for James P. Hart (no relation) when he won a place on the Supreme Court. The 1950 Shivers campaign was not hard, but those in 1952 were strenuous and demanding. Hart said he always worked for pay, but also had to respect the candidate. He helped in the 1952 and 1956 campaigns for Eisenhower and the 1960 one Richard Nixon lost between his service as vice president and his election as president.

Hart's appraisal of Shivers adds up to a conservative who accomplished more liberal goals than any "liberal" ever did in Texas.

"He will go down as a strict conservative, and he spoke and stood for many things the so-called 'conservative' side does stand for," Hart predicted. "But as for being an inflexible one, I don't think he was. Perhaps he was forced to the right more and more by the forces which were operating from the left, as well as the ones pulling from the right. It is next to impossible for a politician to remain in the middle of the road. Moderates don't help in campaigns. Those who get after it are the ones who feel strongly."

Shivers' policy of frequent substitutions on his administrative team was made necessary in part by political developments and by his wish to make sure no one operated in his campaign while on state payrolls.

The same technique was carried over in the secretary of state's office, usually considered the highest honor a governor can bestow,

although certainly not the most remunerative. And politics probably played a part there, too, for even if he did not plan it that way,
several went on to higher office.

Mrs. Jane Y. McCallum of Austin had been secretary of state a
record six years (1927-1935)—four by appointment of Governor
Dan Moody and two by Governor Ross Sterling. Prior to that there
had been three men who held the office four years and four for
three years. But mostly the appointment as chief spokesman for the
governor had gone for two-year terms and often for one.

Shivers changed all that. He had six men in the position in a
seven-year period. And he had a seventh for a six-month holdover
on the appointment he had helped negotiate through Governor
Beauford Jester. He saw four of them go on to higher state office—three of them elective places and one appointive. No other
governor in history had that kind of track record.

Shivers "inherited" Ben Ramsey in the secretary of state post, but
he kept him on for a very good reason. Jester had run afoul of
senatorial "courtesy" when seeking confirmation for a South Texan
to a vacancy which occurred shortly after he promoted Paul H.
Brown, his secretary of state, to what then was called the State
Board of Insurance Commissioners. The controversy became so
heated that there was threat of trouble on confirmation of Brown, as
well as his successor, even though the secretary of state is one of the
offices the Senate usually "gives" a governor.

Shivers, who was friendly to Jester and to former Senate col-
league Ben Ramsey, suggested that the governor name Ramsey and
avoid any possible conflict. Ramsey had served in the Senate for
eight years, and in the House of Representatives before that, and
was well liked. The appointment met with general approval and
calmed the waters in other areas. Jester put him into the office on
January 19, 1949.

When Jester died in July of that year, Shivers left Ramsey in the
office he had helped to get for him, until Ramsey resigned on
February 9, 1950, to run for lieutenant governor. He won a record-
setting six terms in that office, and went on to win consecutive
terms as a member of the Railroad Commission.

Shivers named John Ben Shepperd as secretary of state, February
9, 1950; he served until April 30, 1952. That was when he began
campaigning successfully for the office of attorney general, which
he held until he decided against trying to go for the governorship.

Jack Ross, a former Rio Grande Valley district attorney, then was
appointed by Shivers, and served nine months before Shivers

named him to the Board of Pardons and Paroles. He held that place 12 years.

Another former senator, Howard A. Carney of Atlanta, then was picked by Shivers for secretary of state, in which position he remained 16 months, until May 1, 1954. Shivers then put him on the State Parks Board.

A Lubbock banker, C.E. Fulgham, who later moved to Arkansas, was picked to succeed Carney. He held the post about nine months before returning to the banking business. In later years he became investment manager for former Governor Winthrop Rockefeller of Arkansas.

In Fulgham's place, Shivers named another West Texan, Al Muldrow of Brownfield, who turned out to be another short-termer. He held office from January 21, 1955, to November 1 of the same year.

That was when Shivers chose Tom Reavley, an Austin lawyer and Methodist lay leader, for the secretary of state's job. Reavley served from November 1, 1955, to January 16, 1957. He later was elected to a district judgeship and ultimately to the Supreme Court of Texas.

There had been 60 secretaries of state in the 103 years before Shivers took office. He chose six and part of a seventh in the roughly seven and a half years he served as governor.

No other governor, except perhaps James Stephen Hogg, saw as many of his proteges move on to higher state office. The difference between Hogg and Shivers is that Shivers helped his young men move up, and thus lengthened the influence he held on state government.

Chapter 12

Gas, Gasoline and Roads

Hectic, surprising and unbelievable are the best words to apply to the regular session of the 52nd Legislature which Shivers faced in 1951. It was to produce one of his few legislative defeats.

And it all had started out so quietly, with the usual preludes. State Auditor C.H. Cavness had told the Legislative Budget Board that it would take $65,000,000 a year in new taxes to carry on state government at the 1950-51 levels. Reasons were many: The new Gilmer-Aikin school program, with its automatic appropriations as school enrollments and teacher experience grew; the fact that the State's 30-cent per $100 property tax for general purposes had been abolished; the $15,000,000-a-year General Revenue appropriation of farm-to-market roads under the Colson-Briscoe program; and growing welfare costs had created such a situation that the 52nd would have to tax to pay for what the 51st had spent.

Harry Whitworth, of the Texas Manufacturers Association, had the usual "no new tax" proposal—cut down on spending for highways, higher education, welfare and soil conservation, and balance the budget by economy elsewhere.

Shivers, getting ready to start that term of his own, let it be known that as a general rule he would not reappoint members of the state boards and commissions. Those honors should be passed around, he said, and citizens should not be asked to give more than six years to such posts. However, he found that very few wanted to step down from the non-paying jobs that took up valuable time. One small-town banker actually begged for reappointment; and when Shivers refused, sent a relative, who had been in law school with the governor, to further plead his case.

"I asked him what in the world the banker wanted with such a task, and he very frankly replied that small-town bankers otherwise would not get to be entertained on bond-selling trips to New York and other places," Shivers related. "I did reappoint that particular man."

Many six-year appointees of Governor Coke Stevenson were nearing the end of their terms, and Shivers naturally wanted to put some of his friends in their places. One of his first was Ely H. Thornton, Jr., of Galveston. Thornton had served in the House while Shivers was a young senator, had been a law school friend and was in the Shivers wedding party. He put Thornton in as chairman of the Highway Commission, which was to make him a storm center during the legislative session.

New presiding officers were taking over in both houses, Ramsey of San Augustine as lieutenant governor and Reuben Senterfitt of San Saba as the unopposed candidate for speaker. Both were conservatives, and their committee appointments reflected their views. Representative Edward Dicker of Dallas took his seat as the only Republican in the Legislature, despite the fact that he had failed to pay his poll tax and was being challenged.

The Korean War was under way, and because of the international situation, Shivers told the inaugural committee not to arrange for an inaugural ball.

Ken McCalla for the railroads and Jim Taylor for the truckers were squared away for a fight over higher load limits for trucks. The Texas Social and Legislative Conference called for removal of the $25,000,000 ceiling on welfare. Shivers appointed District Judge Clyde Smith, who had given him the oath of office as governor in 1949, to the Supreme Court, replacing Justice James P. Hart, who had resigned to take a $20,000-a-year job, the state's largest salary, as chancellor of The University of Texas.

The County Judges and Commissioners Association softened its position on rural roads. Under Judge Otha Dent of Lamb County, its new president, the association agreed to a compromise by which the Highway Department, rather than the counties, would build the roads to be financed by a tax on natural gas.

A higher education advisory committee recommended that no money be spent trying to finance professional schools at the Texas State University for Negroes.

The 1950 census, and passage of a constitutional amendment for legislative redistricting every ten years, by an ex-officio board if the Legislature failed to, assured that that hot item would be the topic of much discussion.

Then Comptroller Robert S. Calvert made his official revenue estimates, showing that $55,000,000 in new taxes would be needed to finance just the programs then under way in the state government.

The inaugurations of Shivers and Ramsey were quiet and quick. In his message to the Legislature, Shivers said there were two questions to be answered on each program: "Can we afford it? Can we afford to do without it?"

He recommended a new study of the system of higher education, legislative redistricting, new codes on water, insurance and election laws which interim committees had prepared. He also asked for four-year terms for state and local officials, registration of members of the Communist Party, continuation of the new farm-to-market road programs (but not with financing from the General Revenue Fund), a cost-of-living pay raise for state employees and the elimination of state-owned passenger cars. He had no tax recommendations, except that he was opposed to both sales and income taxes.

Among the early bills introduced was HB 226, by Representative Callan Graham of Junction, with Representatives Dolph Briscoe, Jr., of Uvalde and Clyde Whiteside of Seymour as co-authors. The presence of two rural roads leaders of 1949 made this bill look pretty much like a compromise.

HB 226 was the plan of Highway Commission Chairman Thornton and Ike Ashburn of the Texas Good Roads Association, and had Shivers' as yet unannounced backing. It would have cut off the counties' sharing of the growing surplus in the one cent of the gasoline sales tax which was devoted to paying off county road bonds used to buy rights-of-way for highways which later joined the state system. It would drop the $15,000,000-a-year general fund allocation for farm-to-market roads, and let the Highway Department build those roads out of the road bond surplus money. In addition, it was pointed out by Graham that the counties had the right to re-levy the 30 cent per $100 state tax for road purposes, to be spent locally.

When the county judges and commissioners heard of that, they descended on Austin from all directions, their coat-tails barely hitting the seats of their pants. Briscoe and Whiteside took their names off the Graham bill, and the fight was on. Briscoe—22 years later to be governor himself—incurred Shivers' wrath over withdrawal from sponsorship of the bill.

The Governor said Briscoe had asked to sponsor some of his legislation but that when the county officials protested the highway measure he asked why Shivers had asked him to help pass such a bill. "I reminded him that he had asked to sponsor it and I expected him to carry out his commitment. He did not, of course; he not only withdrew as sponsor but opposed the legislation."

Whiteside's Highway and Roads Committee gave the Graham bill a 15-3 unfavorable vote, and Speaker Senterfitt quickly got it re-referred to State Affairs, a more favorable committee, so a compromise could be worked on by Graham, chairman of that committee. His compromise offer was to let the counties continue to get their share of the road bond fund surplus, but turn it over to the State Highway Department to spend. The results would have cut F-M road building by about $9,000,000 a year, and the counties and Farm Bureau spokesmen weren't about to accept that.

Then Representative Jim Sewell of Blooming Grove, who had lost his eyesight when a Japanese kamikaze pilot crashed on the deck of his ship in the Pacific during World War II, started working the House floor on his bill, a one cent per 1,000 cubic feet tax on the "gathering of natural gas." He would allocate the revenue half to rural roads, a fourth to the cities for street work, and a fourth to the public schools.

He, Briscoe, Whiteside and others continued to organize the House, and when Graham's HB 226 was reported favorably by the State Affairs Committee, Briscoe's motion to re-refer it to the more liberal Agriculture Committee carried 74-62. That House Agriculture Committee, headed by Representative Lamar Zivley of Temple, was to handle also the public welfare amendment, the tax bills, and much other major legislation. It was one committee controlled by the rural group who made up the majority of the House. When it became obvious that the Revenue and Taxation Committee was not going to give the Sewell gas tax bill much consideration, it, too, was re-referred to Agriculture, and quickly reported back favorably.

Meanwhile, the four major appropriations bills had passed both houses and had gone to a free conference committee for final rewriting. There was a $60 million-a-year deficit in sight.

Shivers, smarting at the defeat of the highway plan in the House, called in about 40 of his leaders from over the state to an unannounced meeting at the Mansion. Thornton explained the dire needs of the primary highway system for more money, and Shivers suggested a compromise, laying it out for discussion. It was to increase the gasoline tax from 4 to 5 cents a gallon, to freeze the counties' share of the road bond assumption fund at $7,300,000 a year, with the growing surplus to be used for rural road construction by the Highway Department. The Colson-Briscoe $15 million annual appropriation would be eliminated.

Shivers, as a former legislator, felt that he should not advise the Legislature very frequently, lest they decide he was getting too deeply into their business. But word of his views got around, and the natural gas tax vs. gasoline sales tax fight was on.

In April Senator Jimmy Phillips filibustered for 18 hours against a bill by Senator Dorsey Hardeman to abolish the new Board for State Hospitals and Special Schools, which had had three executive directors in its first year of operation. And the House passed the Sewell gas tax bill, and a tax bill supported by Shivers to make permanent the 10 per cent increase voted in 1950 on all taxes in the omnibus tax law of 1941, a bill about 40 per cent resource taxes and 60 per cent sales taxes.

Briscoe then announced that he would approve the repeal of the Colson-Briscoe program only if the Sewell gas tax bill passed the Senate and was signed by the governor.

Shivers decided it was time for him to speak out. He called his first press conference since the opening of the session three months before. He said he would sign a tax bill with the 10 per cent omnibus increase, a one-cent gasoline tax increase and an added tax on gas pipelines. He also called for some new spending ideas, $9 million for new buildings at the Houston Dental and Dallas Medical schools, some for the prison system and the Gatesville State School, a $2 million emergency fund for civil defense in case of enemy air raids, and pay raises for state employees. He was aided by another international development. A revolution in Iran cut off that country's flow of oil, caused substantial increases in Texas oil allowables, and allowed Comptroller Calvert to revise his revenue estimates which are the ceiling on state appropriations. This reduced the need for new revenue for the coming two years to $76 million, even if Shivers' new spending proposals were included.

Senator Weinert of Seguin was given the job of writing a new version of the tax bill. As his products usually did, the revised bill came out of the Senate State Affairs Committee. It was what Shivers had proposed, and Highway Commission Chairman Thornton had written in the new compromise version of the rural roads program. It included the one-cent rise in the gasoline sales tax, a freezing of the counties' share of the surplus at $7,300,000 a year with $15 million of the state's share of the surplus to be used for F-M roads exactly as the Colson-Briscoe program had provided.

Briscoe and the county judges declared the net effect would be to cut F-M construction $150 million in the next ten years. "We will dig in to fight that one all summer," they announced.

Senator George Nokes of Corsicana, Senate sponsor of the Sewell bill, got it re-referred to the Senate Agriculture Committee where Senator George Moffett of Chillicothe quickly called a meeting and reported it favorably to the Senate, 9-2.

It was becoming obvious that natural gas was to pay the bill in some fashion. Weinert's revision had included the 10 per cent increase on all the omnibus taxes except the gas production tax, which was raised 20 per cent. That brought a new lobby group into the fight—the Texas Independent Producers and Royalty Owners Association. To Tommy Thompson, its legislative lobbyist, it looked as if the gas pipelines were trying to switch their tax to the producer. So he joined the gas pipeline taxers as a matter of strategy.

Shivers read accurately the anti-sales tax strength in the House and backed away from the gasoline sales tax increase, coming out instead for a new idea devised by Clint Small, Sr., lobbyist for Carthage Hydrocol. It was called a tax on dedicated reserves of gas as a sort of property tax, to be levied upon withdrawal from the reserves at the rate of one cent per 1,000 cubic feet. Representative H.A. (Salty) Hull had run with it in the House. Senator Kyle Vick of Waco offered it as an amendment, and after a lot of exemptions were accepted by amendments, it was adopted, along with an increase in the gas production tax from 5.72 to 10 per cent of well-head value.

Senator Howard Carney of Atlanta sent up an amendment, saying, "That other amendment exempted Lone Star Gas. This is one to exempt United Gas Pipeline Co., which operates in my part of the state. . . ." It was adopted, too. This and other amendments led the crusty Weinert to remark: "That wouldn't raise enough money to buy a hat, it's so full of holes."

The Senate then rejected the Sewell-Nokes gathering tax 20-10, and sent the battered tax bill back to the House, where the war was resumed the next day.

The House rejected the Hull-Vick-plus-sales-tax bill, and carefully instructed the five members Senterfitt was to appoint to accept nothing but the Sewell-Nokes tax and a carefully drawn rural roads section. Dent wrote Shivers an open letter with five barbed-wire questions about taxes and roads, and the bill went to conference committee.

Just then, the first 120 days of the session ended, and legislators' expense allowances dropped from $10 to $5 a day. The group which came to be known as the Gas House Gang rented an old boarding house at 1700 Rio Grande Street and many of them moved in to cut expenses. The Farm Bureau sent baskets of groceries "from farm women" to be presented to Sewell and Nokes in the House and Senate.

Sure enough, the conference committee brought back a bill leaving the rural roads program as it was, but raising the gas production tax to 10 per cent. This passed the Senate, 16-15, but the House turned it down, 82-60, with Lone Star Gas and the producers and royalty owners association finding some votes to help the Gas House Gang.

Shivers called a press conference and blistered the House for turning down a bill "which would have assured continuation of a good rural roads program."

Representative George Hinson of Mineola wrote an open letter to Shivers, saying, "The rural road fight is won. The only question now is how to tax gas."

And sure enough it was. This time, Senterfitt appointed tax conferees who agreed with a majority of the House. It brought back a bill which raised the taxes on oil, gas and sulphur 10 per cent, increased corporation franchise taxes, and levied the Sewell-Nokes "gas gathering tax" at the rate of 9/20 of 1 cent per 1,000 cubic feet, with no exceptions.

Shivers got a partial victory in that it did freeze the counties' share of the road bond surplus at $7,300,000 a year giving the Highway Department an ever-increasing share of that one cent of the gasoline sales tax, instead of just half of it. This allocation was still in effect 20 years later.

During the long 151 days of the session, much other legislation which Shivers recommended was passed, and he agreed that the final compromise on taxes was acceptable to the vast majority.

In a session-end statement June 8, Shivers noted that the 52nd Legislature had paid the bills for the reform programs voted by the 51st Legislature, then added:

"The 52nd had many other achievements to its credit, including the first legislative redistricting since 1923 and the submission of an amendment to raise the ceiling on public welfare grants. Ambitious recodification and reform measures were passed, affecting the anti-crime, insurance and election laws. Provision was made for the education of mentally retarded children . . . . Several new laws are intended to make our highways and streets safer. The farm-to-market road program was further stabilized. Inflation-pinched state employees in the lower pay brackets were given a modest increase, while the State's overall expenditures were kept approximately within the bounds of the previous biennium. While no one would say that all the good bills passed and all the bad ones failed, the ultimate results of this session are distinctly to the Legislature's credit."

The proposals for legislative pay and four-year terms for state officials were among those which failed to pass.

One of the first moves toward giving the governor more power came when the making of the executive budget was moved from the Board of Control to the governor's office.

Shivers wanted to veto some riders on the appropriations bills, but Attorney General Price Daniel held that he did not have that authority. Shivers then submitted requests to Daniel for opinions on the validity of all of the 235 "riders," language by which legislators try to control and direct administrative agencies, and often really try to pass legislation. He later modified the request, and Daniel held some 30 riders to be unconstitutional.

But high on the Shivers list of unfinished business was the expanded financing of the state highway program. Less than a month after the Legislature left town, Thornton launched a campaign to sell the public on the need for more money for highways. In a statewide radio speech, and in countless other speeches, Thornton said there were three possibilities: 1. To stop building highways, and turn the Highway Department into a maintenance outfit; 2. To turn over to the Highway Department the one-fourth of the gasoline tax revenue which goes to the public schools and the portion which goes to other non-highway purposes; or 3. To increase the gasoline tax from 4 to 5 cents a gallon. The latter was, of course, the plan Thornton and Shivers had in mind.

Chapter 13

The Piper Plays

Gatlinburg, Tennessee, and Hot Springs, Arkansas, had little to do with early Texas history, with the possible exception of providing some of the manpower that won the state's independence from Mexico.

But in 1951 they were sites of events which set the stage for the most turbulent year since that 1836 engagement. It was in those two towns that Allan Shivers first gave public indication that he might defect from the Democratic Party if President Harry Truman won nomination for another term or if the party chose a candidate amenable to the course Truman had charted.

The Texan had a bill of particulars ready for anyone who questioned his position. He was tired, he said, of Dean Acheson's "bungling" foreign policy; of "communist coddling" in high places; of a trend that is "carrying us swiftly toward socialism"; and of retention and perhaps expansion of the "strange and disturbing" doctrine of paramount rights under which Truman had claimed the Texas tidelands.

Thus, when the 1952 Democratic National Convention in Chicago nominated Governor Adlai Stevenson of Illinois, whom Shivers considered a Truman apostle if not his personal selection, Shivers wanted some answers. He wanted to check with his home folks to see how they felt, but first he wanted to hear something from Stevenson. He went to Springfield and asked the Illinois governor in a jaw-to-jaw session what he would do if the Congress passed another bill to restore to Texas the tidelands it had owned as a republic. And when he got the candid reply that Stevenson would veto the measure as Truman had done for two previous bills, the issue was joined. It kicked off one of the hardest campaigns ever waged. It made political history.

Texas was a bed of discontent, Shivers remembered later, but without the tidelands issue there would have been no "cause célèbre" sufficient to carry the state against the Democratic nominee. Shivers himself had opposed the Truman administration on the handling of the Korean War, on inflation, overall policies and minor scandals, so he entered the fight with gusto.

One close to the battle, though, was less than enthusiastic about the demands it made on the governor's time. Mrs. Shivers was interested in his endeavors, but she also was pregnant. Her husband had been nearby during the births of their other children but this time he was campaigning all over the state most of the time—and even out of the state some. In June, two months before the baby was due, she had to accompany Shivers to Houston to play host to the nation's governors and their wives at their annual meeting (their first in Texas). Next, the governor had to campaign on the delegate seating issue for the convention, go to the convention and then come home to assess the Democratic primary returns which had assured him another term. Also, there was that trip to Springfield which he delayed until after the baby arrived.

Mrs. Shivers possibly sized up the year at the governors' meeting, which, because of presidential implications, included all governors. Governor Adlai Stevenson of Illinois wore white shoes throughout the meeting, and Mrs. Shivers had a particular aversion to white shoes on men.

"No one who wears white shoes will ever be elected president of the United States," she predicted with all the authority of a pregnant woman. It turned out that she was right.

The year 1952 will go down primarily as the first time a Democratic governor of Texas led his party to carry the state for a Republican candidate for president. But in truth it was three campaigns: one to gain control of the precinct, county and state conventions; one to win nomination—and later election—cross-filed on Democratic and Republican tickets for a second elective term; and the main fight to carry Texas for Eisenhower in the general election.

All were bitter struggles, and, for Sam Rayburn of Bonham, pure gall. The one-time speaker of the Texas House of Representatives and later the record-holder in the same post in Washington learned the hard way that fame and power in the nation's capital are one thing and day-to-day attention to the voter pulse at home is something different.

Rayburn touched off some of the fire at Hot Springs, although things had been building up in Texas to the point that it required only some little thing to spark it. "Mr. Sam" was the main speaker at a dinner for the Southern Governors' Conference, which included one Republican and four governors whose normally Democratic states had gone to the State Rights Party in 1948. So Rayburn's high praise for the Truman administration and his warning that Southern Democrats would lose much power in Washington if a Republican should win in 1952 were not too well taken.

The lone Republican—Theodore McKeldin of Maryland—walked out during Rayburn's speech, and several Democrats let it be known that they didn't like the partisan nature of his talk at a supposedly non-political affair. Shivers paraphrased Shakespeare for his comment on Rayburn: "Methinks he protesteth his virtue too much."

Earlier, at the National Governors' Conference in Gatlinburg, Shivers had flatly declared he would not support Truman for re-election unless he changed some of his policies. He did not say so, but implied strongly that the same measuring stick would be applied to anyone sympathetic to Truman or hand-picked by him for the nomination.

A month after the Hot Springs meeting, Congressman Wingate Lucas of Fort Worth suggested that Shivers would make the party an attractive presidential nominee. But the governor quickly extinguished that, and came back with a proposal that Eisenhower be considered by the Democrats. As an alternative, he said Democratic Senator Richard Russell of Georgia, also would be welcome to Texas members of the party.

The situation then developing had a long background. It had begun in 1944, when conservatives, headed by State Democratic Chairman George Butler, picked a delegation pledged against a fourth term for President Roosevelt, and named electors instructed not to vote for Roosevelt even if he won the nomination. Former Governor Dan Moody had headed that group, but loyalist-liberals—under the leadership of Herman Jones, Mrs. Alfred Taylor and Mayor Tom Miller, all of Austin—named a rival delegation bound to support Roosevelt. At the national convention, the issue was settled by splitting the votes.

They returned to Texas to fight over the September convention, and the Roosevelt group won. They selected electors who would vote for Roosevelt. The conservatives set up a third party, the Texas Regulars, with uninstructed electors, but accomplished little. In 1944, Roosevelt got 821,605 votes to Thomas E. Dewey's 191,425 and the Regulars polled 135,439.

In 1948, the loyalists, led by former State Democratic Chairman Harry L. Seay of Dallas, controlled the party machinery in a coalition with Lyndon B. Johnson's forces. They formalized the "party loyalty" issue into party law, and the fall convention adopted a requirement that all party officers and participants in conventions take a loyalty pledge. That purged some precinct chairmen where county chairmen enforced the rule, and the next year, after the Supreme Court upheld the rule, it was enforced widely.

The Texas Regular leaders of 1944, including Democratic National Committeeman Wright Morrow, in 1948 joined the State Rights Party and supported Governor Strom Thurmond of South Carolina against Truman. The third party this time did even worse, getting only 106,909 to Dewey's 282,240 and Truman's 750,700.

Shivers had stayed out of the intra-party fights while lieutenant governor. He represented Texas at Truman's inauguration and was considered a loyalist. When he became governor in 1949 he declined to enter a coalition with Arch Rowan of Fort Worth, Lamar Fleming,Jr., of Houston and other leaders of third party movements. He replaced many of the 1948 loyalists on the State Democratic Executive Committee in 1950, however, explaining he wanted his own friends on his committee.

The loyalist movement got a shot in the arm, though, when Senator Keith Kelly of Fort Worth introduced a bill in the 1951 legislative session to permit cross-filing, or nomination of the same candidates by two parties. What it really meant, of course, was that Republicans, who did not then have to hold a primary, could nominate the winners of the Democratic primaries and thus present a ticket identical with the Democrats, except for the president and vice-president.

Then U.S. Senator Karl Mundt, a South Dakota Republican leader, proposed that Southern Democrats join with his party in nomination of a ticket acceptable to Southern conservatives. Mundt suggested any combination of General Dwight Eisenhower, Senator Harry Byrd of Virginia, Senator Richard Russell of Georgia and Senator Robert Taft of Ohio. He proposed an extension of the technique that had been tried in Texas in 1944 by instructing Democratic presidential electors against Democratic nominees. As alternatives, he advocated nomination of Republican candidates by a Jeffersonian Democratic Party and the cross-filing plan. In an interview, Mundt mentioned that Shivers had signed into law a bill to permit cross-filing. And he said Texas would be a key in the coalition idea.

"I have not been approached by anyone on this sort of alliance," Shivers reponded. "And I have not authorized anyone to say I favored it."

Shivers denied having pushed the cross-filing bill as Mundt had said, and was generally noncommittal about it. But the talk stirred the suspicions of the Roosevelt-Truman Democrats. They remembered the 1944 attempt to do just what Mundt was proposing—fix it so there would be no way to vote for the Democratic ticket. Seay called a meeting in October in the name of the Volunteer Democratic Committee with Austin's Mayor Miller presiding. The 300 who attended condemned the Mundt plan and organized the Loyal Democrats of Texas, with Walter G. Hall, Dickinson banker, as chairman.

The loyalist band was not originated to fight Shivers, but when he began to get more outspoken against Truman, it turned in that direction. Hall said the governor was being used as a stalking horse by the forces which had taken over the 1944 delegation to that national convention. The break became clean on Dec. 7, when Shivers met in his office with third-party leaders Rowan and Fleming; J.E. Price of Houston; Tom Sealy of Midland and former Senator Clint Small, Sr., of Austin, all of whom had leanings toward the Mundt plan. After the meeting, Shivers made clear his views.

"If we say we're going to support the nominees—no matter who they are—we might as well send a letter to the convention instead of a delegation," he snorted.

That brought the Loyal Democrats of Texas into fast action. Fagan Dickson of Austin, a former legislator and first assistant attorney general, was named executive director. He began organizational work to capture the precinct conventions on the issue of party loyalty. He and Hall contended the loyalty pledge imposed by the 1948 convention still was in effect.

Meanwhile, Shivers got busy on the job he knew was necessary for any route he took. He put Weldon Hart to work on a booklet telling inexperienced voters how to organize—and win—a precinct convention. Shivers expressed confidence in the citizens' committee which during the Legislative Interim had rewritten the election code adopted in 1951 and in doing so made it possible for Democrats and Republicans to nominate the same candidates if the candidates were willing.

"There's only one thing which might cause trouble [in the code] and it won't if we work," Shivers said. "The law says any qualified voter can go into a convention—it doesn't say how long he can stay there."

The governor by that time had gotten more specific about his views, saying he not only would oppose Truman or anyone hand-picked by him but would want to "take a long look" at anyone named by the national convention.

"Let's see who it is and what he stands for before pledging support for the ticket," he counseled. "Let's come home from the convention and get instructions from Texas Democrats."

The Loyalists continued their campaign, declaring themselves interested only in the party support issue and disclaiming any interest in running someone against Shivers. However, Dickson indicated more than casual interest in the race when he called public attention to Shivers' trip to one of the governors' conferences in an airplane owned by Arch Rowan.

And Dickson, working on the "birds of a feather" theme, noted that Rowan had been a presidential elector on the Texas Regular ticket in 1944 and a member of the States Rights Party in 1948. He also noted that Wright Morrow of Houston, then Democratic National committeeman, had been a Texas Regular and a States Righter. Dickson tossed out the possibility that Democrats from twelve Southern states might form a third party if unsuccessful in getting nominees of their choice. That group then could align with Republicans in Washington and throw the election into the House of Representatives, he warned.

For the most part, Shivers ignored the critics except for an occasional needling inquiry about where their loyalty lay. He repeatedly said his followers were loyal to "the free and independent Democratic Party of Texas." It was on this predicate that he made one of the turning-point speeches of the year at a State Democratic Executive Committee meeting in New Braunfels in April.

The Committee had met to perfect plans for the May 27 convention in San Antonio, and specifically to act on the pledge requirement at precinct conventions. Dickson and John Cofer of Austin had submitted a legal brief contending that the Texas Supreme Court had held that the pledge was authorized by state law, and was required by party law adopted by the 1948 convention. Senator Kelly submitted a brief maintaining that the election law revisions of 1951 had been intended to repeal the right of a party to require loyalty pledges. After a strong and blistering speech, Shivers was able to get the Committee to declare the 1948 pledge requirement invalid.

Calling the opposition "self-appointed and self-serving serfs of a corrupt national political machine," he said they were seeking under their self-styled label of loyalty to "prostitute the power and pillage the opportunity of our Texas Democratic Party to aid in

ANTI-NEW DEALITIS

Courtesy, THE HOUSTON CHRONICLE

recapturing and redeeming the National Democratic Party from left-wing domination and machine control."

Shivers had nothing but scorn for the suggestion that loyalty demands what he called "an abject, contemptible and unconditional surrender in advance to the whims or the dictates of any absentee overlords of the national party." He reminded the anti-Truman forces that the Democratic Party in Texas nurtured the "still, small light of the party of Jefferson and Jackson for 50 years during which it was extinguished in darkness in the North and East." He said Texans "do not need to go—hat in hand—to anybody's back door to make a blind trade of their heritage for a handout."

Listing his own bill of rights, Shivers said Texans should demand that the party nominees unqualifiedly pledge the restoration of the "confiscated" tidelands to Texas and other tideland states. The Texas party also should oppose a compulsory Fair Employment Practices Code and insist that "sound and lasting progress down the paths of Christian brotherhood and enlightened understanding" be the policy on the issue of race relations.

As a model of what should be in the national platform, Shivers called for an end to "creeping socialism," a reduction in non-essential, non-defense spending by the Federal government, the cleansing of government payrolls of communist infiltration and subversive influence, and a spiritual reawakening "leading to a moral regeneration of government."

Shivers called again for a delegation with no instruction as to the presidential nominee and free to vote as it should see fit. He also suggested the framework under which the Texas delegation could return and report to the state party in the event nominees or platform were not acceptable—advising that delegates come home and confer with party leaders and submit the question of support to a referendum or other special procedure.

Walter Hall of Dickinson, who held his wife's proxy on the committee, had carried the Loyalists cause at the New Braunfels meeting. He pledged that if Shivers would pledge to support the party nominees, he and Dickson would withdraw from convention opposition to Shivers. But Shivers' speech was so strongly against the idea of supporting the nominee without reservations, that there was no ground for compromise.

Shivers' speech at New Braunfels committed the Loyalists to their course. They had had assurances from President Truman to Maury Maverick, Sr., that if the 1948 loyalty pledge was broken by the Texas Democratic convention, the pledge-breakers would not be seated at the Chicago convention.

Recognizing the power of Shivers' appeal, the Loyal Democrats came up with a pattern for their battle plan. Where they could not win precinct conventions, they would set up rump conventions made up of those who would abide by the 1948 rule of pledges to support the party nominees—no matter who they were.

With Dickson declaring that any who refused to take a pledge would be putting themselves out of the party, the Loyalists recommended that if majorities refused to take pledges at the May 3 precinct conventions, the Loyalists would have separate meetings of those who were willing.

Dickson told how to perfect records at rump conventions at precinct and county levels and promised that "The Loyal Democrats will help you out from there on." He said the New Braunfels decision that a pledge could not be imposed was a nullity.

Shivers' reply was that "they don't want majority rule."

It was during all this brawling that the Shivers camp and the loyalists found something on which they could agree. Shivers said he opposed the Mundt plan for an alliance of Southern Democrats and Northern Republicans. Neither side could agree with Mundt's roundabout and far-fetched plan for fighting the "drift toward socialism."

At the May state convention in San Antonio, they agreed on nothing—not even the temporary roll. The state committee submitted its report on organization of the convention, and Maury Maverick, Sr. of San Antonio, former congressman from that city, offered a minority report immediately. It stipulated that no delegate could be seated unless he pledged to support the national ticket. State Chairman J.E. Wheat ruled that report out of order, and Maverick called for his long-scheduled bolt. The Loyalists trudged through the rain to La Villita, a replica of an early-day Mexican village, where there were no adequate facilities for a convention and many had to stand in the rain.

Nevertheless, each convention went through all the motions, adopting resolutions and naming delegates to the national session. Then they settled down to campaigning with friends in delegations from other states, hopeful of backing when the certain fight on seating came up in Chicago.

Also during this period came the Republican intra-party fight between backers of Senator Robert A. Taft and Eisenhower. Such a wave of protests grew out of the GOP convention in Mineral Wells— where Taft supporters ruled in the customary winner-take-all manner—that it got national attention.

And another National Governors' Conference entered the picture, this one in Houston. Republican governors signed a mass "fair play" protest resolution and sent it to their upcoming national convention. It called for barring any contested delegation (such as the Texas group) from voting on its own seating in the convention. Eisenhower got a tremendous boost out of the resulting activity at the convention, also in Chicago, and may have won his race through the fight that began in Mineral Wells.

Shivers in the meantime was conducting his re-nomination campaign against Ralph W. Yarborough and Mrs. Allene M. Traylor of San Antonio, the latter not a factor in the race and Yarborough almost an accidental candidate.

Earlier in the year Yarborough commented to Stuart Long, Austin news writer, that Shivers had just about dried up all the financial help by getting commitments for John Ben Shepperd in the attorney general's race—the one Yarborough wanted to enter. Long asked why, if he was forced to fight Shivers, he didn't run against him instead. "That's funny. That's what Bill Kittrell said," Yarborough retorted. Kittrell, a Dallas lobbyist and close friend of Rayburn, was active in liberal and loyalist affairs.

Loyalists became quickly attached to Yarborough, and gave him something more than token aid just because he was running against Shivers. Labor was in pretty much the same position.

Either Shivers thought the election was in the bag or he considered the national fight more important. At any rate, he left in the heat of the campaign to go to Chicago on July 17, nine days before the primary election. It turned out he had not risked much. He won the Democratic primary with 833,861 votes to 488,345 for Yarborough and 34,186 for Mrs. Traylor—eliminating any need for a run-off and giving Shivers a free hand for the fall campaign.

At Chicago the pre-convention scuffling was rowdy. Maverick charged that the Shivers delegation had no intention of supporting the party nominee and only wanted the prestige that goes with speaking for the party. In reply, Shivers said the Loyalists had no more than a sprinkling of votes and had pre-arranged bolts at every stage of the convention process because they knew they could not muster a majority.

Using a term that had come to be associated with gift-taking by leaders in the Truman Administration, Shivers called the Loyalists "five per centers." He said they had no more voice than that, and did not want majority rule because they knew it would not involve them.

The credentials committee, headed by Calvin Rawlings of Utah, went along with the Shivers group, and recommended that they be seated, 36-13. When the convention got down to approving a roll, the minority report was presented by William Proxmire of Wisconsin, who became senator from that state a short time later. It advocated seating Maverick's group.

Shivers, in an emotional appeal to the convention, asked the delegates "in fairness, honesty and decency," to give the majority of Texas Democrats "their bill-of-rights guarantee of the privilege to speak their minds."

Maverick claimed the seats in Chicago for his delegation on the grounds that Shivers planned to oppose the national ticket unless the party "subscribes and binds itself to the sectional view of their group." He also reviewed the history of Texas politics since President Roosevelt's third-term campaign, saying there had been Texas Regulars, Dixiecrats, State Rights Democrats, and "now Shivercrats."

Maverick, whose family name had become a generic term for unbranded cattle, had coined the term "gobbledygook", to apply to bureaucratic double-talk. He may have also coined the term "Shivercrat". Which may live in American politics as long as "gobbledygook."

But in a series of frantic meetings (including one of three hours' duration) with representatives of all presidential candidates, the Rules Committee headed by Senator Blair Moody of Michigan worked out a compromise. The southern delegations being contested would be seated, if they would subscribe to this language:

"No delegate shall be seated unless he shall give assurance to the Credentials Committee that he will exert every honorable means available to him, in an official capacity that he may have, to provide that the nominees of the convention for President and Vice President, through their names or those of electors pledged to them, appear on the election ballot under the heading, name or designation of the Democratic Party."

When that temporary rule had been adopted, the Credentials Committee report was brought to the floor, with a minority report favoring the seating of the Maverick delegation. Governor Gordon Browning of Tennessee asked for the right to ask Governor Shivers a question about whether his delegation had signed the assurance "without any reservations."

"It did that, Governor Browning, and filed it with the Credentials Committee last evening," Shivers replied, as a nation-wide TV and radio audience listened.

"Without any reservations?" Browning repeated.

"And without any reservations," Shivers replied.

The vote then came on the minority report, and it was turned down by voice vote. National Committeeman Morrow at first called for a roll call vote, but then withdrew the request. The majority report was then adopted, and the Shivers delegation was seated. They remained in the convention, voting the 52 Texas votes for Senator Richard Russell on each of the three roll calls needed for Governor Stevenson to become the party's nominee.

Then Shivers went home to get the thinking of fellow Texans on Stevenson's nomination, as he had promised. But first, he wanted to get the facts, first hand.

Attorney General Price Daniel prepared a brief on the Texas claim to the tidelands, which Shivers sent to Stevenson. It was that August that the governors of Texas and Illinois had their historic meetings in Springfield.

Shivers had talked with the presidential nominee briefly about the tidelands question in Chicago after the convention closed. They talked about a future conference where they would have more time and Stevenson would be able to study the issue more closely. Stevenson suggested they meet in Springfield, and Shivers agreed to arrange a time suitable to both.

So, in August, he flew to Springfield with a brief on Texas claims to the tidelands under the terms on which the Republic of Texas was admitted to the Union. He explained that the Congress in 1845 didn't like the prospects of taking over Texas' public debt, so it voted to let Texas retain both its debts and its public lands. That included the three marine leagues (10.5 miles) into the Gulf of Mexico—and no one then could know that in a little more than a century there would be oil discovered under the tidelands; and, more importantly, ways to recover it.

The two governors had lunch, after which Stevenson asked for time to study the question and, Shivers later learned, to re-read briefs prepared by federal attorneys.

"I went back late that afternoon," he said, "and he told me he would veto a bill restoring Texas' title—just as President Truman had done on two occasions. I asked him to put that in writing, and he did, in a hand-written note."

(The note was to be one of Shivers' treasured possessions two years later as he explained during his third-term campaign why he refused to support the Democratic nominee in 1952.)

It was near dark when Shivers left Stevenson's office, and he was met by newsmen who had been waiting most of the eight hours since the extended talks began.

"I told them just what I had told him—that I couldn't support him because of his stand."

Stevenson told the same newsmen that if he were in Shivers'

shoes he probably would feel the same way and probably would make the same statement. With equal candor, Shivers said he probably would have done as Stevenson did, given the same circumstances.

Shivers returned to Texas and made a radio report on his conversation with Stevenson. He asked for advice on what to do, pointing out that the impending state party convention in Amarillo could do as it pleased in the matter. The Pied Piper was testing his horn.

Rayburn got free radio time to respond to Shivers. He declared that if Shivers and Daniel had gone along with the tidelands compromise he and Truman had agreed on in 1949, Texas would have shared in revenues from the whole 18,000,000 acres of the outer Continental Shelf, instead of just the 3,000,000 acres inside the three league limit.

Shivers said he was waiting for the action of the State Democratic Convention, and there was a time at Amarillo when it looked as though the view of Arch Rowan, Lamar Fleming, Jr., and others would prevail, to put Eisenhower and Nixon on the ballot at the head of the Democratic ticket. But Shivers, true to the pledge he had taken at the national convention in July, took the floor to oppose that resolution, and with the help of delegations held by the Loyal Democrats of Texas, it was defeated. Price Daniel told the convention he would like to see it done, but had concluded it was not legal. However, the convention did pass a resolution urging all Texas Democrats to vote for Eisenhower for the tidelands' sake.

A dissident group of conservatives met the next day in Dallas; ten of them formed the "Texas Democratic Party" and filed a ticket for the ballot, headed by Eisenhower and Nixon and made up of the rest of the Democratic nominees.

But a group of thirteen lawyers headed by John Cofer and Fagan Dickson brought suit, and the Supreme Court held that ten men meeting in a law office couldn't form a political party under Texas law.

So the campaign began, with Stevenson and Senator John Sparkman at the head of the Democratic ticket. But the model ballot sent out to the counties by the secretary of state had a gap to provide room for write-ins of Eisenhower and Nixon in the Democratic column, for those Democrats who just couldn't bear to vote Republican. Attorney General Daniel, in all sympathy, held that ballots so written in should be counted.

And to make correlation of the campaign for Eisenhower simpler, the Democrats chose Wallace Savage of Dallas as state

Governor Shivers: Texas in Revolt

Courtesy of Newsweek Magazine

The Shivers-led revolt against a Democratic ticket headed by Adlai Stevenson got national attention, as this cover page of *Newsweek* magazine illustrates. It came at the height of the Texas campaign and influenced the outcome there as well as in other states.

Democratic chairman. His law partner, Alvin Lane, was state Republican chairman.

Shivers, arranging for his big coup, was like a maestro conducting a symphony. And it worked.

Two close allies, Tom Sealy and Claud Gilmer, went to work almost as soon as the Amarillo convention adjourned. With the help of Hart and Van Cronkhite, who had quit state posts for the year-long campaigns, Sealy and Gilmer put together the Democrats for Eisenhower organization.

Shivers officially took no part in the Democrats for Eisenhower during its formative stages. He still had not made up his mind about voting Republican. For an officeholder, he said, it was a decision that had to be weighed very carefully.

Then in his words: "I finally came to the conclusion that I couldn't *fail* to vote.

"Certainly the governor ought to vote, and I had said I was not going to vote for Stevenson. And if I was not going to vote for him there was only one other person to vote for, and that was Eisenhower, and then if I was going to vote for him I should announce publicly that I would vote for him. And if I was going to vote for him, I might as well support him." And that he did, telling the voters all over the state it was a time "when principles must prevail over party, and the best interest of our nation above all else."

Declaring he first had hoped that Stevenson would "clean up the mess in Washington," he said it had become apparent that "Stevensonism would be nothing more than Trumanism with a Harvard accent." Specifically, he said it would mean retention of the doctrine of paramount rights under which Truman claimed Texas' tidelands. He called it a dangerous doctrine and a brazen action upon which Stevenson already had placed his stamp of approval.

Shivers campaigned exclusively for Eisenhower (Shivers was unopposed in the general election, having been cross-filed by Republicans), and Rayburn worked just as hard for Stevenson. Both candidates came to Texas, and both spoke in storied San Antonio.

Shivers made capital of the fact that Democrats sent seven senators into the state to help Stevenson and six of them had voted against Texas on the tidelands bill.

The Texas governor coined two phrases during the campaign that were picked up by Eisenhower—that it was a "year of decision" and that each voter should "caucus with his conscience." Introducing Eisenhower at San Antonio, Shivers said that 20 years earlier Franklin D. Roosevelt had come on the scene to lead the nation out of economic wilderness. And, he added, the same FDR called on Eisenhower ten years later to lead the nation out of military wilderness.

Stevenson made one statement in Texas which Shivers called "double dealing." He said he was surprised that Stevenson would castigate Texas Democrats for supporting "Ike," yet would say that Senator Wayne Morse, Oregon Republican, was putting principle above party by saying he would support Stevenson.

Shivers got what probably was his biggest pleasure out of the campaign when he discovered that a dismissed "5 per center" had been working in the Texas Democratic campaign headquarters. He said Colonel Lawrence Westbrook of San Angelo, former assistant chairman of the Democratic National Committee, had been "Mr. Sam's [Rayburn's] right-hand man."

Calling him the "biggest 5 per center of them all," Shivers said Westbrook was dismissed for assertedly negotiating a government contract while employed by the National Committee. Shivers said the fee, reportedly $450,000 for three persons, was "a darned good one."

The finding probably did not affect the outcome, for it had been determined before that final week of the campaign, but it gave Shivers a good closing note.

The general election satisfied him immeasurably. He had not had any doubts that Eisenhower could carry the state. The trend was unmistakable in the closing days of the campaign.

All that really bothered the governor was the cross-filing by Republicans of Democratic nominees in all races except that of Agriculture Commissioner John White, who declined the Republican nomination, as did many county officials who were offered cross-filing.

The final canvass removed all questions. Every Democrat who had been cross-filed won his race. Shivers himself posted 1,375,547 votes as a Democrat and 468,319 votes in the Republican column. He led on the Republican ticket in Dallas County. However, the Eisenhower-Stevenson vote was 1,102,878 to 969,228, so some 160,000 voted only for president.

And so, for the first time in history, a Democratic convention had endorsed a Republican candidate for president, and had helped carry the state for the Republican national ticket.

The Pied Piper of Texas Politics had put his mark on Texas history. He felt that since the National Democratic Party had failed to pay its just debts to Texas, he was justified in leading the voters into the Republican mountain.

Photo courtesy of Shivers Museum Collection

General Dwight D. Eisenhower, accompanied by Governor Allan Shivers, laying a wreath at the Alamo during the strenuous 1952 campaign in which Shivers led Texas Democrats into the Republican column and helped elect Eisenhower to his first term as President.

Photo Courtesy of the Shivers Museum Collection.

Personal friendship, politics and the visits a governor must make
were melded at this civic club luncheon in mid 1952. Robert B. Anderson, at left, is shown with Shivers in the heat of the governor's
re-election bid and his drive to elect Republican Presidential
Nominee Eisenhower with Democratic votes. Later he recommended Anderson for the Navy secretary job Shivers turned down. Anderson later became Secretary of the Treasury.

Chapter 14

Teachers' Pets and More Roads

With the 1952 election out of the way and Shivers' greatest political victory assured, thoughts turned to the legislative session of 1953 for which several arrangements had been made. Some were intentional and some were accidental.

Top leadership of Shivers' opposition of 1951 had been eliminated from the Legislature. Representative Sewell of Blooming Grove, just out of law school and needing a paying job, had accepted appointment as county judge of Navarro County when Judge J.D. Huffstutler was offered a better job in Tyler and resigned. Sewell had been the down-the-line leader of the rural roads bloc in the House, despite his blindness. Redistricting had put Representative D.B. Hardeman of Denison in a flotorial district with Cooke County, and he had been defeated in the primary.

Redistricting also had done away with Senator Nokes of Corsicana. He had been put in a district with Senator William T. Moore of Bryan and, like Sewell, Nokes needed to find paying work, so he did not run again in 1952. And Representative Bill Daniel of Liberty, brother of Attorney General Daniel and the liberals' candidate against Speaker Senterfitt, was badly injured in a fall from a horse and felt he had to withdraw from the speakership race.

This assured that Shivers' speaker, Senterfitt, would win a second term without opposition.

Shivers was asked later whether he had anything to do with the creation of the vacancy in the county judgeship to get Sewell out of the Legislature, and with the legislative redistricting which eliminated Nokes and Hardeman.

"You remind me of what the old Baptist lady said to the preacher," Shivers said, laughing. "When he preached against sin, and drinking and dancing, she nodded her head and said, 'amen.' But when he came out against snuff-dipping, she bristled right up and said, 'Preacher, you've quit preaching and gone to meddling.' "

Special-interest organizations were getting their legislative ducks in a row for the session. Highway Commission Chairman Thornton and the Good Roads Association had put on an extensive "educational" campaign with business groups, seeking $100 million more for the primary road system. He and Shivers met with Mayor Armistead Rust of San Angelo, president of the League of Municipalities, and County Judge Ned Price of Tyler, president-to-be of the County Judges and Commissioners Association, trying to develop a unified approach to highway legislation. The judges and commissioners had taken the attitude that, like Greta Garbo, they just wanted to be left alone in 1953, with what programs they had.

This action came despite a speech to their convention by State Highway Engineer DeWitt C. Greer on the need for more state highway money, and after a speech by Representative Briscoe, opposing any increase in the gasoline sales tax of four cents a gallon.

District Judge Jack Roberts of Austin held the Sewell-Nokes gas-gathering tax invalid, after pipeline companies had paid it under protest, and thus tied up the $12,000,000 a year it was supposed to produce. Attorney General Daniel had argued the State's appeal from Roberts' ruling in the Third Court of Civil Appeals in December, so the final decision was to be a question mark across the coming legislative session and its fiscal problems. It was also to be a technique for offering a partial solution to what was to be the biggest issue of the session—teacher pay increases.

The State Teachers Association had elected former Senator Bob Proffer of Denton as its president, and had come out for pay increases from the scale which had the beginning teacher with a bachelor's degree starting at $2,403 a year. The TSTA was asking for $3,000 starting pay, with regular increments for experience and added education. It was estimated to cost $34,000,000 a year. Shivers gave it a generalized endorsement after the teachers' convention at Thanksgiving.

Shivers, who had continued to gain in know-how on executive dealings with legislators, was thus ready to begin the session when he got back from trips to Mexico City, Chicago, and Wichita, Kan., in time for the traditional Senate duck hunt arranged by Jefferson County industries for the Senate, with the local senator as the nominal host. These had been started while Shivers was senator, and had become a traditional December opportunity for senators, the lieutenant governor and the governor to get together and discuss things over a drink after the hunting was done.

Back in Austin, where lawyer Ed Clark was making arrangements for a full-scale inauguration, Shivers played host when Charles E. Wilson, who was to be Eisenhower's secretary of defense, flew to Bergstrom Air Force Base and met with Shivers. What they talked about was a big mystery. Some newsmen speculated that Shivers was to be offered a sub-cabinet place as Secretary of Air. Others thought he might be made ambassador to Mexico.

What really happened was that Wilson offered him the job as Secretary of Navy. Shivers declined it, saying he didn't want a Federal job, and suggested Robert Anderson of Vernon, manager of the Waggoner Ranch and chairman of the State Board of Education. Anderson had been president of the Texas Mid-Continent Oil and Gas Association, and, since the Navy holds considerable oil resources, Shivers felt he would be well qualified. The offer was made. Anderson came to Austin to talk to Shivers about it, and accepted. It moved Anderson into the national arena.

January 1 was coming up, and Shivers recouped on a bet he had lost to Governor Gordon Browning of Tennessee in 1951. That year Shivers lost the Brazos River when Tennessee beat Texas in the Cotton Bowl, 20-14. But this time he bet the Alamo and Maury Maverick, Sr. (hedging his bet a bit because he wanted to lose Maverick) against the Brazos River and Silliman Evans, a Texan-turned-Tennesseean. Texas came through, 16-0 over Tennessee, so Shivers won back the Brazos, but didn't get rid of Maverick.

(In Washington, Congress organized with a Republican majority, and two Texans, Sam Rayburn and Lyndon B. Johnson, became minority leaders instead of speaker and majority leader.)

As legislators, new and old, began gathering for the opening of the session, Shivers decided to take the initiative on the school financing problem. Stressing his belief in more local responsibility, he proposed that the 1949 Gilmer-Aikin formula (by which local districts paid a flat $45,000,000 and the State the rest of the Minimum Foundation Program) be revised to a 75 per cent State, 25 per cent local basis. Growth of school enrollments was increasing total costs each year, and Shivers could see the State portion zooming steadily throughout all time. In the 1951-52 school year, the State had paid 79 per cent and local districts 21 per cent. He wanted it frozen at 75-25. He also proposed that $15,800,000 of the taxes then going into the Available School Fund be put instead into the General Revenue Fund, to thus reduce the amount being allocated to the school districts on the basis of the head-count of children of school age. This, Shivers explained, would free more money for allocation to school districts on the basis of need under the Minimum Foundation Program, money which was going in part to rich districts which didn't need it. In fact, he maintained that this fund switch would make oil-rich districts pick up $20,000,000 more of their own costs. And finally, Shivers proposed that the teachers settle for less than the $600-a-year increase they sought.

Charles H. Tennyson, executive secretary and lobbyist for the State Teachers' Association, said Shivers' formula would provide less than half the $600-a-year increase. The battle was on.

In his message to the Legislature, Governor Shivers suggested that the rural road program be left as it was, just as the County Judges and Commissioners Association had asked. But he proposed that the gasoline sales tax be raised from 4 to 5 cents a gallon to provide $20,000,000 a year at the start, toward the $100,000,000 the Good Roads Association wanted for primary highways. Out of the $28,500,000 anticipated surplus in the General Revenue Fund, Shivers urged emergency appropriation of $6,725,000 for new tuberculosis hospitals at Harlingen and San Antonio, for which Federal Hill-Burton construction aid funds had already been allocated by the State Board of Health. He asked for cost-of-living pay raises for state workers, the creation of a Texas Toll Roads Authority to build a Fort Worth-Dallas toll road and possibly others, for a tax on water use to help finance reservoir construction, and for reorganization of the new Board for State Hospitals and Special Schools to make a medical man the top administrator. The board had had continued trouble keeping doctors because it felt the top man should be a businessman, not a medical man.

Shivers also recommended a building program for the School for the Deaf, M.D. Anderson Hospital, the University of Texas medical and dental branches, and (in his budget, the first ever to be submitted directly by a governor) a start on a system of state parole supervision, improvements to state parks and other improvements. The rival budget, that of the Legislative Budget Board, proposed spending $4,500,000 less than Shivers' did.

At the formal inaugural address preceding the festivities, Shivers suggested modernization of state government on a piecemeal basis, suggesting that small policy-making boards with a full-time executive director seem to work better than large boards.

Observers could see him comparing the highly efficient Highway Department, with its three part-paid commissioners, to the nine-member, unpaid hospital board which seemed to be continually in a stew.

Arrangements were being made to keep the House under better control, too. Speaker Senterfitt was ready with a rules revision requiring six days' written notice of a motion to re-refer a bill from one committee to another. The many new members, plus careful organization of the conservatives, made it possible to get this rule adopted and thus handcuff the anti-administration forces in the House. It was the start of a process of giving more and more power to the speaker that culminated in the 1971 Gus Mutscher affair.

Representative Joe Kilgore of McAllen introduced the Shivers school finance plan, modified a bit. It would have provided a $240 pay raise for teachers instead of $600; Tennyson sent out a message to the teachers that the fight was going to be rough, the understatement of the year. Shivers started releasing a series of newspaper articles explaining his side of the argument, and why he thought local control should be preserved by having local school taxpayers provide a larger share of the money. Tennyson hired Jimmy Banks away from The Dallas Morning News to be his ghost writer, in order to counter Weldon Hart's efforts on the other side. Tennyson's articles began to appear. The battle for the public's mind was on.

But there were other things for the busy governor to do. He called in all the sixteen state college and university presidents to work them over because they had not come up with a plan for "coordinating" the higher education system to eliminate as much duplication of special fields of work as possible, and thus economize on higher education. He had suggested in 1951 that this be done, but it hadn't been done voluntarily. He threatened to set up a high-level board. The presidents set up a 16-member Higher Education Study Committee, which was to recommend in short order that a 41-member committee be set up with a $200,000 appropriation to study the need for coordinating higher education.

When Senator A.M. Aikin, Jr., of Paris finally called the hearing in his Senate Education Committee on the full $600 teacher pay raise, some 2,000 school people and Parent-Teacher Association members packed the Senate and its galleries and halls.

The committee heard the testimony, and reported the bill favorably. Senators knew that they, and Shivers, probably were not going to finance such a program, but they were engaged in the old game of "putting the monkey on the other House." The bill could not be acted on under Joint Rule 9b until the major appropriations had been acted on by both houses, so Aikin let it sit on the Senate calendar for a time.

Meanwhile, the single general appropriations bill, being used for

the first time instead of the four-bill system of the past, was put
together by the Senate Finance and House Appropriations Committees. The first break in the hold-the-line idea on new spending
came when the House voted 86-49 to increase the allocations to
junior colleges by $1,400,000 a year. That may have been inspired,
in part, by the Third Court of Civil Appeals' opinion by Associate
Justice Robert G. Hughes holding the Sewell-Nokes gas pipeline tax
constitutional, overturning the lower court.

That same, week, Shivers flew to Chicago to speak at a Chicago
Club lucheon given by two men with military titles, General Robert
Wood of Sears Roebuck and Colonel Robert McCormick of the
Chicago Tribune. They were looking over this precedent-breaker
who had led Texas out of the Democratic Party. Talk started at that
luncheon was to appear in another conservative bastion, the *Saturday Evening Post,* a few months later. It was widely assumed that
President Eisenhower would serve only one term, so the *Post* article
proposed Shivers for president in 1956.

But the governor hurried back. There was work to be done with
the Legislature. Tennyson had turned out another 2,000-teacher
crowd for the House hearing on the Shivers "compromise" plan, in
which Representative Kilgore had raised the pay raise offer from
$240 to $360 a year.

But the State Teachers Association was adamant, and in mid-
April, Shivers told a press conference, after the Senate had passed
the full $600 pay raise: "It's just an empty gesture. Nothing can be
done about it this late."

He said he was not against a pay raise, but with the 120th day of
the session on May 12 drawing near, he thought it best to wind up
the session with no new taxes and no teacher pay raise at all.

He called in Senterfitt and Kilgore to plan the action on the rest of
his program. The eight bills in his water program were moving
slowly. Senator John Bell of Cuero simply was not going to get approval of the plan for a tax on water to provide a guaranty fund for
dam-building bond issues, a proposal which had come out of an interim study committee headed by J.B. Thomas of Fort Worth. The
Shivers proposal for four-year terms for county officials had been
approved, to be voted on in 1954. But it appeared that the opposition
(by Briscoe and others) to the increase in the gasoline sales tax had
killed Thornton's highway program for this session.

Senterfitt went back to the House with a "monkey killer" idea on
the Aikin teacher-pay bill which was being sponsored in the House
by Representative Lamar Zivley of Temple. Since the big appropria-

tions bill had been passed and certified, there was not enough money left for the $34,000,000 needed to finance the pay raise.

Senterfitt jammed the bill through the House, So it went to Comptroller Robert S. Calvert, who certified that the money was not in sight to finance it, and sent it back to the Senate, in effect, vetoed.

Shivers then publicly proposed a compromise. He coupled this offer with an attack on Tennyson for "costing the teachers their pay raise" because of his "arrogant, unyielding attitude." Tennyson fired back that it was a "half-way, maybe-so" pay raise Shivers was offering. Tennyson called a meeting of TSTA leaders, who rejected the Shivers proposal. That ended all efforts for the session on teacher pay.

Shivers and his lieutenants did a lot of week-end work because there was a lot more of his program which was stalled in one House or the other.

Both Lieutenant Governor Ramsey and Speaker Senterfitt were thinking strongly that they would be candidates for governor in 1954, and that Shivers would step aside after his two and three-quarters term, the longest in Texas history.

So Shivers called a press conference to "re-plant the rumor" that he might run for another term, especially if he didn't complete his program in the nine days remaining of the session. Of course, there had to be some more name-calling between Shivers and the teacher bloc during those nine days, but, for all practical purposes, he dropped that subject, and concentrated on other things.

His threat to run again seemed to unify the Senate. Ramsey's friends pitched in to help Shivers' friends pass their bills. The Senate passed eight water bills, everything except the water-tax amendment, and Senterfitt, anxious to show his cooperation, passed six of the water bills on a local and uncontested calendar. From Thursday to Saturday, Shivers was able to raise his tally-card on passage of his program from 25 to 50 per cent, and by adjournment time, he had it up to 75 per cent.

Creation of a statewide toll road authority, which had been bogged down for weeks, sailed through when 20 House votes were switched in a week. This was an important one to Shivers, because it enabled the construction of a badly needed expressway between Fort Worth and Dallas by means of revenue bonds, without tapping the Highway Fund. It also permitted the same method to be used on proposed Dallas-San Antonio and Dallas-Houston toll roads, but they never materialized.

There were major accomplishments in that session of the Legis-

lature. Eleven constitutional amendments were submitted to the
voters, some being important changes in State government. All of
them were approved by the voters in the election Nov. 2, 1954.

They included an increase in the ceiling on public welfare, requiring women to serve on juries, allowing municipal employees to
have social security, a $25-per-day expense allowance for legis-
lators for 120 days of a regular session, permitting the Legislature to
set the salaries of the governor and other constitutional state officers, four-year terms for county officials, allowing teachers and
state employees to interchange their retirement credits between
systems, and the creation of the State Building Commission with a
statewide two cents per $100 property tax to finance state office
buildings.

Shivers considered the water program a major accomplishment.
It reorganized the State Board of Water Engineers into the three-
member board with a chief engineer, modeled after the Highway
Department, and gave it added duties and powers, including planning for water development. It put tighter state control on the use of
surface water, allowed the cancellation of water permits which go
unused for ten years, and created still another study committee on
water laws. The program took the first state step toward water
pollution control by setting up a Water Pollution Advisory Council
to correlate the work of the five state agencies which had power in
that field.

A 40-hour week for state employees became statutory policy in
that session. By appropriations bill rider, the governor was given a
vast new power. He was authorized to move in on any state agency,
and, with the advice of the Legislative Budget Board, require it to
submit quarterly or semi-annual budgets for his approval. Creation
of the Commission on Higher Education to undertake the coordinating role he had envisioned was the first of many efforts
toward that goal, none of them very successful as yet.

The stalemated teacher-pay fight was left hanging as the session
ended. The solution worked out that spring in the press box at
Memorial Stadium by former sports writers Hart and Banks would
not be moved onto the center stage until fall.

Legislators got home to find that in the opinion of many people,
Shivers had won the battle for the public's mind. Most people told
them that the Legislature offered the teachers the $300 pay raise,
and the teachers turned it down.

Shivers said that if the Sewell-Nokes gas tax were upheld, he
would consider calling a special session for financing the needed

state buildings and state employee pay raises. But, still smarting under blasts from Tennyson and H.W. Stilwell, Texarkana superintendent and the TSTA's legislative chairman, he would not say that he would include teacher pay in a special session, even if the money should become available.

Shivers turned to other matters. A serious drought, which was to continue until 1957 in much of West Texas and to spread eastward as well, had created crisis conditions among ranchers particularly. Shivers pressed his Republican friends in Washington for an aid program, already authorized by Congress but needing administrative action. Secretary of Agriculture Ezra Taft Benson came to Texas for a first-hand look at the parched pasturelands. Benson seemed reluctant, so Shivers prevailed on President Eisenhower to come in person, and to meet with a number of Southwestern governors at Amarillo.

Eisenhower promised help, but said the federal government could not do it alone. The federal program was instituted in most of Texas and Oklahoma, and Shivers asked his protege, Attorney General Shepperd, for a ruling on what the State could do. Shepperd produced a 30-page legal opinion, much of it based on the new power given the governor to change agency programs by requiring them to submit quarterly budgets. Shivers put a group of agency task forces to work on programs of drought relief as suggested by Shepperd's opinion, and some of them were put into effect. He also pressured Eisenhower to make Benson soften the pauper's oath required of ranchers to get reduced freight and feed prices for their hungry cattle.

Shivers was also getting his water program moving. Interestingly, he named County Judge Otha Dent of Littlefield, who had headed the County Judges and Commissioners Association in its bitter fight against Shivers in 1951, to the State Board of Water Engineers.

To his Water Resources Committee, he named former Mayor Gene Klein of Amarillo, who had been bitter when Shivers forced "states' rights" amendments onto a bill creating the Canadian River Municipal Water Authority. These amendments conflicted with Federal Bureau of Reclamation policies and law for the construction of Lake Meredith on the Canadian to supply eleven Panhandle and South Plains cities. By giving Klein a hand in recommending state water policy, he gave the committee a point of view it might not have had otherwise.

Shivers had generally sided with those who opposed Bureau of Reclamation projects in Texas, and had helped block the Oakville

Courtesy, THE DALLAS MORNING NEWS

project at Three Rivers, which was to help supply Corpus Christi's future need for water.

And Senator Johnson had just had federal water agencies produce a "mock up" plan for water development in Texas, under the

direction of Harry Burleigh, then area planning engineer for the
bureau, and later, in 1970, to become executive director of the Texas
Water Development Board.

Johnson had been pushing for state action in the water field.
When he released the report urging strong moves to conserve water
when it was available, he asked for state comments so he could go
to Congress with a proposal for studies and action. Shivers, preferring that rivers and dams be developed with local and state agencies, was pushing for action at the state level.

Governor Shivers vacationed in Colorado en route to Seattle for
the National Governors' Conference of which he was chairman.
There he learned that Eisenhower would sign the Continental Shelf
management bill which had passed the Senate, 45-43, with Senator
Johnson voting against it. Attorney General Shepperd urged a veto,
since it would remove state taxation of oil and gas produced from
the federal areas in the Gulf. But Eisenhower signed it anyway.

This was a period of consolidation, and of the education and
negotiation which precede legislation. The State Teachers Association, burning from its defeat by Shivers, announced that because
of low pay, 33,000 Texas children would be in half-day classes that
fall, and many classes were being taught by teachers without
degrees. Thornton renewed his drive for an increase in the gasoline
tax, so Texas would have the added money to match an expanded
Federal-aid program Eisenhower was pushing. Mayor Jim Wright
of Weatherford, president of the League of Texas Municipalities,
was campaigning for a city share of state road money.

And there was a harbinger of things to come. District Judge Harris Gardner ruled that Texas Mutual Insurance Co. of Beaumont
had been organized fraudulently and had never had the $200,000
capital to issue non-assessable policies. This was to become the case
which broke the first of the insurance scandals after Associate
Justice Robert Hughes of the Third Court of Civil Appeals wrote a
blistering opinion when the case came up on appeal.

It was during this time that Shivers took on J. Edgar Hoover of the
FBI. At the governors' conference, there had been complaints that
Hoover's men were coming into state prisons and mental hospitals
to investigate complaints of violations of civil rights, without in-
forming state authorities. Governor Dan Thornton of Colorado was
especially bitter about it.

Speaking off the cuff at the East Texas Peace Officers Association convention, Shivers made a vague reference to FBI agents'
snooping around Texas. Hoover snapped back at him. Shivers told

a press conference that he and other governors were complaining because the FBI investigated state agencies without notifying the governor or the Department of Public Safety, but merely told the head of the institution being investigated.

"There have been a hundred instances of this in Texas institutions," Shivers declared. "And my comments were meek and mild compared to what some other governors are saying about it."

All of this was embarrassing to Maurice Acers, the Shivers aide who had been an FBI agent-in-charge at San Antonio. But there was no way Acers could soothe the irritated feelings of his two friends.

Hoover said there was just 16 investigations in Texas instead of 100, and he turned some national columnists to writing on his side, laying down quite a barrage. One of them published an instruction sheet purportedly from the Communist Party, telling members to use the governor's attacks on Hoover as widely as possible.

Finally, Hoover wrote Shivers a four-page letter which, among other things, charged that Acers had asked the FBI to delay its investigation of Gainesville Training School for Girls until after the primary in 1952. Acers denied this hotly, saying he could substantiate that it was not true.

Acers was well known to have continued to use the FBI technique of recording all phone conversations. Wags suggested a radio "battle of the disc jockeys" between Hoover and Acers, with each producing his recording of the conversation. But since federal regulations then prohibited recordings without a beeper on the line, neither ever did, and the fuss subsided.

It was in August that the teacher pay raise "send it to a committee" idea, worked out by Banks and Hart as they watched spring football training from the press box at Memorial Stadium in Austin, got under way. When Hart and Banks figured it out, there was too much bitterness between Shivers and Tennyson to talk about a peace conference. President Proffer of the TSTA and Shivers met with other TSTA officials and agreed to set up a 25-member study committee with Education Commissioner J.W. Edgar as chairman, and with each side naming twelve people. Shivers named Senator Ottis Lock of Lufkin as his leader on the negotiations. Lock knew when to listen, and when to talk, and had a knack for working things out. The tall, balding Lock had been a school teacher at Zavalla in Angelina County when he first won the Senate seat, so he could speak the language of the opposition. It was he who cooled the situation enough to find a solution both sides could accept.

The agreement led Traxel Stevens, then a Capitol newsman and later editor of the teachers' *Texas Outlook*, to conclude: "The romance between Governor Shivers and the school teachers, which waxed so warm in 1952, has cooled, but they are continuing to appear together in public, for the children's sake."

The 25-member committee of school people, legislators and citizens began meeting Sept. 21, and, true to the custom, appointed a subcommittee to work up a proposal. Tennyson said TSTA would accept any reasonable pay raise offer in order to cure the problem. A check of school openings found 38,000 children in part-time classes, and 75,000 being taught by teachers with no degrees. At Thanksgiving, the TSTA convention went along with the "no set figure" idea on pay raises, and thus cleared away the $600-or-fight stand of the previous convention.

That very hot pot, which had boiled over repeatedly all year, was put on the back burner to simmer.

Photo Courtesy of the Shivers Museum Collection

Probably the happiest of his four inaugurations was that of 1953, coming on top of his first hard campaign and his leadership of Democrats into the Republican presidential column. Here he is shown with wife Marialice and mother, Mrs. R.A. Shivers at right.

Chapter 15

But There Aren't
Any Keys!

The interlude in teacher-pay wrangling found Shivers busy with national affairs—primarily concerned with President Eisenhower.

Eisenhower had appointed Shivers to the Commission on Intergovernmental Relations, a body designed to work out problems of the relations between the federal and state governments. Shivers took an active part on the commission, with an admittedly selfish goal of getting the U.S. to relinquish its motor fuel tax so the states could levy it to bolster their highway programs. That didn't come to pass, of course, but Shivers was trying.

And, on Oct. 19, 1953, Eisenhower was coming to Texas to dedicate Falcon Dam on the Rio Grande. He was to be the Shiverses' house guest at Sharyland, and it was to be a whangdoodle of an affair both because few Texans have ever hosted a president, and because President Adolpho Ruiz Cortines of Mexico was to join Eisenhower for the dedication of the international dam at the precise point of the international boundary—the center of the huge dam.

As Mrs. Shivers prepared the house for receiving the president, she decided that it needed a ninth bathroom for the downstairs bedroom to be occupied by Eisenhower. So she added one. Word around the Capitol was that Senator Johnson was adding a ninth bathroom to his home at the LBJ Ranch, so Shivers wouldn't get ahead of him.

There was one problem. Like so many rural families, the Sharys and the Shiverses never locked their doors. There just were not any keys. They had been lost a generation before.

The Secret Service wanted all locks on the big house changed and all the new keys delivered to them. The Shiverses told them the doors never had been locked and there were no keys; and they thought there was plenty of security, anyway. The agents finally agreed, but increased their personnel. They insisted on interviewing all the help, despite word that most had been born on the property and worked there all their lives.

The President and the Governor gave the Secret Service a hard time on the Sunday afternoon after Eisenhower's arrival. Shivers asked if the president would like to shoot some doves. He knew "Ike" wouldn't have a Texas hunting license but figured he could get by with it.

The president didn't care to shoot doves, but said he had a new rifle which had been given him shortly before and he'd like to try it out. So they drove ten miles to the farm headquarters, with Secret Service cars before and behind them, and got the foreman to take a pickup truck loaded with bales of hay to meet them in a pasture where there were no cattle.

"He and I shot up an entire box cf ammunition, and he turned out to be an excellent rifle shot," Shivers said.

The protocol of the visit, the joint preparation of guest lists by Shivers' staff and that of Jack Porter, Republican national committeeman, the preparation for feeding and housing, and the sheer detail took many hours and days. Mrs. Shivers and Mrs. Shary sailed through it all, having the entire house repainted and redecorated for the occasion. Dawson Duncan of he *Dallas Morning News* scoffed at Washington reporters' stories that Eisenhower would visit on "a ranch near McAllen." It's "a mansion without a cowboy in sight," Duncan wrote, "admist an 800-acre citrus orchard." And besides, he went on, Sharyland adjoins Mission, not McAllen.

The visiting news media representatives were hungry for every detail, and Mrs. Shivers tried to cooperate. She did pretty well on menus until she mentioned that chukars would be served at one meal. Few of the news people knew what kind of bird it was, some not even sure it was a bird; and she had to explain it is an Asian bird similar to the American quail, only larger, and is raised domestically in this country.

Three formal meals were served for the president and staff. The one which made the news had as guests, in addition to the official party and Mr. and Mrs. Shivers and Mrs. Shary, this group of important Texans related to oil: Sid Richardson, Mr. and Mrs. Amon Carter, Sr., Mr. and Mrs. Robert Kleberg of the King Ranch, Mr. and Mrs. Leonard F. McCollum of Continental Oil, Mr. and Mrs. Clint Murchison of Dallas, and Mr. and Mrs. Harvey Baum of New York. (Mrs. Baum was the mother of the hostess who had introduced the Shiverses in 1935.)

If what was published about the meeting was correct, it may have changed Eisenhower's cabinet. Reports were that the Treasury Department was thinking of recommending that the oil and gas depletion allowance be cut from 27.5 to 15 per cent. Texas oil allowables had been cut 340,000 barrels a day because of increasing supplies of foreign oil, and the further threat of a substantial tax increase must have been shocking news for Richardson and the other oilmen at the dinner to hear from President Eisenhower himself.

National oil writers picked up the story and confirmed that a study which could lead to such a recommendation was indeed being made by the Treasury. But it was not long before the problem was corrected. Robert Anderson, who had resigned as Secretary of the Navy to go into private investment banking in New York, was enticed out of retirement at Richardson's suggestion to become Secretary of the Treasury. And there were no such proposals from the Treasury during the years Anderson served as secretary.

President Eisenhower and the Shiverses went to church together that Sunday, and on the way home Shivers directed the driver to take a route which would bring them by a small home. He had received word that the crippled son of a friend of Shivers wanted to see the president, but his mother could not get him to the street where the car was to pass.

"I told the President about this boy, Tommy Robertson, and he told me to have the driver go by their home," Shivers said. "The Secret Service was upset with him, but we went where he said. And when he stopped the car and got out to talk with the boy on his front porch, the Secret Service was even more upset. But for the little boy it was a memory of a lifetime—the President had come to see him."

Shivers likes to remember another human touch which Eisenhower demonstrated on his motorcade ride of about 40 miles through Rio Grande Valley cities. It seems that Jack Porter was riding in the car with Eisenhower, and Shivers was with Sherman Adams, the president's chief of staff, as they passed the many thousands lining the streets and highway. Many of the spectators waved bouquets of flowers, and one woman tossed a rather large one into the car with the president. Porter, thinking it might be an explosive, threw it right back, and in doing so, hit the woman who had thrown it to the president.

Eisenhower was disturbed about the event—and that he didn't get to keep the flowers. He asked Shivers to get the woman's name for him, which Shivers did from the newspapers the next day. A few days later, Shivers got a copy of the president's note of apology to the woman.

A humorous note occurred on the way to the formal dam-dedication ceremony.

Eisenhower and Shivers walked to the Mexican side of the dam to meet President Ruiz Cortines and other Mexican officials. The Mexican president, who had been a friend of Shivers long before his election as president, greeted Shivers with the traditional Mexican *abrazo*, in which men throw their arms around each other and whack each other on the back.

Eisenhower asked the meaning of this activity. Ruiz Cortines explained simply, "He and I both enjoy Dos Equis cerveza." He was referring to their mutual enjoyment of a Mexican beer with a name meaning "Two Xes."

The dam was dedicated by President Eisenhower and President Ruiz Cortines as one designed to end forever the floods which had ravaged the Lower Rio Grande Valley. While there was drought in much of Texas, there had been floods that year on the Rio Grande, and Falcon Reservoir was full. The Treaty of 1944 reserved to the State of Texas, rather than the International Boundary and Water Commission, the right to say when the Texas share of the water was to be released. There was no law permitting the creation of a watermaster, so Shivers designated the Board of Water Engineers to order the releases, when needed for irrigation. It was not until 1971, after long and costly litigation, that the successor agency, the Water Rights Commission, was able to name its own watermaster for the section of the Rio Grande below Falcon. From 1956 until the litigation ended in 1971, a court-appointed watermaster controlled the releases.

It was during this period that jockeying among potential candidates for governor and other offices was at starting-gate tempo. Speaker Senterfitt, Attorney General Shepperd and Lieutenant Governor Ramsey were all being talked of as possible candidates. Former Senator Howard Carney had been working as secretary of state, hoping to follow Ramsey into the Senate presidency. The thinking was that Shivers wouldn't run for a third full term. Senterfitt announced that he wouldn't run for re-election to the House because it was his intention to run for governor, but he hadn't talked with Shivers.

Apparently Shepperd had. In November, he launched a crusade against a union at Port Arthur, claiming it was communist-dominated. Then he handed Shivers the ball, and the governor named an industrial commission to investigate the union. It had hearings, and finally concluded that it could find no communists. But its lawyer members, L.N.D. Wells, Jr., for labor and Martin Harris for management, recommended a carefully drawn communist-control law, which Shivers said he would submit to the coming special session.

Shepperd, obviously getting the inside track, renounced his candidacy for governor and said he would run for another term as attorney general. But it was not until the following April, just before the deadline, that Shivers made it official that he would run again in 1954. Other candidacies were up in the air until then.

"They had threatened me, saying I couldn't win because I had supported Eisenhower," Shivers said. "I decided that they might beat me, but they weren't going to run me off."

Meanwhile, there were other things to get cleared up. Shivers called in 40 of his campaign leaders to get moving on organization for the 1954 Democratic precinct conventions. He assured them that he would retain leadership in the convention, even if he did not run for re-election.

In the fall of 1953, word was that Eisenhower would not run again, and Shivers was taken under consideration by some leading business elements. They "looked him over" by inviting him to speak to the Executive Club in Chicago, the Southern Club in New York and to another executives' club in Pittsburgh. His speeches were scholarly and thoughtful, pressing his view that the states had rights, but also had responsibilities, and some of the functions taken over by the federal government should be returned to the states.

He frankly analyzed his political feelings by asking a question which he admitted he could not answer: "What if the reactionary Old Guard marches the GOP off the road to the right, into the primeval marshes of the Dark Ages—and the Walter Reuther faction hustles the Democratic Party out of bounds on the left? Where, then, will the conservative Democrat or, for that matter, the liberal Republican, find a flag he can follow?"

It was widely assumed that no one could prevail on Eisenhower to run for a second term, so the possibility of Shivers as a presidential candidate in 1956 was taken seriously in high Republican quarters in the 1953-54 period. What he said about the problems of left and right led the *Saturday Evening Post* to propose Shivers as the Republican candidate for president if Eisenhower did not run for a second term.

In the fall of 1953, Shivers realized that Ralph Yarborough had more color, and more following, than either Senterfitt, Ramsey or Shepperd, and that Yarborough probably would win over them. Shivers felt that he was the only one who could defeat Yarborough and the growing liberal-loyalist movement which had now formalized into the Democratic Advisory Committee (DAC) to the Democratic National Committee—a formally organized branch of the national party in Texas. County Judge (formerly Representative) Sewell of Corsicana headed the DAC after he had managed the 1952 Stevenson-Sparkman campaign in Texas.

But Shivers knew that the teacher-pay issue had to be handled, and that was the first order of his 1954 campaign—long before he said publicly that he was going to be a candidate.

Chapter 16

The Lobby Takes
A Tax Plan

Ottis Lock and the teacher-pay subcommittee had labored all fall, and had come up with a proposed compromise. It gave the teachers a $402-a-year pay raise, set the formula for financing the school program at 80 per cent state and 20 per cent local, but gave an additional $100-per-teacher payment to each school district from state funds, to be used for buildings, maintenance or anything else the schools needed. This latter item eased the local cost of the 80-20 formula, which was the one thing Shivers had insisted on.

The full 25-member committee approved it unanimously, so Shivers called special elections to fill legislative vacancies, and said he would call a special session for teacher pay, state employees pay raises, the building program, paid state parole supervisors, and outlawing the Communist Party. Before the session opened March 15, 1954, Senterfitt, hoping to line up conservative support, came out against part of the teacher compromise, and was to wind up vainly advocating a watered-down program which could be financed with no new taxes.

In February, the U.S. Supreme Court held the Sewell-Nokes gas-gathering tax to be an unconstitutional burden on interstate commerce, so the air was cleared for the proposal Shivers made to the special session when it opened:

"At this point it might be the discreet thing for me to say that money raising is the prerogative of the Legislature—and that I don't want to infringe on your prerogative. Perhaps because I served in the Legislature myself, I look at it a little differently. When the governor recommends the spending of money, I think he ought to recommend the means of raising that money. When he puts you on the spot, I think he ought to have the courage to get on it with you."

Shivers could well say that, because he had already worked out a tax plan. On March 8, he called in top executives of oil, gas, sulphur and other businesses for cocktails and dinner at the Governor's Mansion. He preferred to go to the head men, rather than their lobbyists as he had done as a fledgling governor.

The executives had had their meeting in the Austin Hotel earlier, to plan how they were going to stand together, or at least to talk about it over a few drinks. When they got to the Mansion, they had a few more, then a good dinner, and finally they were gathered in the big blue room on the northeast corner of the Mansion.

Shivers presided, of course, calling on Ed Clark to outline the political situation. Clark made it clear that conservative legislators were going to be in trouble with the school folks if something wasn't done about teacher pay. "We are going to lose some of our best men," Clark told them, his San Augustine accent rolling his words for emphasis.

Then Senator Lock outlined the needs in dollars and explained the compromise which would cure the political troubles of the conservative legislators. He might even have threatened the executives with Ralph Yarborough.

Next Shivers went through his tax proposals. "We need a new gas-gathering tax to replace the old one which you pipeline people knocked out," he said. "It is my judgment that we can get by with one which won't cost you more than $14,000,000 a year. Then we need to raise the corporation franchise tax to produce about $9,000,-000 a year. We can get the other $3,000,000 by raising the tax on beer to $2 a barrel. And remember, Representative Joe Pool has a bill to raise the beer tax to $10 a barrel."

Then Shivers called on a couple of executives he had previously primed to endorse the plan. That made it harder for others to object, but everyone there had his chance. Shivers called on them one by one, and got their comments.

One of those there was Harry Jersig, president of the Texas Brewers Institute. Homer Leonard, their lobbyist, had told Shivers that if he put a beer tax increase in the package, he would block the entire tax bill. And he added that he had the votes in the House to do just that. Leonard, a former speaker, did have many friends in the House, and his provision of free beer for candidates' rallies or parties, plus his catfish luncheons every Wednesday, cemented those friendships.

Shivers had called Jersig at San Antonio and said: "Harry, either I'm in trouble or you beer people are in trouble. I'm not going to let Homer block this whole program. I'm not going to let beer be taxed double what we are proposing, but if the brewers fight this little tax increase—their fair share—we're going to have to run over them."

Jersig came to the meeting at the Mansion, agreed to accept beer's "fair share," and while Leonard testified against it in the House Revenue and Taxation Committee, it was just for the record.

And, on the other side of the street, Shivers had to mollify the Women's Christian Temperance Union and the United Texas Drys. They were opposed to having beer pay teachers' salaries, thinking it would lead teachers to laud beer to their students. Shivers called in some of the leaders for a lecture on how the state fund system works. The money would go into the general revenue fund, and would not go directly for teacher pay. So they withdrew their opposition.

"But one of my biggest jobs was to call in businessmen and convince them that spending was necessary," Shivers, the Pied Piper, explained.

Shivers had some other loose ends to tuck in. Attorney General Shepperd was battling George Parr in court actions of all kinds. The Supreme Court removed District Judge Woodrow Laughlin, clearing the way for the court to name retired District Judge A.S. Broadfoot of Bonham to preside over trials and name grand jury commissions in Duval County. Parr was to be made an issue in the coming campaign, and Shepperd was Shivers' Jeb Stuart, harassing the enemy with his legal cavalry. And there was a phone call to make to Senator Lyndon Johnson, assuring him that his re-election bid in 1954 would not be troubled by Shivers in that race.

The Legislature got its hearings under way, and Comptroller Calvert announced happily that he could see a surplus of $11,900,-000 in the General Revenue Fund. This led Senator Jimmy Phillips of Angleton to quip: "That's just enough to finance the Governor's building program of $10,600,000 and hold out a little ray of hope to the boys with those little appropriations that they'll get to pass them if they'll vote down the line with the Program." Late in the session, with filibuster and threats of filibuster, and by an unusual (for Phillips) use of the rules, the Angleton senator was able to block the special appropriations bills for which Shivers had traded votes.

Speaker Senterfitt was balky, so Shivers went personally to the House Revenue and Taxation hearing on the tax bill. When gas pipeline witnesses attacked the new one-half cent per 1,000 cubic feet tax, Shivers sent word to Representative Joe Kilgore, author of the bill, to amend it for an increase in the gas production tax, shifting much of the cost to producers and royalty owners. The bill came out of committee, and despite a speech and a "no" vote against it by

Senterfitt, passed with 90 votes, 30 of them delivered by Shivers from the no-tax voters of the previous year.

The Senate passed all of the spending bills the second week of the session. Ramsey was "using the calendar," the all-but-forgotten system provided by Senate rules to let the majority prevail. Thus, it did not take 21 of the 31 senators to suspend the rules to take up bills out of their regular order.

Ramsey and Shivers had agreed on this technique, because they feared the gas lobby might be able to muster eleven votes and block consideration.

All along, as legislators went to Shivers asking that he open the session to consideration of bills to create courts, regulate fishing or provide more money for junior colleges, Shivers agreed to do so only after "the Program" was passed, and after the supplicant had agreed to vote for the "Program" bills.

One minute after the Senate accepted the minor House amendments to the final Shivers bill, a message from the governor reached the Senate, opening the session to a long list of other subjects.

Before Reading Clerk Carl Hardin, Jr., finished reading the message, 20 senators were standing, waving bills they wanted to introduce as soon as they could get recognized. The Senate pages, junior high school boys, had a busy afternoon carrying bills to Hardin for "first reading" and referral to committee.

And at the press table, reporters looked out the window and saw that it had begun to rain, breaking a long drought in Austin. "Shivers is even controlling the Weather Bureau," one of the reporters said.

A measure of that control was found when Senator Warlow Lane of Center offered an amendment to the gas tax bill, exempting condensate from the tax. Clint Small, Sr., had cleared the amendment with Shivers, but word hadn't reached the Senate yet. Senator A.M. Aikin, Jr., got the amendment tabled. Small, sitting in the gallery, went to the phone booth and called his clients. The calls then came back to the governor's office, and within five minutes Read Granberry, one of Shivers' assistants, glided into the Senate and whispered to Aikin at his front row seat.

Aikin went to the podium and told Ramsey what Shivers wanted. Ramsey recognized Aikin for a motion to reconsider the vote by which the amendment had been tabled. It was reconsidered, and the amendment went into the bill.

Three days later, Shivers told a press conference that there were still lots of problems to solve in Texas, and while he would like to be a part of the solution, he owed a duty to his family. They were going to Sharyland for the weekend and talk it over, and decide whether he would run for another term.

Secretary of State Carney knew what the outcome would be. He resigned and went home, giving up his hope of running for lieutenant governor. Ben Ramsey knew, too. He announced for re-election for Sunday release, without waiting to hear about the family conference and its outcome.

They knew, as did Allan Shivers, that Marialice would again give him that "extension" on his promise to quit politics in "just two more years."

Sure enough, they came back to Austin and Shivers announced for the unprecedented third term, and then went off to Washington for a governors' conference, ready for the hardest fight of his political career.

Photo Courtesy of the Shivers Museum Collection

Governor Allan Shivers and Lieutenant Governor Ben Ramsey are shown at the 1953 inauguration. First recommended by Shivers for Secretary of State, Ramsey left that post to run for the
second highest job. He won a record six elections as Lieutenant Governor.

Chapter 17

The Mean One

Allan Shivers probably was the only governor ever to hold a union card—certainly the only one to join during an election campaign and in a year when he was battling union leadership.

It was a typical touch of irony in the Shivers Story that he was called to play a bit part in 1954 in *Lucy Gallant*, which starred Charlton Heston and Jane Wyman. He was to play the Governor of Texas, a part for which he was by then eminently qualified.

But to get on the set, he had to join the union, which he did. Then, when he got his check for scale pay of $87 for the day, he endorsed it over to the Actors' Equity benefit fund.

Shivers bore the working men of Texas no malice, and contended that labor had fared better under his administration than under those of previous governors. And, by indirection, that statement asked them why they were fighting him.

But fight they did, remembering the 1947 anti-labor laws, and Shivers' backers gave as good as they took by publicizing the "Port Arthur Story" of how one union moved into town and tried to force the organization of clerks in retail stores. It still is hard to tell which side struck the first blow, but the fight went on for months. And the fierce tenor was no surprise to either group.

Long before it was time for the 1954 campaign, Shivers realized it would be tougher than that of 1952. And, where he had ventured into that one gingerly, he was ready for the re-run. The opposition had aroused all his fighting instincts by boasting that no Democrat who helped the Eisenhower campaign in 1952 would ever hold office in Texas again. At the same time, he was realist enough to know that the loyalists had a stronger case against his third-term bid than they did when they were simply predicting in July, 1952, what he would do in November. Now he had done it.

At one point he had had serious doubts about seeking a third term, about going through all the bitterness again—and about leaving his growing family alone as much as campaigning and holding the office demanded. But the smoke had no sooner died from '52 than he knew deep down that he was going to have to renege once more on his biennial promise to Mrs. Shivers that he would not run again.

When the State Democratic Executive Committee met in Mineral Wells in September of 1953, Shivers laid down his challenge to the members: "If 1952 was the year of decision for the Democratic Party of Texas, 1954 will be the year in which that decision is ratified or rendered empty and meaningless."

The governor told a mostly friendly meeting that the question of 1954 would have nothing to do with national politics; it would, he said, be the same question that had been recurring every two years—"Who's going to direct the affairs of the Democratic Party of Texas?" For three years, he reminded them, it had been the majority of Texas party members. He asked that the majority prevail again.

Before Shivers made his third term announcement, close friends knew that he would stand and fight; and they urged him to soft-pedal the Eisenhower support while doing it. But he told them, as he had proclaimed in numerous speeches, that the apologist's role was not for him. He had contended from the time of the election that Texas had not gone Republican in 1952—it had simply found a way to tell Democratic leaders that the state no longer wore the party's brass collar. And, in spite of his personal regard for Eisenhower, Shivers read the results as being as much an anti-Truman expression as one for "Ike." Shivers, incidentally, had supported Truman and all of the ticket in 1948.

But he had no idea of backing away from his help for Eisenhower—particularly in the face of threats from the opposition that no one who had helped in that movement ever would hold office again.

"I decided I'd rather get beat than let them say they ran me off," he explained.

Some were playing down the Eisenhower campaign. Price Daniel, who had been elected to the United States Senate at the same time, was one of them. He had helped, at the Amarillo convention which urged party members to support Eisenhower, in the drafting of a resolution to bar Stevenson's name from the ticket, and then had backed away from it. But in 1954 he was telling Democrats the fight was all over—and that he had passed the tidelands bill and Eisenhower had signed it and that was what it was all about in the first place.

Shivers went right ahead on his record—conceding the Eisenhower aid was as much a part of it as his outstanding success with the Legislature in 1953.

He did encounter one feature which he had not anticipated. He learned that some of his long-time backers were opposed to a third term for him almost as solidly as they had been against one for Franklin D. Roosevelt in 1940. Possibly they did not like the idea that it might lead to a fourth, as it had done for FDR. He found it hard to argue against the third-term prejudice because it fitted in with his assessment of the 1952 revolt: that Texans support a strong central government in time of emergency but when it comes to standing for domestic practices they don't like it.

Actually, Shivers had let out hints before the 1953 session of the Legislature that he might not be a "lame duck." His opponents had organized an unofficial parallel to the state party organization, and school teachers were upset with him because he would not go along with their proposal for a raise unless they would help find taxes to finance it. In essence, he told both of them to "come and get it."

The liberal-loyalist opposition was centered at first in the Democratic Organizing Committee and later in a Texas Advisory Council of the Democratic National Committee. National Chairman Stephen Mitchell appointed 55 to the Texas group, and some Shivers backers doubted any other state was getting the opportunity to give that much advice. Mitchell later came to the state for a six-day tour of reconciliation that was something less than a success. Naturally he was working with the group trying to oust Shivers supporters from party offices, and got little help from the formal organization.

Mrs. H.H. Weinert of Seguin, who had been a national committeewoman before the fight and was to be after, was the only one in authority to greet Mitchell. She told him and his welcoming audiences that Democrats who left in 1952 had no idea of staying with the Republican Party. But very few of the state Democratic committee members appeared for his talks. The Loyalists put out a folder explaining that a majority of the state's Democrats had stayed with the ticket and that they should be in control of party affairs instead of Shivers' followers.

Accordingly, they met at Lake Buchanan one Sunday in May, 1953, to organize the Democratic Organizing Committee. They elected Byron Skelton of Temple state chairman, Mrs. Jud Collier of Mumford, vice chairman, and Creekmore Fath of Austin, secretary-treasurer. Those three were told to pick committee men and women from each of the 31 senatorial districts to serve until a "convention" could be held.

By formal statement they repudiated party officers who "have betrayed our party" and dedicated themselves to their removal from office. Fagan Dickson of Austin told the group that independent voters have the privilege of picking the party with what they consider the best platform and candidates but added "this is not true of candidates and political leaders—their sins of infidelity will never be forgotten." His guarded welcome to those Democrats who might return was in the pattern of Mitchell's, who had said, "We'll welcome them back to church, but not as deacons."

Shivers said, before the 1953 session ended, that he might run again—in spite of the teacher lobby's opposition over the pay-raise stalemate and the liberal-loyalist organization against him. The *Fort Worth Star-Telegram* applauded the prospect, saying there had not been a crisis during Shivers' administration, and adding that he had planned carefully, looked ahead astutely and handled relations with the Legislature adroitly. He soon had support of other newspapers, including the *Dallas Times-Herald, Houston Chronicle, Beaumont Enterprise, Marshall News-Messenger, San Antonio Express, Dallas Morning News, San Angelo Standard-Times, Corpus Christi Caller-Times* and *Beaumont Journal.*

Claud Gilmer of Rocksprings, who had headed the Democrats for Eisenhower, got to work on the third term bid, aided by John Van Cronkhite.

Setting a theme of "States' Rights versus a Dominating Central Government," the Shivers campaign began running against the Congress of Industrial Organizations, and its Political Action Committee, the Americans for Democratic Action, the National Association for the Advancement of Colored People, and one other initialed enemy—PARR. That stood for George Parr, "Duke" of Duval County, who gave Shivers' opponents fantastic but customary majorities in the 1950 and 1952 campaigns.

It was a campaign based on initials. "Nobody is against me," Shivers would say on television, "except the CIO, PAC, ADA, NAACP and PARR."

A complete indictment of Parr was contained in Shivers' campaign material. A brochure stated that when he first became governor, Shivers began trying to rid Duval County of "boss rule, fear and intimidation, 'lost' records and ballots and misappropriations of public funds." It said some see nothing wrong with the "serf system" used by Parr, but quoted Shivers as saying Parr had 26 deputy sheriffs and 300 to 400 special deputies, all armed. "If there isn't anything wrong, why is it necessary to have a private army?" Shivers asked.

Shivers' material made a pitch for the rank-and-file union member, saying labor had prospered during his administration and would continue to do so as more industrial expansion was achieved to create more jobs. "No law which harms in any way the rights of the laboring man has been passed during Allan Shivers' administration, and he is determined to see that no such law is passed," his brochure stated. It added that union leaders were opposing him because of his opposition to bossism in any form.

At this point, just after the Supreme Court of the United States had ruled against compulsory segregation, Shivers stuck to a theme of local control of schools, and promised to "use every legal means at my disposal to maintain the public schools of Texas as they now exist."

Perhaps with a bit of foresight, the 1954 campaign platform told how Shivers had been asking since 1951 for stronger insurance laws. It said action was being taken to weed out unsound companies and promised the cleanup would be continued. As if in anticipation of the failures that produced a scandal the following year, Shivers said, "The great majority of Texas insurance companies are sound, strong and honest. But we are going to continue vigorously our campaign to rid the state of the 2 or 3 per cent which are unsound. We are working against the roadblocks thrown up by those who want to preserve such companies and let them continue to gyp the public."

Shivers campaigned on that basis and kept his second-time opponent, Ralph Yarborough, off balance with charges of mud-slinging and fronting for minority groups and Parr. Yarborough countered with charges that Shivers had "flip-flopped" on supporting the Democratic nominee for president in 1952 and on the teacher pay-raise issue (which had been settled in special session by then). Yarborough also tried to make capital of a $425,000 profit Shivers made on a Valley land deal, referred to in Chapter 10.

One reason he failed was that Shivers frankly acknowledged he had made a profit on a land deal. And he made repeated references to the fact that Yarborough did not mention that the transaction had occurred eight years earlier—before he was lieutenant governor and three years before he became governor.

Shivers virtually baited the Loyalists by saying in 1954 that he wouldn't support Stevenson in 1956 any more than he had in 1952.

Asked what the former Illinois governor would have to change, Shivers said "a lot of things—including his name." He refused to debate Yarborough on the latter's charge of insurance scandals that were about to break. Aides pointed out to him that part of the trouble had been due to prolonged illnesses of two members of what then was the State Board of Insurance Commissioners, but Shivers said both had died and he did not want to subject their widows to charges in a political campaign.

Key issue of the campaign was the widely circulated "Port Arthur Story." Shivers had charged that his opponent was backed by national labor organizations and was being financed by them. This turned labor to Yarborough to a certain extent but some union men stuck with Shivers because of his opposition to the Supreme Court decision that separate but equal schools did not meet the test of segregation. Shivers said "we are going to keep running the public schools of Texas as they are today," so some of the labor force was divided.

The "Port Arthur Story" was presented as a "road show" in other cities by a group of merchants from Port Arthur, who tried to show the way business had been crippled by a campaign of "organization by intimidation." It depicted efforts to force unionization through picket lines outside stores which had no labor troubles and never had had.

When the Austin public relations firm of Syers, Pickle & Winn came into the campaign, Ed Syers and Ed Potter of that firm hit on the idea of making a television show of "The Port Arthur Story." Bob Heller and Bill Moore of their staff went to Port Arthur to film it.

"I had to take 30 minutes of film to get a few seconds when there was no smoke coming out of the smokestack at one plant," Moore said later, after he had left the advertising firm. He also said he took pictures of a deserted hotel coffee shop on a Sunday morning.

J.J. Pickle (later U.S. Congressman), Windy Winn and Heller (later a partner in a major Houston firm) disclaimed responsibility for the decision to make the film in that fashion. Shivers did not even know it was being made.

One Sunday, Shivers and other top campaign staff members viewed the finished product at the P-K Restaurant on East Seventh Street in Austin. They saw the story of a city immobilized by the strike of the retail workers. They adjudged it effective, as indeed it was, and authorized its showing.

"Shivers just saw the finished product," one of those at the meeting said. "He didn't know some of the pictures were faked." But its showing on TV and at the "road show" drew attacks of "fake" and "fraud." Another group of Port Arthur people set out to follow the other group around as a "Truth Squad."

Shivers used the issue heavily, charging that out-of-state labor leaders were supporting Yarborough, and that the Port Arthur strike headquarters was in the same building with Yarborough's local campaign office. A folder distributed by the "road show" in East Texas showed a picture of a Negro carrying a picket sign which also had a Yarborough sticker on it.

The going got rough, with Yarborough and his backers calling the traveling presentations and TV film a deception, using fake photography and trick pictures. One Yarborough supporter, State Senator Kilmer Corbin of Lubbock, denied Shivers' charges that labor unions were assessing their members to aid the Yarborough campaign. Yarborough himself tried to turn the tables by calling it a Shivers failure. He said the governor was claiming to be powerless to act in a strike that had cut his home town into two camps and was using the strike as a political pawn.

"Maybe he approached the Port Arthur situation as he approached the burning drought of the past five years," said Yarborough. "Maybe he'll study Port Arthur as he now says he will study the drought—or maybe he'll be too busy, along with other Republican governors, recommending trade with Communist China, as he did back in July after that trip the taxpayers paid for, the trip he made to the Far East with two other GOP governors."

Shivers stuck to the Red issue, saying that a Communist-tainted union clamped a paralyzing strike on small businessmen of Port Arthur, and saying he and the attorney general scuttled its plans to spread all along the Gulf Coast and to other parts of the state. He said responsible Texas Labor members approved of the cleanup but that when the CIO took over the striking union, their representatives assailed the governor for "meddling" in its affairs.

The first primary showed Shivers some 23,000 votes short of a majority. J.J. Holmes had received 15,591 votes and Arlon B. (Cyclone) Davis, 16,254. Shivers got 668,913 to Yarborough's 645,994. And the runoff began at the same speed at which the first campaign had closed.

Shivers claimed the tabulations proved his charge that Yarborough was the captive candidate of the CIO and NAACP. He said Yarborough carried every county where the CIO had strength and "every Negro box in Texas by 10-to-one to 20-to-one." He blamed overconfidence on the part of his backers for the failure to win without a run-off. For example, he pointed out that he got 24,000 fewer votes in Harris County than he had received in 1952, but that Yarborough's total was 2,000 higher.

In the run-off, business picked up—literally. Jim Taylor, lobbyist for the Texas Motor Transportation Association, tried a new idea. He enlisted—possibly drafted is a better term—the aid of almost all trade associations in the state. He asked the loan of their top executives and the names of their top ten members in each county—where that many were available.

Then Taylor, who had served two legislative sessions in the Senate with Shivers and who introduced Shivers when he announced for lieutenant governor, set up a separate campaign headquarters, completely divorced from the official task force. The association executives would hold county or senatorial district meetings and be assured of up to 100 enthusiastic backers. They stressed getting out the vote, and they did. The Port Arthur story was re-told many times in an effort to get local businessmen interested.

Obviously they did, for Shivers got more than 100,000 additional votes in the run-off and Yarborough nearly 40,000 new ones. Shivers won—775,088 to 683,132. Then, with practically no campaign effort, he defeated Republican Tod R. Adams in the general election—569,533 to 66,154.

That fall, 1954, Shivers, Senator Daniel and Senator Lyndon B. Johnson declined invitations to a dinner in Chicago honoring Adlai Stevenson. All pleaded prior engagements.

And a new wrinkle was put into the state party fabric after the fall convention. State Chairman George W. Sandlin, Jr. announced appointment of a long list of "old pros" as advisors to the state committee. At the time there was a prohibition against having state officials on the committee, but Sandlin—and Shivers—wanted the help of all when time for the 1956 campaign came around. The list included James M. Windham of Livingston, member of the Board for State Hospitals and Special Schools; Wendell Mayes of Brownwood, State Parks Board; E.H. Thornton, Jr., Galveston, State Highway Commission; and Tom Sealy, Midland, Board of Regents for The University of Texas.

Also on the list were Kermit Dyche of Alvin, husband of a committeewoman and brother of Eddie Dyche of the Public Safety Commission, and former Speaker of the House Claud Gilmer (head of the Democrats for Eisenhower in 1952); Howard Carney of Atlanta, former senator and secretary of state; Howard Hartzog of

Port Lavaca, former representative. Several of Shivers' district campaign managers were named in the list of 27, which Sandlin said might be expanded to sustain the zeal developed during the third-term race.

The stage was well set for the fight of 1956. But Shivers had survived his Pied Piper role of 1952, narrowly, but as Senator Carlos Ashley once said of a close race, "Any's enough."

Chapter 18

1955—A "Troublous" Year

Because memories of 1952 still were fresh, and prospects for 1956 were enticing speculation, the legislative year of 1955 was interlaced with politics from start to finish.

Shivers stuck defiantly to the guns of party independence he had manned in 1952 and was promising to fire them again in 1956 if necessary. And his opposition hit on every hint with hope of rallying support for a fight on any position he took.

In addition, scandal and inept administration began to threaten public confidence in his leadership. It developed that the Veterans Land Board, of which he was a member, had been used for fraudulent purposes that brought on investigations and indictments. And failures of insurance companies were pointing up weak or indecisive supervision by Shivers' appointees. Later they were to underline questionable and illegal activities as well.

Still Shivers had a highly successful session of the Legislature, which he commended on adjournment for having solved 85 per cent of the problems it faced. It raised taxes, always a chore, following in general the recommendations the governor had made.

All of the year's activities—even the legislative and political—had their inception in 1954.

Senate Majority Leader Johnson showed he was not as vehement about defections as some Democrats were. He held on to his position by promising to restore to Senator Wayne Morse all the committee assignments he had as a Republican before he joined the Adlai Stevenson camp in 1952 as Shivers' opposite number. But he didn't get Shivers' backing that way. Shivers said in an interview he might support Ohio's Governor Frank Lausche for a spot on the 1956 presidential ticket, but he changed the subject when asked about Johnson. Shivers may not have figured he had to cater to Johnson, since the latter had defeated his Republican opponent by 406,000 votes while Shivers was beating his by 460,000 that fall.

And at a governors' conference in Boca Raton, Florida, Sam

Wood of the *Austin American-Statesman* overheard Shivers and Governor James E. Byrnes of South Carolina in a late-evening discussion of politics. Shivers was contending Lyndon Johnson was the Democrats' best chance for 1956. Byrnes said he had not thought much of Johnson as presidential ticket material, and dismissed the subject with the comment that if 1956 were a re-run of the Eisenhower-Stevenson race, "I'll vote for Ike and so will you." Neither had any comment on the Wood story after they returned to their offices, but Shivers sent Wood a stepladder to imply that Wood had listened through a hotel room transom. U.S. Senator Daniel was enthusiastic for Johnson—and thinking of the possibility of running for governor in 1956.

Paul Butler succeeded Stephen Mitchell as Democratic National Chairman, burying plans for the 1956 loyalty oath Mitchell had announced he planned to push.

The Veterans Land Board took note of the rising public clamor and called for a full investigation of any large-scale deals. Shivers recommended to a Senate committee that he and the attorney general be removed as ex-officio members of the board and replaced by two citizen members. He said neither the governor nor the attorney general had time to attend regular meetings and usually had to send assistants—in Shivers' case, Maurice Acers, and in John Ben Shepperd's, Robert Trotti. The Legislature agreed, and removed them both from many boards of which they had been ex-officio members.

Also adding to the task facing the Legislature was the fact that the "Port Arthur Story" didn't end with the 1954 election. Retailers in the coast city refused to attend a "peace" meeting with CIO officials, and the union retaliated with threats to continue the strike ten years if necessary. Shivers later recommended a ban on picketing or striking to compel recognition by an employer unless the union represented a majority of the employees affected. The Legislature was to pass it in just about that form.

Another incident that was to produce legislative effort was the failure of two insurance companies—one of which had been found solvent by virtue of having sufficient cash on hand at annual report time but in the form of $60,000 in checks which later "bounced" and changed the picture.

So the 54th Legislature convened with a number of problems in addition to the new money demand created by rising costs of the Gilmer-Aikin program for public schools and increasing enrollment at college level. The comptroller estimated $26 million had to

" I CAN LICK ANY MAN IN THE HOUSE ! "

Courtesy, *WASHINGTON STAR-NEWS*

be raised to maintain existing levels of spending. But higher education was estimated to need $12 million a year; state hospitals, $5
million; welfare, $7 million; water and insurance supervision, $1
million each. The Department of Corrections needed more money
for custodial care or for parole supervision, and more money was
needed for the extra employees being added to serve a growing
population.

Shivers recommended a two-cent-a-gallon increase in the
gasoline tax, as had the Highway Commission. He also asked a
higher rate on cigarette taxes, an increase in college tuition and a
revision of school financing to put a heavier burden on "wealthy"

school districts. He also advocated switching from a per capita allocation of school funds to one based on average daily attendance. He said the gasoline tax would help school income some but would have the added virtue of assuring funds on hand if the federal government initiated a nationwide program to share road costs with states (as it did).

Shivers offered a broad program for insurance reform, including a change from the system of three commissioners representing various phases of the industry to an "Insurance Board" composed of three men to supervise all aspects jointly. Shivers also suggested that more capital be required for organization of new companies, that the board be given more supervisory employees and better salaries for them, and that the board be authorized to regulate sale of company stock.

Senator George Moffett announced plans to ask another $100 million for the veterans' land program, saying there had been comparatively few misdeeds. Three aides to Land Commissioner Bascom Giles resigned, as he had done. Senator Dorsey Hardeman, chairman of the general investigating committee, called a halt to its probe, but Senator Jimmy Phillips started one of his own and revealed some findings not publicized by the official studies.

Meanwhile, the Legislature was moving with very deliberate speed on the revenue-raising measures. Shivers urged the opposition to offer alternate plans if they were not ready to go along with his gasoline and cigarette hikes. And talk was started—possibly at the governor's suggestion—of raising rates on items in the omnibus tax bill which covered just about everything. That got the attention of the business "lobby" and created more interest in the single-shot bills.

Shivers signed a bill in which he had a personal interest. It was one by Representative Maury Maverick, Jr., to do away with authority for cross-filing of candidates, and left Shivers as the only cross-filed governor to that time. His two-party candidacy in 1952 created the first such governor—and the only one.

Shivers, Shepperd and new Land Commissioner Earl Rudder voted to hike royalties on school land leased from the state from 1/8 to 1/6, and raised the minimum bonus from $5 to $15 an acre and annual delay rental from $2 to $3 an acre. It assured considerably higher state revenue and put rates at the same level as those the federal government charged on tidelands leases. The number of indictments in the veterans' land program rose to 264.

The House of Representatives, which has to originate tax

measures, finally took action on a bill by Representative Stanton Stone. It proposed raising the tax on gasoline by 1 cent a gallon and that on other motor fuels by 1.5 cents. It called for an increase of 1 cent a pack on cigarettes, and on beer and wine dealers' annual license fees from an average of $30 to $105 a year. Shivers applauded the move but said more taxes would be necessary unless appropriations were cut down.

Shivers won out on his water fight—getting a water commission appointed by the governor but with geographical limitations on residences of the commissioners. The Senate had wanted an appointive board; the House, an elective one. The legislators cut down the higher requirements advocated by Shivers for creation of new insurance companies, but did raise them some. His suggestion of higher driver's license fees—from $1 to $2—passed the Senate.

In a political interlude, Shivers made his first peace gesture toward the party loyalty Democrats. He urged Democrats to buy tickets to a Washington dinner honoring Sam Rayburn. His action came at a time when an advisory committee headed by U.S. Senator Hubert Humphrey and former Virginia Governor John S. Battle made its report. It said it would be "assumed" that state delegates would try to assure that national nominees be put on ballots but that loyalty would be "required" of members of the national committee. This was a slap at Texas' Wright Morrow, who did not support Truman in 1948 or Stevenson in 1952. He resigned in order to support Eisenhower but his resignation never was accepted by the state committee. However, the national committee had recognized it, and his status was in limbo. Shivers was to accept the latter view later in the year.

The governor paid little attention to Democratic party efforts to raise $100,000 as the state's quota of national expense; or to Stephen Mitchell's repeated statement that Southern Democrats would help in 1956 to bar seating in the national convention of Shivers, Byrnes and Governor Robert Kennon of Louisiana.

He turned back to the Legislature, where a lawmaking crisis of sorts had developed over the addition of snuff and other tobacco products to the tax bill. The House bill was promptly put into a free conference committee by senators who knew the sanctity of snuff and chewing tobacco. Then, too, the bill was $17.6 million short of spending plans for the coming biennium and Shivers wanted even more.

The governor tried to "sell" his 2-cent gasoline increase by giving one-fourth of the additional money to a right-of-way fund to help cities and counties. His campaign manager, Senator Lock, was on both the state affairs and finance committees, giving him a voice in both taxing and spending.

Shivers himself worked the floor and secured passage of a bill by Senator George Parkhouse which would bar picketing by any union unless it represented a majority of the affected workers. It won passage as a means of "preventing another Port Arthur," though union leaders protested loudly. But Representative Wade Spilman, House sponsor, said nobody should be able to tell better than the unions whether they represent the majority. Labor opposition to Shivers was increased by his approval of several other bills, including the "Ford Bill" to outlaw strikes at operations owned by firms affected by strikes in other states.

A "way out" was offered the hard-pressed lawmakers, who had gone past the constitutional limit and no longer were drawing their per diem allowance for expenses in Austin. Shivers offered them a chance to adjourn and come back in special session at $25 a day. But the members knew that if they did, there would be no chance for their pet "local" bills which were in various stages of passage..One such local bill was a pay raise for District Attorney Tom Moore of Waco, later to become a representative. Shivers vetoed the measure on the grounds such pay raises should be in a general law. Moore claimed the veto was his punishment for having supported Yarborough against Shivers.

On the political front, Shivers was softening his stand. Democratic National Chairman Paul Butler came to Texas but declined an invitation to have lunch with Shivers. This gave Shivers an opportunity to return to form and charge that Rayburn and the Democratic Advisory Committee influenced Butler. He publicly called on Butler to assure Texans that the delegation representing the majority of Texas Democrats would be seated at the 1956 national convention. The only response was that Butler believed in majority rule and would keep hands off in any delegate fight. Rayburn served notice of the 1956 battle by sending out booklets on how to organize conventions, somewhat similar to the ones Shivers had prepared in 1952.

Later, at a press conference, Shivers said he could not argue with Butler's contention that the new national committeeman from Texas should be one who always had supported the party's nominees. In an unexpected declaration, the governor said he always had felt the state committee members should be friendly to the state administration and the national committee had a right to expect the same fealty. That was the death knell for Morrow, although it was a while before it was formalized. At a meeting of the state committee, Shivers advocated that Morrow be jettisoned because the two of them were too heavy for the state party organization to carry and Morrow had the public admission of his 1952 guilt through his resignation. Even though the resignation had not been accepted at state level, it was recognized by the national committee on the basis that Morrow had helped raise money to assist Eisenhower in defeating Democratic nominee Stevenson.

A short time later, Shivers said at the national governors' conference in Chicago that he would vote against Adlai Stevenson again if he were the nominee in 1956. He didn't say what nominee might keep him in the party. There was talk at the national level about pushing Rayburn for the presidential nomination, but those close to Shivers saw no possibility of that so long as the governor controlled the state committee. Stevenson came to Texas in October of 1955 but ignored Shivers. He talked with Rayburn and Johnson and made two campaign speeches.

In October, the state committee met and picked Lieutenant Governor Ben Ramsey as national committeeman. He had the backing of Shivers and was acceptable to Rayburn and Johnson because he had supported the Democratic ticket in 1952 and promised to do so again in 1956. Ramsey went to a national committee meeting in Chicago and was seated. However, Rayburn was not satisfied with the situation at home. He let it be known that he planned to challenge Shivers for control of the 1956 delegation to the national convention.

Shivers made one more concession to the veterans' land program scandal that fall. A vacancy in the district attorney's job at Cuero arose, and Senator William T. Fly of Victoria had a suggestion, which normally would have controlled the governor's thinking. But Shivers appointed County Attorney Wiley Cheatham, who had helped break the original case by questioning Negro veterans who told him of getting money for signing papers they did not understand. Shivers explained that he didn't want anyone to be able to say he had done anything to block full discovery and prosecution of wrongdoing.

But no sooner did it look as if the land scandal had simmered down than an even bigger one, about insurance, broke into the open.

The non-legislative aspects of 1955 had not helped the governor's plans in 1956.

Chapter 19

Scandals

It wasn't all a downhill, wine-and-roses route for the Shivers administration. Like all governments, this one had its minuses along with the pluses. And Shivers was first to admit that if governors are to be credited for the good, they should also be blamed for the bad.

In fact, he argued that theory as the reason for his plea for appointment of most state administrators, for reform and modernization of state government. The Constitution calls for statewide election of many officials—yet the governor gets criticized for their faults and credited for their achievements. It should not be, he contended. If a governor is to be blamed for what happens while he is in office, he should be allowed to pick up the officials who may make it happen—or who may allow something bad to happen now and then.

An example was the serious Veterans Land Board scandal which resulted in a six-year prison term for Land Commissioner Bascom Giles. (He served all of it except that portion waived for good behavior, blood donations, etc. Price Daniel, who succeeded Shivers, had been brushed by the land scandal, too, and would not release Giles earlier.)

At the close of World War II, when he was thinking of running for governor, as he had for several years, Giles suggested that the Legislature honor returning veterans with an opportunity to buy land on long-term, low-interest loans.

The Legislature submitted a constitutional amendment to authorize a bond program and, after a hard fight, created a board to take charge of the plan. It named the Commissioner of the General Land Office (Giles) as chairman of the board and the governor and attorney general as ex-officio members, with the commissioner as the chief administrator.

The first board was made up of Giles, Governor Jester and Attorney General Daniel. Later it included Giles, Shivers and Daniel, and still later, Attorney General John Ben Shepperd replaced Daniel.

"We set up guidelines for the loans, but we had no way of check-ing," Shivers explained. "Every time deals would come up, we'd ask if they met the guidelines and Giles always said 'yes'."

Shivers added that of course he and the attorney general fre-quently missed meetings because of other official obligations, and sent stand-ins.

Without seeking to escape blame, Shivers offered the explanation that he had little reason to suspect wrongdoing of a man who had been elected nine times to a statewide office and who had con-sidered running for governor several times.

But Shivers didn't consider himself really responsible for the veterans' land scandal—which actually involved wrongdoing on a grand scale, but which, in the end, may wind up with a profit for the state when all of the "block deals" are paid out.

The "block deal" operation began to come to light when County Attorney Wiley Cheatham of Cuero and Ken Towery of the *Cuero Record* learned that Negro veterans were being paid "to sign some papers" by a local land dealer. They began inquiries, and Towery's published reports of his suspicions began to get attention from larger newspapers like the *Houston Chronicle* and the *Fort Worth Star-Telegram.* Ultimately, Towery won a Pulitzer Prize for dis-covering The Scandal.

Late in 1954, the Senate General Investigating Committee took note of the matter, on the insistence of Representative Tom Cheatham, Wiley Cheatham's father, and began perfunctory in-vestigations. Enough had begun to appear that on Jan. 1, 1955, Giles announced, just before the Cotton Bowl game was about to start, that he would not qualify for the ninth two-year term as land com-missioner to which he had just been elected.

Shivers chose Mayor J. Earl Rudder of Brady, one of his cam-paign managers and a World War II hero, to replace Giles as land commissioner, and the investigation began in earnest. Oddly, Rud-der had been associated in business with B.R. Sheffield of Brady, who was to become the only one, besides Giles, to serve time in prison for making the fraudulent land deals.

State Auditor C.H. Cavness and Attorney General Shepperd began investigations. So did a House Investigating Committee. What they found was the literally dozens of "block deals" had been made by a dozen or so promoters.

Judgments were obtained against them all, with court orders sell-ing the promoters back the land at the same inflated prices at which the Veterans Land Board had bought it. They were given ten years to pay them out, with interest, and by the fall of 1973, the board had collected more than $900,000 in principal on the judgments. All but five had been paid off. The balance on pending judgments was only $169,084, and payments were up to date.

So, while the State may eventually recover all the money it invested, the deals deprived hundreds of veterans of land purchases at the 3 per cent interest rate in effect when the promoters were selling the land to the State at inflated prices.

In the process of shaking down the scandal, Shivers, Shepperd and Rudder met as the board, and "corrected" minutes of a number of meetings at which block deals had been approved. Shivers and Shepperd said that some of the deals were put into the minutes when they were not actually acted upon by them or their designees as board members. The Senate committee found Shivers and Shepperd guilty of absenteeism. The House committee decided that the board minutes did not reflect what had happened, so the governor and attorney general could not have discovered what was going on.

The lawmakers then tilted the decision in favor of the veterans' land program by submitting another $100 million bond issue to the voters. It was approved by the voters, and other issues were approved in 1967, 1972 and 1973, bringing to $600 million the total authorized.

Since 1955, two citizen members named by the governor have served on each board, with the elected land commissioner still chairman and still making the loans, but under restrictions designed to prevent any future "block deals."

While Shivers didn't feel he was responsible for the land scandal, he did take full blame for the faults of the Board of Insurance Commissioners. Although there was a matter of two long-time illnesses of appointees not his own, there was a time when his appointees were in full charge.

The time was ripe for such a situation when Shivers took office. Texas laws had not kept up with the industry, nor with the promoters of the 1940s and 1950s. It was possible to start a life insurance company with $25,000 and sell to everyone from whom you could get a commitment. The number of companies had risen astronomically since World War II.

First, Shivers appointed Garland Smith, who had been his office "greeter" in both the lieutenant governor's and governor's office, as casualty commissioner. He conceded Smith was not qualified, but said he relied on industry spokesmen who said they would help him get hold of the job.

It was in the final month of 1955 that the insurance blockbuster struck. United States Trust and Guaranty and its subsidiary, U.S. Automotive Service, failed almost simultaneously. What shocked many in state government was that the two had been under surveillance for 16 months and that a report six months earlier had showed them to be insolvent. A hearing on cancellation of charter had been held, but was recessed because the question of solvency assertedly turned on the size of real estate appraisals.

At first, A.B. Shoemake, head of the two firms (and of three others later discovered to be part of his empire) would say only that the operations were very involved. Thousands of investors had bought certificates from U.S. Trust with assurance of a good interest return. The money then was funneled into the other firms for investment in a wide range of enterprises but with little obligation to the parent company and the investors. U.S. Trust apparently had about $800,000 in cash, a $100,000 mortgage on a home in Waco that was later valued at much less, and $6 million in 10-year bonds of U.S. Automotive. A farm valued by the company at $1 million was appraised at $400,000, which would have entitled the parent company to list it at $240,000. Another property valued at more than $1 million was found to have been bought for $30,000 cash and a $150,000 note. The insurance board recessed first one, then a second hearing on cancellation, and Chairman Smith was quoted as saying he would never again "try to save a company."

Shoemake shot himself before being questioned, and lived despite a bullet through his brain. But he never could be questioned, and investors had to take their losses.

A former counsel for the board, Renne Allred, Jr., said he wrote the board in 1954 that the real estate assets of U.S. Trust were so overvalued that it might be insolvent. During the follow-up investigation it turned out that numerous senators and representatives and one former senator were on a list for whom legal expenses had been authorized out of an unexplained $50,000 outgo for that purpose. A $10,000 item was listed for Senator Carlos Ashley, and $3,000 for Senator William T. Shireman (both of whom later agreed to repay the fees).

Peeks into what had been happening in the Board of Insurance Commissioners' transactions began to appear at the Travis County Courthouse as early as 1953. District Judge J. Harris Gardner, assessing $200,000 against policyholders of the Texas Mutual Insurance Co. of Beaumont in late 1953, said flatly that the company never had the authority to issue non-assessable mutual policies,

because it never really had the $200,000 in capital required by law
to issue such policies.

Two promoters who organized the company borrowed the $200,-
000 for three days and got a certificate from a bank that the money
was on deposit and belonged to the company. This qualified them
for a license to operate in Texas; the next day they paid the $200,000
back to the bank with three days' interest, and started writing insurance policies with no real capital to back the policy reserves.

Judge Gardner was mild. A year later, crusty Associate Justice
Robert Hughes of the Third Court of Civil Appeals "told it like it
was" in an opinion upholding Judge Gardner. This got attention
from the Capitol Press Corps, and the insurance scandal revelation
was on.

And in early 1954, District Judge Charles O. Betts of Travis County, in a case granting the receivership of two similar phony El Paso
companies, had spoken up about it. The headlines were about
Governor Shivers' trip to Korea with other governors for President
Eisenhower. Few people noticed it when Judge Betts said that the
insurance laws were "misleading" and were "going to blow the
Capitol higher than a kite" because they were "an invitation to promoters."

Travis County's highly important district courts, which handle all
cases involving the State, are seldom covered by reporters, either
for the Austin newspapers or for the wire services or Capitol
bureaus. So, the people of Texas were late in finding out what had
been happening in the insurance business. They learned when
they presented claims for damages or bodily injuries, and never got
replies from the companies. They learned it when their lawyers got
judgments which could not be collected. They learned it when they
"put their trust in U.S. Trust" as Drew Pearson recommended on
television commercials.

Governor Shivers had been worried about the insurance
situation, because Chairman George Butler of the Board of
Insurance Commissioners (the life insurance commissioner) had
been ill and out of the office for eight months before he died. Fire
Commissioner Paul Brown, who had been Governor Jester's
secretary of state, had been in a coma, and could neither act nor
sign a letter of resignation. There is no way a governor can remove
a state official unable to perform his duties. So Smith, a country
newspaperman, had been running the department with a deputy
named by Chairman Butler.

When Butler died, Shivers called in his law school friend, J.

Byron Saunders of Tyler, and asked him to accept the job as casualty commissioner, since he planned to move Smith to life insurance commissioner and chairman.

"I can't afford to take the job at what it pays," Saunders told Shivers. Saunders had been serving on the unpaid Board of Public Welfare, which requires only a day or two a month. But the insurance job was full time.

"You are a lawyer," Shivers told Saunders. "If you will do the outstanding job that I think you are capable of, and if you keep your nose clean—an old East Texas expression about not getting into trouble—you can either become general counsel of a major insurance company or retire into private law practice and have the experience that would justify a good and lucrative law practice."

At that time, members of the insurance board were paid $7,200 a year. Men of great ability couldn't be attracted to a job of that kind without the possibility of future improvement, as Shivers explained it. He also recognized the alternative, the temptation to yield to pressure, and for that reason added the "keep your nose clean" warning.

This is, perhaps unfortunately, the way men are recruited for major state jobs. It is a promise of future improvement, of a delayed return from investment in time.

As long as Texans believe that policymakers should not be paid at all, and public administrators be paid as little as possible, the huge businesses which underpaid public employees supervise will have the upper hand.

So it was in this period. Slack insurance laws, and even slacker enforcement of the laws on the books, made it "the decade of the promoters."

To explain this more simply, it may do for the moment to leave out names, although some will be mentioned later.

In the 1950s it was possible for a promoter to organize a casualty insurance company with no money at all. He needed a front, enough money and prestige to borrow $200,000 from a bank for three days, and a banker friend who was willing to sign an affidavit that the $200,000 was the promoter's property free and clear. Dozens of them did it, and went into the insurance business with no assets except a lying banker, a brash front, and the gall to entertain and sometimes pay off an examiner for the Board of Insurance Commissioners, or a commissioner, long enough to "plant" some agents and start piling up business.

Then it came time for the year-end statements, under oath, required by law, of the assets, liabilities and other claims. All the promoter had to do was to go back to his friendly banker, pay him a high bit of interest for a year-end, three-day "window-dressing loan" to show on his books that he had the reserves to cover his liabilities and to maintain the $200,000 he needed to remain in business.

Dozens of them flashed across the horizon in the 1950s, crashing finally because they had to pyramid to stay in business. They had to get enough new premium income to pay off old claims, or to use the old walnut shell game of reinsurance with other insolvent companies scattered from the Bahamas to the camel market in North Africa where one promoter's assets were invested in "bearer bonds." Some went to phony subdivisions in Missouri or Kentucky which issued worthless sewer bonds which trailed their red ink across the books of a score of promotion insurance companies.

One such company was General American Casualty of San Antonio, a craftily chosen name close to that of American General Insurance Co., of Houston, headed by Gus Wortham, himself a former board worker who had built a great insurance empire.

BenJack Cage of Dallas had scouted General American Casualty for an international promoter, and had advised him that while the kind of auto risks it was taking were "sure death" because they were drivers no one else would insure, there was "profit for the management" for a time. A South Dakota promoter took it over, and when examiners from the Texas and other boards started finding things wrong, the company management hired a lawyer and public relations man. The lawyer was Hubert Green, Sr., Shivers' campaign manager in Bexar County. The public relations man was John Van Cronkhite, Shivers' former staff member and campaign worker in 1952, now in private enterprise.

Their appeal to Chairman Smith was that if the board would hold off, they could "save the company." Their payments of $1,000 a month each to Green and Van Cronkhite came to light, among other things, in the 1954 campaign, but it was just before the primary and had little effect. Later, when Smith put the company into receivership, much more came to light.

There were dozens of company bankruptcies, all of them because of fraudulent organization without the required assets. But the stunner was ICT Insurance Co. and its dozens of affiliates.

BenJack Cage was a handsome, blonde, fast talker who formed The Insurance Company of Texas in 1951, and talked leaders of the Texas State Federation of Labor into selling and buying stock in the company, which would be owned by AFL union members. Cage held out great hopes for working people, and got more than $300,000 in union and individual investments in stock.

Cage probably had a good idea, but he could not stop pyramiding. He hired Lone Wolf Gonzaullas, the famed but then retired Texas Ranger, to head a company which sold alarms for women to carry in their purses to set off sirens if they were assaulted. (It could be that this 1953 idea was 15 years ahead of its time.) He subdivided his family farm near Houston into "ranches" one inch square, and sold them as "Texas Ranches" at $2 each in newsstands over the nation. He probably ruined forever the title on the Cage family ranch, if indeed the deeds were ever recorded. And, week after week, he was busy with big reinsurance and merger deals which dazzled the plumbers, printers, longshoremen, carpenters and others from the unions who made up his board of directors. He always opened board meeting with prayers by Freeman Everett, the devout Negro who headed a Houston longshoremen's local. And he closed the board meetings with parties at swanky country clubs at company expense.

Honest examiners for state agencies in Texas and elsewhere knew what was happening. But Cage had visited often with Chairman Smith and Commissioner Saunders and other board officials. They, too, were impressed by the young man who at 34 was a member of the Young Presidents' Organization.

Cage, like Shivers, told Saunders that the pay for his important job was too low. But Cage had a quicker solution. He proposed that to make up for this oversight by the Legislature, he would just put Saunders and Smith's son-in-law on his management company payroll at $7,500 a year.

This leaked out, and came back to Jerry Holleman, who had become executive secretary of the Texas AFL when Cage hired Paul Sparks, the secretary of the Texas State Federation of Labor, to work for Jack Cage & Co., the management company.

Somewhere Shivers had picked up a hint that Cage might not be the All-American boy he sounded and looked like. When he went to St. Louis in 1954 to speak to a Baptist convention, Shivers was offered the use of the private car of the president of the Katy Railroad to make the trip. He accepted, but insisted on paying for the use of the car. Byron Saunders went along on the trip.

"Byron," Shivers told him as they enjoyed the luxury of the private car, "you'd better watch this BenJack Cage. I hear that he's doing some pretty fancy dealings."

Saunders listened, and seemed to agree. What could have been his thoughts while the train clicked its way across Texas as he heard this warning from Shivers?

By then, ICT had expanded into industry, and had bought National Bankers Life Insurance Co. from P. Pierce Brooks, taking over its building in Dallas, and promising to pay Brooks far more than could be made from the vanishing ICT assets.

Brooks was also one with a Texas political background. He had been often a bridesmaid, never a bride. He got into the run-off with Coke Stevenson for lieutenant governor in 1938. He got into the run-off with Olin Culberson for Railroad Commissioner in 1940, and with Ben Ramsey for lieutenant governor in 1950. But he lost them all.

Then he turned to insurance full-time, and built up a fairly substantial company.

Someone, still unknown to the authors, began to give weekly reports to Stuart Long on what was happening about BenJack Cage at the Board of Insurance Commissioners. The information was checked, and Long, who for a time in 1952 had been sponsored on a statewide radio network by ICT, took it to Holleman, who called a special directors' meeting and fired Cage as president.

Again, efforts were begun to "save the company." Holleman's lawyers found Brooks holding a revival meeting on a Caribbean island (he was also a missionary in his spare time) and waited until he had baptized nearly 400 converts in a sluggish river to ask him to accept a large profit to reverse the sale of National Bankers Life to ICT, because ICT simply could not make the payments.

But there had been too much "window-dressing"; it was impossible to salvage the ICT. And in the investigation which followed, the payments to Smith and Saunders came to light. Both were indicted, but Saunders' conviction was reversed, and Smith's indictment was never brought to trial.

But by the time of the indictment, Saunders had left the board, and, as Shivers had predicted, was general counsel of a major Dallas insurance company, making more than the State and Cage together had been paying him.

Smith was replaced as chairman by John Osorio, Shivers' executive assistant, who was later to serve as president of National Bankers Life, and then to become involved, and indicted, on the money shiftings connected with the Frank Sharp affair of the 1970s.

Insurance laws were tightened in 1955, but were loosened in 1961. And the state charge on which Osorio was indicted in 1971

was for violating the 1961 law against filing false information with
the Board of Insurance. District Attorney Bob Smith of Austin had
already persuaded the Legislature to revise the false-information
law, saying it was unconstitutionally broad. So the Osorio indictment, like that of his predecessor Garland Smith, was questionable.

National Bankers had been through a few more hands before
Governor Shivers bought 53 per cent of its stock in 1963. He in-
stalled Osorio as president, and they built the company up to substantial size, so that the book value of the Shivers holdings was
nearly $8,000,000 when Will Wilson came to see him in 1968. This
former attorney general (who had unsuccessfully run for governor
and senator) approached Shivers on behalf of a "client" whom he
did not name.

"What will you take for your National Bankers stock?" Wilson
asked.

"Book value," Shivers replied, "and that's $14.56 a share."

Wilson took the offer under consideration, and later returned,
bringing Frank Sharp of Houston and revealing that he was the
client.

"Whatever you and Will agree on is all right with me," Sharp said
after they had haggled a bit.

Wilson offered $7,500,000 for the Shivers stock, saying he would
write a contract that day.

"All cash," Shivers said, "and I'll take it."

They shook hands on the deal, but later Wilson asked for amendment, to pay $4,000,000 cash and $3,500,000 six months later, at
seven per cent interest. Shivers agreed to the change, but insisted
that he would retain voting rights on the stock until the final payment was made.

When it was later contended that cash "and other assets of National Bankers Life" had been used to pay off the final $3,500,000,
Shivers said that wasn't possible.

"I was running the company until the day they transferred the
$3,500,000 from the Republic National in Dallas to my bank, the
Mercantile National in Dallas," he recalled. "There was no way
they could have used the company assets to pay me, because I was
in control of the company assets until I got the money."

National Bankers went into receivership after the Sharp owner-
ship sold and bought stock right and left in the series of operations
which led to the 1971 Securities and Exchange Commission lawsuit, and the convictions of Speaker Gus Mutscher, Representative
Tommy Shannon, and Rush McGinty, Mutscher's administrative

assistant. They were charged with accepting loans from Sharpstown State Bank in return for helping pass legislation for a state
system of bank deposit insurance.

The bills passed, but Governor Preston Smith, who had also
made a profit trading in National Bankers Life stock with a loan
from Sharpstown State Bank, vetoed them. One of the men who
urged Smith to veto the bills was Shivers.

With BenJack Cage in Brazil, fugitive from a 15-year embezzlement sentence, and two high-ranking legislators and a former state
insurance chairman convicted because of it, National Bankers Life
has left its tracks on Texas politics and business.

RIVAL PIED PIPERS

FORT WORTH STAR TELEGRAM 4/12/56

—By Harold Maples, Star-Telegram Staff Cartoonist

The 1956 battle for convention control got wide play from cartoonists. Here is one using the theme of this book's title.

Chapter 20

Lame Duck Can Still Pipe

Tribulation came to the Shivers administration in 1956.

Faults of subordinates caused a loss of support that was compounded by the governor's retirement announcement, and the combination allowed those of little faith or of much political opportunism to jump on the lame duck.

But even in defeat, Shivers was able to punish the Democrats who had ousted him from Democratic Party control through a temporary coalition that self-destructed later in the year. Once again he led the state into support of President Eisenhower against Democrat Stevenson.

The year opened with typical acrimony. State Democratic Chairman George Sandlin charged that anti-Shivers forces were bringing in out-of-state labor oganizers to help "steal" the party conventions. The Democratic Advisory Committee retorted that such talk was a smoke screen to evade the issue of "corruption."

Insurance company liquidations were rampant. Talk about legislators calling themselves into special session to investigate alleged bribes proved to be only talk. A Senate committee asked the State Bar to draw the line between a fee and a bribe for a lawmaker. Garland Smith resigned from the Insurance Board because of health. A Waco grand jury learned that A.B. Shoemake once had been making weekly reports to Smith on how much U.S. Trust was taking in on the "certified drafts" it was selling, when it had no license to sell securities.

At about this time Shivers announced he would not seek a fourth term, as many had urged, but would continue his fight to get a voter expression on interposition. He said it would not be a stand for segregation or integration but a move to strengthen local authority and protect it from federal interference.

Interposition was the shibboleth which Shivers used to rouse his backers, who warmed to it even though few understood it. Shivers said states should get together and interpose their views when federal courts or agencies made decisions on matters left by the constitution to the states. He wanted to invoke its vague power in such questions as school desegregation and the tidelands issue—and to put the opposition on the defensive by the old political trick of asking how they stood on it.

Sandlin sent out letters asking that local conventions draft Shivers for head of the delegation to the national convention.

This drew prompt counteraction from Rayburn, again speaker of the House. He suggested that Senate Majority Leader Johnson be given the twin honors as delegation chairman and favorite son candidate for the presidential nomination. Rayburn had quarterbacked favorite son campaigns for John Nance Garner in 1932 and 1940—and had held out just the right length of time in 1932 to get Garner on the ticket as Franklin D. Roosevelt's running mate. No newcomer to the national political scene, Rayburn knew he had a drawing card. He also knew liberals would join him in support of Johnson, even though many did not completely trust him. Johnson was, after all, in office for another four years, while Shivers was on his way out. And because Jake Pickle, later to become congressman, had helped set up campaign organizations for both men, lots of Texans were to feel the heat of taking one at the expense of deserting the other. Shivers knew the exigencies of such a situation, and knew that most political animals stay close to the feed trough.

Mrs. Hilda Weinert, national committeewoman, suggested that Johnson take the favorite son role and leave the delegation chairmanship to Shivers. But she got no response from the Rayburn-Johnson camp. Shivers demanded almost daily that long-time friend Johnson—now an opponent—take a stand on interposition and the Southern manifesto signed by many Southern congressmen. He said Texans might understand why the majority leader of the Senate might refuse to get involved in the manifesto controversy.

"But we're talking here of a majority leader for Texas Democrats," Shivers pounded. "I don't see how Senator Johnson or any other aspirant for that honor could avoid taking a stand on interposition."

He also asked that Johnson state his stand on federal aid to education, restoration of the two-thirds rule for nominating at national conventions, on repeal or weakening of the Taft-Hartley Act and how he stood on Adlai Stevenson for the nomination. Shivers said Texans needed to know if Johnson was traveling under the sponsorship of the people who put up his name—and whether he had adopted their platform. He said Rayburn was seeking to divide conservatives through use of Johnson's candidacy.

Whatever the strategy, it worked. The Rayburn-Johnson forces won about three-fourths of the delegates to the state convention in Dallas, and Shivers conceded, saying a majority had expressed themselves in favor of principles "with which I am not in accord." Talk immediately started about possible removal of state committeemen and women who had supported Eisenhower in 1952.

The frailty of the winning coalition was demonstrated at the state convention. Delegates spent 13 hours deciding how unified they were. They gave Johnson both the chairmanship and designation as favorite son, and picked Mrs. Frankie Randolph and Byron Skelton for the national committee posts. After long debate they decided against ouster of committee members who had supported "Ike," but they called on all to resign if they had any doubts about supporting the next Democratic ticket. Before the convention adjourned, there were wounded feelings on both sides. Johnson was unhappy because the liberals rejected Mrs. Lloyd Bentsen, Jr., wife of the congressman who later was to become senator, for the national committee. Loyalists were irate because they had been unsuccessful in their drive to purge the "infidels," the Ike supporters of 1952, from party offices.

At the convention, Robert Cargill of Longview filed petitions asking the State Democratic Executive Committee to seek primary election voter views on interposition, intermarriage and integration. A check was ordered to see if enough names were on the applications.

As might have been expected, Attorney General Shepperd was pushing for a stand on interposition because he wanted to block oil and gas price fixing by federal agencies. James P. Hart, Austin attorney and Senate hopeful, said interposition was a futile effort to nullify the decision of the Supreme Court of the United States. He said he didn't think people should use such a "devious" method to get around a court decision because it would do little more than raise false hopes and stir up bitterness and distrust. His argument did that with Shivers.

Reuben Senterfitt, former House speaker who wanted to be governor, said Daniel, Shivers and Shepperd were not really worried about infringements against state and individual liberties except where oil and gas companies had financial interests. He said citizens should demand legislative action, since some places needed protection from integration while others didn't. About this time, U.S. Attorney General Herbert Brownell visited Shivers at Woodville and revived talk that Richard M. Nixon might be dumped for Shivers as Ike's running mate in an effort to get back the oil and gas support lost by Ike's 1955 veto of a bill to modify federal gas price controls. The visit wasn't centered on that point in the first place, and producers had no choice except to stick with Ike or go to the liberals—which was not attractive.

The insurance board ran a "solvency test" on active companies, and found some 120 about on the brink of shutdown. When it was over, 99 out of 1,318 did not seek re-licensing. For the most part, they were small companies, usually in the category of the under-financed sort that Shivers had sought to prohibit.

The governor's race—rather, the contest for Democratic nomination—got under way with Senterfitt, Yarborough and Daniel, as top candidates, with former Governor (and senator) W. Lee O'Daniel trying a comeback, and unknown J.J. Holmes and right-winger, J. Evetts Haley, filling out the ballot. Shivers took no part, but during the campaign, and before the national convention, announced he would be unable to support a Stevenson-Johnson presidential ticket or any ticket containing Stevenson.

Daniel and Yarborough led the first primary returns, with Daniel ahead by 628,914 to 463,416. In the run-off, Daniel won by 3,171 votes—most of it from the Duval County lead he got in the George Parr county which had turned thumbs down on Shivers in his races with Yarborough.

Daniel, however, faced the prospect—which turned out to be a very real threat—of a liberal-controlled Democratic September convention known as the "governor's convention." Shivers' forces, recalling the liberal instructions for their group to hold rump conventions at precinct and county levels and plan on help from there on, got set to contest eleven counties which had enough votes to switch control of the convention to the conservatives and Daniel. The governor went to the Southern Governors' Conference and left his lieutenants and Daniel in charge of the Fort Worth Convention.

They took charge, and one of their first moves was to replace Kathleen Voight, San Antonio organizer of the fight that had helped Johnson and Rayburn defeat Shivers in May. She was replaced as Bexar's committeewoman by Mrs. Spike Brennan, wife of Daniel's Bexar County campaign manager, in a concession granted by Johnson and Rayburn. The new state committee of 62 members was estimated to have at least 45 who had backed Daniel—and 45 to 50 who had supported the Democratic ticket in 1952. Picked for officers were Jim Blundell of Dallas, chairman; Mrs. Marietta Brooks of Austin, vice chairman; and Jake Jacobsen of Austin, secretary.

The convention endorsed Stevenson and Kefauver, but Daniel said he didn't. So, he won and lost. And he infuriated liberals by letting Mrs. Randolph, the national committeewoman who was on an unseated delegation, sit outside the convention hall with other Harris County liberals. National Committeeman Skelton got in, but as a delegate from Bell County.

Daniel recalls that a few days before the September convention, he conferred at the Governor's Mansion with Shivers, State Chairman Sandlin and Weldon Hart.

Daniel wanted to work out a coalition with Shivers, but it broke down quickly when Daniel said he wanted to have Fagan Dickson as the state committeeman for the Austin district. Dickson had been a leader of the Loyal Democrats of Texas and was persona non grata to Shivers. But he had been Daniel's first assistant attorney general, and had supported Daniel in the 1956 primary.

However, Daniel did make an accommodation with Speaker Rayburn and Senator Johnson, who were miffed because the liberal-loyalist forces had made them accept Mrs. Randolph as national committeewoman at the June convention in Dallas. And the Shivers people in the convention joined up with Daniel against their old liberal enemies.

For the Daniel-Shivers-Rayburn-Johnson coalition to win, it was necessary for the El Paso delegation, which had barely been challenged, to be tossed out in favor of a conservative group. Woodrow Bean of El Paso, who had been "going along with Rayburn," had to be sacrificed to give Daniel the convention majority, so he was.

Each district elected its members of the committees, so the resolutions committee refused to report out Daniel's platform. It had to be brought out on minority report, and then was gaveled through the convention without being read.

The outrage felt by the Loyalist group led to the formation of the Democrats of Texas, which became the best-organized liberal Democratic group in Texas until it was shattered in 1960 by division over the favorite-son candidacy of Senator Johnson. The labor-liberal-black-Mexican-American coalition dissolved, and was never revived. The DOT group was responsible for Ralph Yarborough's election as senator in the special election of 1957 and in 1958, and that gave the liberal movement new life until it fell apart over the LBJ candidacy.

And, as a footnote, Fagan Dickson of Austin was elected to the

Courtesy, *THE HOUSTON CHRONICLE*

state committee. But Shivers didn't have long to mourn over that.

Segregation came back into the picture when school opened that fall. Trouble arose at Mansfield (Tarrant County) and Shivers sent a Texas Ranger to the scene to preserve the segregation most citizens seemed to want. His explanation was that he'd rather have segregation and peace than integration and trouble (such as had occurred a few days earlier in Tennessee). Federal attorneys studied the situation to see if the governor had violated the law, but did nothing.

Shivers announced again for Eisenhower and against Stevenson, saying he was not satisfied with the latter's statement that the tidelands issue was settled and that he would oppose use of federal troops in the integration matters. Shivers said he wanted a statement from Stevenson about whether he "would use troops, bayonets and tanks to bear on children and people who gather around schools." Daniel said he was satisfied with Stevenson's statement on the tidelands and would support him. Weldon Hart resigned again to head the "Texas Democrats for Eisenhower," and Blundell resigned from the state committee chairmanship but not over Stevenson. House Speaker Jim Lindsey was chosen to replace him. W.R. Smith of San Antonio was named to head the Democrats for Eisenhower campaign, while Tom Miller of Austin and Warren Woodward of Dallas headed the Stevenson drive.

Daniel resigned as senator, effective Jan. 15 or such earlier date as his successor should be elected and qualified. Shivers said that made it impossible to have a senator there for the Jan. 3 organizational meeting of the Senate at which Johnson's razor-thin margin as majority leader would be at stake.

Shivers called it a "post-dated" resignation, and asked for a legal brief on the question. Thad Hutcheson, Houston Republican, said the resignation was effective and an election should be held on Nov. 6. However, Secretary of State Tom Reavley refused to accept his filing for the office. Shivers took two of his sons and left for Alaska on a hunting trip. It was on their return that the governor heard that Rayburn and Johnson had said he and Eisenhower both were politically "dead" and that the Democrats would win. That put him to campaigning in earnest. Yarborough campaigned for Stevenson, and the final count was 1,080,619 for Eisenhower vs. 858,958 for Stevenson.

The Pied Piper could still play the tune the voters liked.

After the returns were in, the mail started pouring in asking Shivers to run for Daniel's U.S. Senate seat and give the Republican administration the Senate majority leadership. He said "no."

Shivers held that the law would not let him appoint a successor to Daniel before Jan. 15, 1957, and then it would take 60 to 90 days to elect a new senator. Talking like a Democrat, he said Johnson's job was at stake, and called on Daniel again to resign without the "post-dated" feature. The arguments continued, with numerous lawyers taking varied positions on the question. But Shivers knew he was the only one who could settle it, and he held Daniel's feet to the fire for an out-and-out resignation.

There never was much friendliness between Shivers and Daniel, either when Daniel was attorney general or when he was senator. So theirs could well be called an arms-length relationship. During this period, they were farther apart than that.

Daniel's position was that he had submitted his resignation in such a way that Shivers could have called the special election for Nov. 6, general election day. Daniel had pledged during his campaign that neither he nor Shivers would appoint his successor.

Shivers contended that Daniel's Jan. 15 resignation was timed to let him control both offices. Since the election had not been called, if Shivers failed to act, Daniel would vacate the Senate seat by taking the oath as governor, and thus make the appointment. Daniel countered that Shivers wanted to appoint a Republican, and give that party majority status in the U.S. Senate. With Daniel there and voting, the Democrats had a 49-47 majority. If Daniel's replacement were a Republican, it would be a 48-48 tie, and Vice President Nixon could cast the deciding vote to let the Republicans organize the Senate and move Senator Johnson from majority leader to minority leader.

Inaugural morning, Shivers appointed Dallas Oilman-Rancher William A. Blakley, a Democrat. Johnson's job was safe. Daniel was properly inaugurated, and went to the Mansion for the hot lunch the outgoing First Lady traditionally leaves for the incoming family.

At long last, Allan had made good on that promise to Marialice of getting out of politics.

In retrospect, Shivers said the 1956 events were the only really serious disagreements he and Johnson had had, adding, "I shouldn't have been there in the first place." Johnson agrees that he shouldn't have been in the 1956 fight, either. Shivers said he tried to tell Johnson that his allies in the spring fight never had supported him and were as opposed to Johnson as to Shivers. It was a mistake to get into the fight, Shivers said. "We never wanted to control the Democratic faction—we were trying to control the Eisenhower faction."

Shivers said he and Johnson never had been in conflict over the 1952 situation; that Johnson did not make much of a fight in 1952 and even in·1956 didn't stump the state as Rayburn did. Rayburn remained hostile to Shivers to his death. Rayburn could have blocked the seating of Shivers at Chicago in 1952 if he had wanted to do so. Shivers had told him he would make no promise to support just any nominee, but Rayburn apparently did not think he would go so far.

In his swan song—a report to the 55th Legislature—Shivers noted that some problems he had helped solve early in his seven and a half years in office were back for solution again. He again urged revision of the state's tax laws. And in a surprise statement of moderation, he suggested the use of common sense in integration of schools—a much less belligerent tone than he had used when in office.

In 1925 Governor Pat Neff had started a tradition by leaving a Bible marked at a passage which he considered good advice for his successor. Shivers marked for Daniel the 6th verse of the 4th chapter of Philippians:

"Be careful for nothing; but in everything by prayer and supplication with thanksgiving let your requests be made known to God."

That first clause translates in the Revised Standard Edition to, "Have no anxiety about anything." That was good advice for Daniel, who was by nature a worrier.

Photo Courtesy, *TEXAS PARADE*

Governor and Mrs. Shivers at Woodlawn, with Samantha and
Peaches.

Chapter 21

Woodlawn

Tears and wine flowed the day Marialice Shivers got the historic Pease mansion, Woodlawn, which she was to restore and enlarge for a family home. And meeting the strict timetable set by the seller almost kept her husband from performing his last formal function as governor.

Most of the tears were shed by Niles Graham, for the home of his grandparents had been his own home most of his life; but Mrs. Shivers made her contribution to the tragi-comic scene.

The wine was provided by the eccentric Mr. Graham, who once had been known as quite a friend of the bottle but who in years preceding the sale had been a teetotaler. He had it served by a Negro butler, Link Thompson. And he had arranged for his long-time Episcopal rector, the Reverend Charles A. Sumners, to offer a prayer for the occasion.

Plans for the rector's part had been made weeks in advance, and Graham called at 6 a.m. on the day the house was to be turned over to remind him of the hour.

Things got off to a shaky start when the rector arrived. The door was swung open for him by Thompson, and Graham, in top hat, frock coat and gray formal trousers, bowed low to welcome him. But when he removed the hat, the Reverend Mr. Sumners could not restrain a bit of laughter—which understandably hurt the seller's feelings. The pastor then had to explain that Graham had been wearing the hat backwards and the red bow from the sweatband had stuck to his forehead. That settled things for the time.

The Shiverses drove up, chauffeured by a state highway patrolman, and were welcomed by the butler and by Graham, who told them about his life in the storied old colonial mansion and his reluctance to leave.

Shivers had to be on the platform in front of the Capitol in an hour to see his successor, Price Daniel, take the oath of office, so he was just as anxious to end the ceremony as Graham was reluctant. But he and Mrs. Shivers listened.

"He cried as he told how he'd slept on the floor of the vacant house the night before," Shivers recalled. "He said the house had never been without its owner before that morning.

"He told us he had looked at the walls, searching for the faces in pictures which had kept him company over the years," Shivers added. "He said that when he had been drinking they were the greatest conversationalists he ever knew because they never talked back or interrupted."

By this time both Graham and Mrs. Shivers were weeping. In a few minutes Graham turned to the rector and said, "Charles, you better get to praying."

The Reverend Mr. Sumners had prepared his contribution carefully, and opened with a request for blessings on the former statesmen who had occupied and visited the rooms. Then he asked blessings on the Shivers family moving in, and moved on to his benediction about Graham and his long residence there.

"Niles and Marialice both started crying, and I cut that part short," he recalled.

It was then that Graham called for more glasses of wine, and Shivers attempted to break the solemnity of the occasion by asking, "Does the boy go with the house?" Thompson said that he didn't wait for Graham to reply, but assured Shivers himself that he was not part of the deal. He also said he did not partake of the wine, explaining, "I don't drink."

The affair turned back to a lighter vein a few minutes later as Graham went to the big front door to hand Mrs. Shivers the large hand-wrought key. It turned out to be wired to the doorknob and she could do no more than reach down and touch it.

"I had two keys until I had a party here for the seminarians," Graham explained.

He had given a party a short time before for students at the Episcopal Theological Seminary of the Southwest, and in mock seriousness implied one or more of them had not been trustworthy.

But it gave a humorous ending to the transaction, allowing the nervous governor and his wife to leave for the Capitol ceremonies they had to attend.

"We just made it to the Capitol," Shivers said.

Shivers knew the reason for Graham's adamant stand on the timing of the house turnover, but the Reverend Mr. Sumners did not learn until fifteen years later. It was 100 years to the day and hour since Governor and Mrs. E.M. Pease had left the governor's office and moved to Woodlawn, which had been built in 1853 by Abner Cook, who built the governor's mansion two years later.

Graham had surprised the Shiverses by getting out of the house by his self-appointed deadline, for he had a lifetime's accumulation of keepsakes—some of them the product of a wry sense of humor, such as a "slightly used" casket.

Among the memorabilia in the Pease Mansion were hundreds of pictures of dignitaries (and some of lesser estate) which lined the walls of the century-old house. Graham had moving vans gather them up and take them to storage, and was ready for formal transfer of the home at 11 a.m. on Jan. 15, 1957.

When Shivers had realized the deadline was to be met, he pleaded for a short delay, explaining that he had to sit on the inaugural stand at noon and that he and Mrs. Shivers by tradition had to leave a hot lunch for the incoming residents of the Mansion and their families. Mrs. Shivers had inquired about the number expected, and was told 150, so she and those preparing a beef Stroganoff lunch were as nervous as the governor. But Graham sentimentally explained that his time of transfer had governmental implications, too, and he wanted the change made on the dot of the one-century mark.

So it was that Shivers went to his office early that morning to attend to some final details of his administration, including appointment of Blakley to the U.S. Senate. Then he put through a call to Senator Johnson to inform him and to assure him that the replacement in Daniel's Senate seat would vote with the Democrats in organization of the Senate and enable Johnson to keep his post as majority leader.

Then the governor dropped by the Mansion to pick up his wife and they hurried to the big old house a short distance from the tiny apartment they had rented when they came to Austin for the first legislative session after their marriage. She was to add a wing and completely remodel the house, while at the same time preserving its original colonial design.

Mrs. Shivers redecorated, rearranged and refurnished the home, even to installation of an elevator to the second floor. She directed as thorough a project as she had undertaken while living in the Governor's Mansion and was later to do at Magnolia Hills (the Shivers home) and at her own Sharyland home.

The Shiverses' acquisition of Woodlawn had not been easy. The couple had been to Houston on a series of house-hunting expeditions while the governor considered a bank presidency offer in

1955. They had not found anything suitable, so when Shivers decided against the bank proposal, they started looking again in Austin.

When they heard the Pease home was going on the market, both
thought it would be an ideal place for their family. But Shivers
made mental notes of the cost of structural strengthening and
redecorating, and decided the sale price was too high. Things
rocked along until 1956 when Shivers was in Florida on an Eisenhower campaign trip. Weldon Hart called him to say that he thought
if Shivers telegraphed the offer of a certain amount, he would get
the house. Shivers sent the offer to Tom Graham, son of the owner,
and talks got underway.

The first disagreement came when Niles Graham wanted to keep
the mansion's old slave quarters and a small plot on which it was
located. Shivers said he wanted all of the four-acre grounds or
nothing. Graham said he couldn't have all of the half-block for the
mansion because he had sold an eight-foot strip on the west border
to two adjoining landowners, Fred Sharp and H. Ted Read.

"I asked him why in the world he had done that," Shivers said,
"and he replied succinctly that 'they wanted it and I didn't need it.'
Then he added 'and you don't either.' " Details were worked out at
last.

Shivers couldn't help wondering what Graham was going to do
with the casket he had bought "after only short use." The story was
was that a Scotsman had died in Austin, with a meagre estate. But
his will provided that as soon as his estate earned enough, his body
was to be shipped back to Scotland for final burial.

As Graham told it, the estate built up the necessary funds after
only 17 years, so the body was dug up, put in a vault, and shipped
back to Scotland.

The "slightly used casket" was sold to Graham, his story went,
and he planned to use it for his own burial. But it turned out, according to his daughter, Mrs. James Harman, that he sold it to Paul
Rogers for a museum at San Marcos.

It is somewhat symbolic that Shivers bought the Pease mansion.
Pease was a native of Connecticut who came to Texas early, and
was one of those volunteers at Gonzales who fired the first shots of
the Texas Revolution. He was secretary of the Committee of Safety
at Mina (later to be named Bastrop) in 1835, then became secretary
of the General Council, and attended the 1836 convention at which
independence from Mexico was declared.

Pease served in various clerical jobs during the remainder of the

Revolution, and was offered the postmaster generalship of the Republic by Sam Houston. He turned it down to resume the study of law, was admitted to the bar in 1837, and successively became comptroller, district attorney, and then Brazoria County's member of the first Legislature of Texas. He became a senator in 1849, and was elected governor in 1853 and again in 1855. Pease, like Shivers, was a progressive in conservative times, but he was a staunch Unionist. He left the governor's office after being the first to live in the Governor's Mansion, built in 1855, and moved to Woodlawn.

In 1866, he was the candidate of the Union Party for governor, but was defeated by J.W. Throckmorton, the Democratic candidate. When the radicals in Congress refused to recognize Throckmorton, martial law was invoked, and Pease was named military governor of Texas. But he was a moderate—called at that time a "conservative Republican" as opposed to the "radical Republicans" of that day. He resigned in protest of the Reconstruction policies, and continued to fight within the Republican Party for easier treatment of the Confederates. He became collector of customs at Galveston for a time, then returned to Austin where he was vice president of the First National Bank of Austin when he died in 1883.

So Pease and Shivers had similar careers—operating within both the Democratic and Republican parties, and winding up in banking.

Woodlawn had been built for Comptroller James B. Shaw in 1853, and was soon on the market. Shaw, a native of Ireland, had been a money man for Sam Houston, and had established Woodlawn as a 200-acre estate in what is now Enfield and Tarrytown. Pease bought it, and his heirs later subdivided much of it, but retained the four-acre Woodlawn which Shivers acquired in 1957.

Mrs. Shivers' renovation work took her time, and that of a dozen craftsmen, for more than a year. The Shiverses lived in a rented home during that period. Mrs. Shivers took advantage of the interval to select such things as lighting fixtures, candelabra and furniture for the new-old home—some of it from Sharyland, and some from the French antique markets of New Orleans. It was restored as a Southern Colonial mansion of the 1850s, with full integrity for that period.

The family was often to recall the pomp and ceremony of the transfer of the key, and to have many happy hours and some sad ones, but they weren't entirely free of politics.

GOLF
BOB HOPE

U.S. Open Champ. CARY MIDDLECOFF

GOVERNOR ALLAN SHIVERS
DOAK WALKER

SUN. OCT. 28-2 P.M.
RIVERLAKE COUNTRY CLUB

ADMISSION

$1.00

PUBLIC INVITED

ALL PROCEEDS TO

CEREBRAL PALSY

ASS'N. OF DALLAS

Courtesy of the Shivers Museum Collection

Being governor had chores which, for Shivers, were more pleasant than cutting ribbons, crowning beauty queens and leading the line at barbecue dinners. Here is an example of liking his work, which also was his favorite recreation.

Chapter 22

Postgraduate Work?
No, Thanks!

When Shivers left political office, he didn't mean to leave all politics behind—either specifically or generically.

But in the period immediately after his "retirement," he was asked (1) to join the Republican Party as a state leader — with national potential; (2) to help create a third national party that would seek to get rid of the extreme "right" and "left" elements of existing parties; and (3) to help feel out public sentiment on better relations with Red China.

He rejected the first two proposals, and turned in a negative public reaction, headed by his own, on the Red China idea.

The Republican feeler came soon after Shivers closed out his 7 1/2-year administration and Eisenhower began his second term. Shivers had just bought an interest in E. Gary Morrison's Western Pipeline Company. Jack Porter, then National GOP committeeman from Texas by virtue of his active roles in "Ike's" two campaigns, came to Austin to talk with Shivers about what he called a plan of mutual benefit to Shivers and the party.

Porter offered to resign, and virtually guaranteed election of the former governor as national committeeman in recognition of his leadership in carrying Texas twice for "Ike." That, Porter argued, would solidify Shivers' position as a king-maker in the state and also would put him in a strong position with the national policy makers. It also offered the possibility of getting the Texan on the GOP ticket to succeed Eisenhower.

But, attractive as it was and knowing his days of leadership in the Democratic Party possibly were over, Shivers turned it down. He was to wonder for years what might have been if he had accepted (as he did about other things he had passed by, beginning with an appointment to the U.S. Military Academy and running through offers of cabinet posts, presidencies of two banks and one university).

What most got his attention during his post-politics period was the overture from Eisenhower about a third party. It's not easy to argue with a president.

The first mention came during one of the golf games they usually arranged when Shivers got to Washington. Shivers enjoyed them more and more as he got used to Secret Service "caddies" carrying side arms in shoulder holsters and others with rifles in golf bags keeping spectators at a distance from the players. At the first discussion, Shivers listened but was politely noncommittal.

It came up again and again during later golf contests, and although Shivers never had agreed with splinter movements, he listened carefully. Eisenhower had the idea that if such an organization could be set up, it could nominate and elect someone of the stature of Robert B. Anderson, the Texan, who had been Secretary of the Navy (on Shivers' recommendation) and at that time was Secretary of the Treasury.

"He [Ike] was disgusted with the extreme right and the extreme left," Shivers said. "He also was disgusted with the self-seeking businessmen and labor leaders whom he called 'Selfish Bigots,' and he thought a third-party election of someone from the middle of the spectrum would be good for the nation."

Eisenhower talked with numerous friends over the country, and asked that they get together for conferences. Shivers met with everyone the President suggested, even while arguing that he had a horror of splinter parties turning the country into a political spider web such as France had been. He contended more good could be achieved by working within existing parties than by siphoning off members into a third party.

Shivers marveled that in spite of the fact that there were many participants in the discussions—some of them well-known in the newspaper, radio and television fields—the word never leaked out. Any of the group could have "spilled" the story to a favorite news gatherer, and there were a variety of business executives who could have done so without incurring suspicion.

The story has not been told until now. In 1972, Shivers was playing golf at the Augusta National Golf Club in Georgia, where he had played often with Eisenhower, when he encountered a mutual friend who had taken part in the conferences. "He asked if I remembered the talks, and of course I did, but I had not discussed them with anyone until he brought up the subject," Shivers said. "And I'm sure no one else had."

Shivers met with leaders in Texas and in many places in the East about the third party idea, but it never got the spark for which Eisenhower had hoped.

The Red China idea also was Eisenhower's, and while it also "wouldn't fly" at the time, it was later to come to fruition through President Nixon.

"Ike" had an idea that this country could make a gesture of economic friendship toward the Red Chinese that might lead to ultimate recognition. He sent a trusted lieutenant around the country to talk about the possibility in the late 1950s, and Shivers was host at a luncheon in Austin at which the emissary met with Texas friends. They were given assurance it was something the President wanted—if not all at once, at least on the piecemeal basis Nixon was to adopt.

Shivers remembers that it was the consensus at the luncheon—"and certainly my opinion"—that it was not politically feasible at the time for the United States to give any sort of recognition to the Peoples Republic of China.

"But I think it is interesting that Eisenhower had the idea then that this was something that was going to be done some time in the future and possibly should be done as soon as possible."

Shivers thought Nixon's approach was the best possible solution, "and of course he has not yet caused the U.S. to actually recognize Red China or have diplomatic relations with it," he said in 1973.

But the Texan thought it a step in the right direction to have Red China in the United Nations, to recognize its ping pong players in this country, and for Nixon to visit in Peking.

Maybe "Ike" could have done it that way. Maybe he was just ahead of his time. But at the time, Shivers was more interested in winding down his public activity and expanding his personal interests.

Just as he had turned down presidents and their staff members on job offers while governor, he had to reject one by a former cabinet officer when he was leaving office.

When the family discussed the transition from public to private life, the governor wasn't exactly sure what he wanted to do or where to do it.

The late Jesse H. Jones of Houston, the towering Democrat of the Franklin D. Roosevelt era, offered one solution. The former Secretary of Commerce and chairman of the Reconstruction Finance Corporation suggested that Shivers become president of the National Bank of Commerce of Houston.

Consideration went as far as house-hunting in Houston and discussions of the effect of such a move from Austin on the four children. Nothing jelled immediately, and Jones died, so the project was shelved by the governor. Later, he was offered a place on the bank's board of directors, and took it.

Shivers also began serious additions to the business interests he had maintained on a more or less part-time basis while he was in office. In partnership with W.E. Dyche, a Houston lawyer who had been a classmate at The University of Texas, Shivers acquired interests in banks in the Houston area. One of their projects was a "first" in the Texas financial world: the Houston First Financial Group, a holding company for the Houston First Savings Association and the Bank of Texas. They converted First Savings, a mutual association, into a stock company, then formed the holding company so as to put both the savings company and the bank into a single firm.

Similar financial holding companies have since been formed, and the idea has been expanded to provide a roundabout way for branch banking in Texas. In late 1972, the Austin National Bank, of which Shivers was chairman of the board, followed that route to financial flexibility. Shivers was also a director of the Texas Bank of Commerce of Houston, Citizens State Bank of Woodville and of the First Financial and Houston First Savings of Houston.

Shivers' other financial-area interests included advisory directorships of the Chemical Bank & Trust Company of Houston, Galeria Bank of Houston, Capital National Bank of Houston and Peoples National Bank of Spring Branch. In 1973, he was a director of the Texasgulf Company of New York; Global Marine, Inc., of Los Angeles; Celanese Corporation of America, New York, and Lone Star Industries of Connecticut. He and Mrs. Shivers had some private holdings and interests in family corporations related to citrus production acreage around Sharyland.

They owned the 600-acre place called Magnolia Hills which Shivers' great-grandmother bought when she came to Texas as a widow in 1846.

It was there that the "keepers of memories" instincts of both Allan and Marialice Shivers could be seen so clearly. Here, in front of the lake which lies in front of the home are the six liveoak trees which Marialice planted while he was overseas in 1943.

Around the house are the magnolias, some native and some transplanted, which give the estate its name. Adjoining is the Woodville golf course, which ranks with Augusta National and the

Austin Country Club as places where Shivers can be looked for when he is wanted.

The original "log cabin" they built with peeled pine logs, when they first got the piney woods "farm" back in the family, has grown extensively. The second enlargement was completed in 1972, adding two guest bedrooms and converting a patio into an enclosed playroom. The former front porch is now a pleasant, sunshiny sun porch, overlooking the lake. The giant rock and log living room with wagonwheel chandeliers is filled with trophies of African hunts bagged by Allan and son, Brian. Elephant tusks, a cape buffalo head, a lion-pelt rug and stools made of elephants' feet decorate the walls and floors.

But everywhere are those memories. Here are pictures of the annual meetings of the members of Augusta National Golf Club, with Shivers at the center of the group each time. This, like everything in the home, recalls a story of golf.

One sketch has Tommy Armour, the pro at Boca Raton during a Southern Governors Conference, sitting with a glass of gin instructing a Brooklyn tourist on how to drive.

"I'm one of golf's immortals," Armour shouted to his student, "and I can't hit the ball if I don't look at it."

The cape buffalo recalls what the "white hunter" leading their safari advised Brian, who asked what to do if the first shot at the buffalo, the world's most fearsome game animal, should miss.

"Look for a tree, laddies," was the sage advice.

Framed on the wall is an "agreement" between two of the Shivers children at fifth- or sixth-grade level, in which they solemnly pledged to "be nice to each other" and signed their names in affirmation. Other family mementos crowd Magnolia Hills with the memories the Shiverses look back at and treasure in close family fashion.

As often as they can, the Shivers family goes to Magnolia Hills, always finding time to visit Woodville to see what's happened to the place which will always be their home town, despite the fact that most of their married lives they have lived in Port Arthur or Austin.

Shivers, a sentimentalist about family homes, bought "Peachtree Village" in 1959. It was the famous John Henry Kirby place near Chester. Kirby had been a plunger, and saw his life's love go on the auction block. G.W. Armstrong of Fort Worth, Shivers' equal on sentiment, bought the 6,000 acres and gave it back to his friend, Kirby. After Kirby died, Shivers was fearful that it would be broken up, so he bought it from a surviving relative. He sold it a few years

The Shivers family near the end of his second record-setting administrative tenure. The Governor and Mrs. Shivers with sons John Shary (left rear), Robert A. Jr. (Bud) (front, left), and Brian (front, middle), and daughter Marialice Sue (Cissie) (front right), later Mrs. Dillon Ferguson of Houston.

later to Temple Industries, but not before Mrs. Shivers got some "remodeling" done. She leaves her mark on every place she owns. She put a chapel on the grounds, just as there is in that ebony grove at Sharyland. She got the chapel fenced in, and she also got the home place remodeled. And then she got the Chester Lions Club to make a museum of it—just so a little more of Texas could be preserved.

But mainly, the Shivers family lived in Austin at Woodlawn during the years after he left the governor's office. He was concentrating on business affairs, and on golf when he found time. Mrs. Shivers was active in her civic undertakings, and practicing her belief that a wife's duty is to "provide a good home for her husband and children." So they were busy and productive in the first ten years they were back in their public sort of a private life.

Chapter 23

Something To Remember Us By

Oct. 1, 1966 was a big day for Allan and Marialice Shivers—and for Tyler County and the surrounding area. It was the day of dedication for the library the Shiverses had given the Woodville Independent School District, and the adjacent Allan Shivers Museum. Jasper and Diboll had smaller libraries, but the new one was the biggest thing "this side of Beaumont."

Typically, it embraced a bit of Mrs. Shivers' penchant for redecorating and some of her husband's nostalgia.

They heard that the old Robert A. Cruse home was going to be demolished in the name of progress—to make way for a new motel for Woodville. Mrs. Shivers liked the 1881 architecture of the home and wanted it preserved. The former governor had a soft spot for the Cruse family because he had "jerked soda" in the drug store owned by the son of the man who built the two-story home.

So they bought a lot a block from the original site (and no more than a good golf shot from Woodville's Wheat Junior High and Kirby Senior High Schools) and moved the Cruse home.

Mrs. Shivers completely restored it to top condition and furnished it in keeping with styles of its time. Three chandeliers were found in New Orleans to complete the renaissance. To recall the early-day privations of the area, the men's room at the museum was papered in Civil War newspapers printed on wall paper because of the shortage at the time.

The library, a completely new structure, was planned just as modern as the museum was post-bellum. And a patio connecting the two has on the wall a tile mural by Woodville artist Clyde Gray depicting the life of the Shivers family from the time the governor's great-grandmother settled at the Magnolia Hills farm he considers "home."

It portrays her son's return to Mississippi to fight in the Civil War

and brings the family through Shivers' father's service as lawyer
and judge and Shivers' own service as senator, lieutenant governor
and governor. One scene shows the 1949 swearing-in at the family
farm, with the ladies of Woodville ready to serve "dinner on the
ground" when the oath had been taken.

The museum, dedicated by Governor John Connally, has its own
library of books that must be examined or read inside the building.
Nearly all existing books on former Presidents John F. Kennedy
and Lyndon B. Johnson are there, most of them autographed by the
authors.

There is an original letter from Sam Houston (to a girl friend,
Anna Raguet), a panel of Republic of Texas currency and a bond of
the Confederate States of America.

There is the American Good Government Society's annual award
to a member of each major party (Shivers got it in 1954 along with
former President Herbert Hoover).

And there is the 1971 designation of the Shiverses as "Mr. and
Mrs. East Texas" at the annual Tyler County Dogwood Festival.

Hundreds of memorabilia line the walls, including an appreciation plaque given Shivers in 1972, quoting from Genesis that "there
were giants in the earth in those days."

There is a letter from President Eisenhower, explaining to
Shivers how it happened that Ike's attorney general was filing suit
against Texas over the tidelands after they thought that issue was
settled. It reflects the exasperation of a military man at the quib-
blings of the lawyers, but concedes that Attorney General Brownell
had his own constitutional responsibilities.

There are the scissors used in long-forgotten ribbon-cuttings, the
cuff links and other tokens given governors on ceremonial occasions, his college diplomas, notable letters—each of them recalling
a happening during the busy life the museum portrays. Keys to cities, honorary degrees, photographs of ceremonies and of Shivers
with other officials—Eisenhower, Johnson, Nixon, Rayburn and
many, many others—a memory lives and a story accompanies each
for those lucky enough to have Shivers as guide on a tour of the
museum.

Upstairs are gowns Mrs. Shivers wore at each of her husband's
inaugurals, and some worn by their debutante daughter (Marialice
Sue, now Mrs. Dillon Ferguson) at coming-out parties over the nation.

And one wall contains original drawings of editorial cartoons
from over the country, and photographs made on special occasions

during his more than seven years as governor. The old home also contains a room that is used for public meetings, with chairs considerably more comfortable than the Victorian sofas and seats in other rooms.

A hallway contains the Freedom Shrine pictures of the 28 most important documents in U.S. history—a gift from the Exchange Club of Beaumont.

Outside, to preserve the 1880s touch, is a well with bucket on a rope; the kind the governor used as a boy.

There was good news awaiting Mr. and Mrs. Shivers the day we visited the museum and library with them. Mrs. Doretta Gilchrist, president of the auxiliary board of the library, was just back from a meeting of the Tyler County Commissioners Court.

"We got some more money from the county," she reported.

The library was built and donated to the Woodville Independent School District, but both Tyler County and the City of Woodville contribute to its operation, through a six-member board.

Every time the Shiverses come to Woodville, they bring more books for the library—some they have bought, and some gifts from friends. Other friends, knowing of their interest, buy a new book, read it, and then donate it to the library. Many of the Shivers books on golf have found their way to the Woodville library once he has read them and gleaned their ideas on how to improve his golf game. And, the librarians say, the golf books are being read.

People come from outside Woodville to see the museum, and to use the library. But it's treasured by Tyler County people, as well as by Mr. and Mrs. Shivers who felt it was a way for them to say "thanks" to the homefolks who supported him through the years, who in 24 hours got enough signatures in 1960 to put him on the ballot for United States senator, and who still consider him and his family as neighbors, friends and homefolks.

So it's something for Woodville to remember them by.

Photo Courtesy of the Shivers Museum Collection

Senator and Mrs. Shivers with Governor and Mrs. W. Lee O'Daniel at Port Arthur in 1940, when O'Daniel was winning a second term and purging many legislators who had opposed his tax plan.

Chapter 24

A Lyndon Johnson Man—Sometimes

"Say it isn't so, Allan."

That was the tone of hundreds of letters and phone calls in 1964 when Allan Shivers told one of these authors for a newspaper article that he would support Lyndon B. Johnson for president that year.

Many of his companions of the 1952, 1956 and 1960 campaigns for the Republican ticket for president and vice president just couldn't believe that Shivers would support Johnson.

"I began to get letters from old Johnson haters who had been supporters of mine," Shivers said. "I believe I got more bitter letters than I had received during all the turmoil and strife of my own campaigns. But I felt that I should support Johnson in his bid for re-election and that he deserved my support. As a matter of fact, I think he made a good president.

"I believe he is doing a good job, and while I do not agree with all of his legislation, I believe he will be better for the country than Barry Goldwater," was the way the former governor put it in 1964 in his office in the Austin National Building.

These two powerful Texans, whose careers in public office ran parallel for years, never did have but one serious crossing which, as Shivers described it, "shouldn't have happened, because I shouldn't have been there in the first place." That was in 1956, when they contested in the Democratic conventions for leadership of the national convention delegation, and Johnson won, going away.

Johnson felt the same way—that he shouldn't have become involved in the convention fight.

Trying to put together the relationships of these two Texans who between them dominated Texas politics for two decades or more recalls what Hubert Mewhinney wrote in the *Texas Spectator* in the later 1940s. It was designed as a criticism of the then current attitude of Texas newspapers—that you quote what the man says, and that's all.

"If Jimmy Allred says it's raining, and W. Lee O'Daniel says it isn't raining," Mewhinney wrote, "Texas newspapermen quote them both, and don't look out the window to see which is lying, and to tell the readers what the truth is at the moment."

The truth, of course, will never be known, because what these two powerful men said and thought about each other in private was and still is veiled. Mind-reading is not the profession of old-time newspapermen like these authors, although it seems to have come into style in later years among younger, better-educated reporters.

Take, for example, the situation when Johnson was nominated for vice president in 1960. He had told all who asked him that he didn't feel that he had done anything to justify his demotion from majority leader of the Senate to vice president.

"Every morning I tell the vice president what the Senate is going to do that day," he said. "Why should I sit up there and have the majority leader tell me what is going to happen?"

Yet, when the time came, Johnson accepted the nomination, and won, with the opposition of Allan Shivers.

Here is the Johnson version of how that reversal came about:

Joseph P. Kennedy called Senator Johnson at his Biltmore Hotel suite in Los Angeles the night Kennedy's son had won the nomination for president.

"I'm for you for vice president," the elder Kennedy said.

In a few minutes, Speaker Rayburn called to say that Johnson was going to be offered the vice presidential nomination.

"Don't take it," Rayburn said.

"Don't worry, they won't offer it," Johnson replied.

The next morning, Johnson was still asleep when John Kennedy called and told Mrs. Johnson that he wanted to come to the suite and talk with her husband. Johnson dressed hurriedly. Kennedy came in and asked him to accept the vice presidency.

"I remember what happened to Al Smith," Kennedy said. "We need you to help out, and after all you did get the second highest vote for president."

Johnson demurred, and Kennedy went on. Johnson would unify the party. He had the experience. The Senate would support such a ticket. He owed it to the party to accept, and not let Shivers carry Texas for the Republicans again.

Johnson thought he would be more help to Kennedy as majority leader than as vice president. But he had no objection when Kennedy said he wanted to talk with Rayburn.

Kennedy talked with Rayburn, and swung him over by stressing what kind of a president Richard Nixon would be. Rayburn never had any use for Nixon. After that talk, Rayburn came to Johnson's room. He recalled how Al Smith, a Catholic like Kennedy, had lost the South.

"You ought to go on that ticket," Rayburn said.

When he was asked how he happened to reverse what he had said earlier, Rayburn replied that he was a damn sight wiser now than he was at 2 o'clock in the morning.

Robert Kennedy made three trips to the Johnson area in the Biltmore. First he tried to dissuade Johnson himself from taking the nomination. Next time he talked to Rayburn. The third time he talked to John Connally, getting lower on the chain of command. By then, Johnson had agreed to make the race.

He did not agree with the view of Governor Daniel, given in Jimmy Banks's *Money, Marbles and Chalk*, that he did not expect the Kennedy-Johnson ticket to win when he accepted the vice presidential nomination.

"I wouldn't be on a ticket, even for public weigher, if I didn't expect to win," Johnson's comment went.

Shivers had promised to support Johnson for president if he got the nomination. But when it was John F. Kennedy at the head of the ticket, Shivers opposed LBJ for vice president, and campaigned for the Nixon-Lodge ticket, and against Kennedy.

"Johnson called me up from California when he accepted the place on the ticket with Kennedy and asked me to support the ticket. He said: 'You promised me you'd support me if I was nominated.' I said, 'You haven't been nominated. Kennedy has been nominated. I can't support him.' He [Johnson] finally said, 'Well, I'm like that fellow up that tree—if you can't help me, don't help that bear.' I said, 'Well, I can't answer that right now. I am very fond of Nixon and I probably will support him.' But then when Johnson himself was nominated in '64 I supported him—although, again, he didn't need any help."

Actually, Shivers and Johnson had talked about Johnson's presidential possibilities in 1960, at a party given by Secretary of the Treasury Bob Anderson on a Treasury boat in the Potomac. Johnson had just had the word from Arizona, where John Kennedy's organization, headed by Representative Stewart Udall, had won the Arizona delegation. Johnson's organization had sent State Senator Dorsey Hardeman of San Angelo out to Arizona. Jerry

Holleman, president of the Texas AFL-CIO, who was working in
the Johnson-for-president organization, laughed about that.

"I'm too conservative to talk to those miners in Arizona, and Marvin Watson sent out Hardeman, a real conservative," Holleman
said.

At any rate, Shivers asked Johnson whether he would accept the
vice presidential nomination. Johnson said he wouldn't, that the
Senate majority leader was far more important.

"I agreed with him," Shivers said, "but I also told him that if he
were offered the vice presidential nomination, he couldn't refuse.

"He just laughed."

But it turned out that way, much to the consternation of many LBJ
people.

"A lot of people, as you will recall, got mighty mad about it when
Johnson accepted the vice presidency," Shivers said. "I told every
one of them that there wasn't any question in my mind—he had to
accept it. He would have been in a very embarrassing position later.
There's no question in my mind but that Johnson on the ticket was
responsible for the Kennedy-Johnson election. You'll get lots of
agreement on that. If he had not been on the ticket and Kennedy
had been defeated, then the party people would have blamed him
for it—for not taking the vice presidency. That shows how smart the
Kennedy people were in selecting him."

After Shivers had told Johnson that he was inclined to support
Nixon, Earl Clements of Kentucky called Shivers, trying to get him
to go along with the Kennedy-Johnson ticket.

"I don't think I can support Kennedy," Shivers told Clements.
"No, I've got to research him a little more, but I don't think so. I'd
like to have Lyndon, but I don't think I can support Kennedy."

Under the law, you can't divide the presidential and vice presidential candidates, so Shivers voted for Nixon and Lodge that fall.
After the Clements call failed to switch him, no more calls came his
way. And, as far as Shivers recalled, there was no personal reaction
from Johnson over Shivers' decision of 1960. Some of the Kennedy
campaign people who were personal friends of Shivers did contact
him but that was all.

The relation between Johnson and Shivers was tenuous at the
beginnings of their careers, but it was natural for them to be drawn
to each other.

Shivers was elected to the Senate in 1934, and shortly thereafter
Johnson became the Texas director of the National Youth Administration, one of the few officials in Texas who had money to shell out

for creating jobs for the thousands of unemployed young people.

They were similar in appearance—tall, thin, black-haired, fast-moving, talkative, friendly—and both were biased a bit toward dark-haired people. They met occasionally in the Austin political-social circles, the parties to which politicians are invited.

"Our relationship was very friendly personally, while he was in the House of Representatives, the Senate, minority leader, majority leader and vice president," Shivers said.

That friendship made it possible in 1957 for Johnson to retain the cherished Senate majority leadership. Shivers recalled it this way:

"When I announced the appointment of Bill Blakley, I immediately telephoned then to Senator Johnson and advised him of it, told him that I wanted him to know that I had appointed Blakley, and that Blakley as a Democrat would support him as majority leader. He was very appreciative and said Blakley was a very good friend of his. That was surprising; although he knew Blakley, very few other people knew him, including Tom Clark, who was from Dallas."

Shivers had talked with President Eisenhower about that appointment, after Daniel's nomination for governor made it clear that there would be an interim senator, and then a special election, despite Daniel's insistence that the special election be held in November.

"Ike asked me what I was going to do about it, and I said, 'Well, we've been debating it and discussing it with lawyers to see what the situation is,' " Shivers said. "I think I'm going to appoint someone."

"Well, I'm sure you're going to get a lot of pressure to appoint a Republican," Eisenhower said, "with the situation in Washington like it is."

"I don't think I can do that," Shivers replied, noting that this would change the organization of the Senate from Democratic to Republican, and demote Johnson from majority to minority leader.

"I'm glad to hear you say that," Eisenhower said. "Actually, I know you can't afford to do it."

"I never did give a thought to doing it," Shivers said. He had told Johnson that, earlier, without telling him he was going to name Blakley.

In 1948, when Shivers had had an easy race and Johnson had his toughest one, the 87-vote victory over former Governor Coke Stevenson, one of the 87 votes was Shivers'.

But there were times when the two were wary of each other.

Their political paths crossed again in 1952 at Chicago, when the Maury Maverick delegation of Loyal Democrats, made up largely of those who had helped Johnson win the Senate race in 1948, was challenging the Shivers delegation.

President Harry S. Truman had promised Maverick that his delegation would be seated, but did not come to the convention. The Texas fight raged hot and heavy, and was finally turned when Senator Richard Russell, who was favored by Shivers for president, warned Adlai Stevenson that if the Shivers delegation were ousted, he [Russell] would walk out of the convention. Johnson served as the liaison man between Shivers and Rayburn, who was inclined to support the Maverick group, and the three met at Johnson's hotel suite for the conversation Rayburn and Shivers always remembered differently. It had to do with whether Shivers would support the party ticket that fall—regardless.

Rayburn thought Shivers had said he would support the nominees, and took his word as Governor of Texas.

Shivers was equally certain that he did not.

"I made no commitment to support the nominee and he made no commitment to have my delegation seated," Shivers put it bluntly. "I told Mr. Rayburn that I had been kicked out of conventions, but I had never bolted one, and that I had always supported the party but that I would not promise to do so in this case regardless of whether we were seated or not."

The third person in the room never said how he remembered it.

Johnson and Shivers campaigned for different tickets that fall, when Shivers had the winner and Johnson the loser.

Then in 1954, Johnson was coming up for re-election as senator, and Shivers was expected to wind up his term as governor. Rumors naturally developed, and newsmen speculated that Shivers might decide to go to Washington as a senator to help President Eisenhower whom he had helped elect.

In January, Shivers made up his mind to run for governor again, and one of the first calls he made was to Johnson, to assure him that there would be no conflict between them.

Johnson had only nominal opposition in Dudley Dougherty of Beeville. While there was no indication that Johnson was helping Shivers in his tough primary battle with Ralph Yarborough, they did talk by phone occasionally.

The two later met head-on in the 1956 precinct conventions, when Johnson teamed up with the liberals and loyalists to smother Shivers. Rayburn, never forgetting Shivers' bolt in 1952, forced the confrontation which both men said in retrospect they should not have been in.

"We were opposed to him on that—not on his being favorite son, but to Mr. Rayburn's proposal that he [Johnson] control the delegation and be favorite son, too," Shivers said. "I talked to Lyndon about that on two or three occasions, and told him we would support him as favorite son; that if he would join us instead the liberals, we could keep the control, and we'd go along with him for favorite son. But his long ties with Mr. Rayburn were so much stronger than his ties with me."

Johnson was trying a coalition with the loyalists in 1956, saying he was trying to hold the party together. Shivers agreed that this was Johnson's purpose, but:

"My point to him was that the people he joined up with in that particular fight against me were never for Johnson. They had always fought Johnson. They were almost as opposed to Johnson as they were to me. But he joined up with them in that fight against me, and of course beat the socks off of us. They won handily."

The night of the precinct conventions, Weldon Hart came back to the Shivers headquarters from his convention in Highland Park in West Austin.

"We've lost," he reported. "If we can't win by more than three votes in Highland Park, we're whipped."

"My group should never have been in that fight," Shivers declares. "We were supporting Eisenhower and had no business trying to control the Democratic faction, because we were going to control the Eisenhower faction."

But the Shivers-Johnson fight left no permanent scars, since they were both political pros.

"I think both of us considered it just another political campaign," Shivers said. "It did get pretty rough at times. We referred to each other in uncomplimentary terms."

But a year after Ike and Allan had defeated Adlai and Lyndon for the second time in Texas, Shivers was in Washington on business, and Johnson was majority leader. Shivers called him up from the Sheraton-Carlton and asked Johnson to come down and have a drink on his way home.

"He asked who was there, and I told him, and he knew all of them," Shivers recalled. "And I said I had called Bill Francis [of Houston who was then working for Eisenhower at the White House on Shivers' recommendation] and he's coming over here also."

Johnson wanted Shivers and his guests to come to his office for a drink, but Shivers insisted.

"He came by and not only had a drink, but spent the evening and had dinner with us," Shivers went on. "And he has been a really good and very generous friend since then."

Asked about Johnson, who was considered anti-conservative because he was against Shivers, and anti-liberal because some Texas liberals would not accept him, Shivers gave this insight into Johnson:

"Let me say this for him in defense of that kind of charge. People all over the United States have often asked me, knowing that I knew him and that a lot of political office-holders are called 'wind riders'—and they say, 'Is Johnson a wind rider?' And I said, 'No, he isn't. He can smell the wind changing and he changes before the wind does. He's ahead of it.' "

That is perhaps the most careful explanation of LBJ yet given, and it comes from one who experienced the same sort of change, but in a different sequence. It is based on the innate feelings of both Shivers and Johnson, that a politician—a successful one—represents his constituency. Both changed, as they went through their careers, and in each case, they could say in good faith that they were representing those who had elected them—their constituents.

And it is worthwhile to note that Johnson lost only one race; Shivers lost no political contest, except the time he and Johnson tangled in the precinct conventions.

"He was FDR's fair-haired boy, even to packing the Supreme Court (which LBJ then called 'unpacking')," Shivers recalled. "But he supported Roosevelt, and it helped him immeasurably, of course.

"Then in his Senate race against Coke Stevenson, he began to take that turn toward the more conservative because he saw that shift in power from the Roosevelt era on down to a more conservative approach to politics. He began to cast a lot of conservative votes in the House—Taft-Hartley and others—there were a lot of others.

"But when it was necessary to make a change for his good, he lined up with the liberals, despite the fact that he and I had always supported each other.

"But he always managed to win. I call it being ahead of the wind. He could smell the change, and he'd change very easily."

Johnson would never agree with that analysis of his political views. Like his father, who was a Texas legislator, President Johnson always had Populist views. He grew up in a hard and droughty land, had to work hard, had a hard time getting an education, and from those experiences came his leadership in landmark education laws and programs. He was certainly far "ahead of the wind" when he took on Austin's business establishment to build the first public housing project in the nation. Rural electrification, low-cost yardstick public power and other programs which brought him undying opposition from the private power companies, would seem to illustrate Johnson's long-time "corporation hating" background.

And when he got into positions of real power as Senate majority leader and as president, he was quite often creating the wind which led to civil rights, education, health and welfare programs.

Johnson saw himself as a lifelong liberal and would point to the censure of Senator Joe McCarthy to show that he was one when the going was toughest.

When Johnson was majority leader and Eisenhower was president, Shivers thought Johnson was one of the main contributors to Ike's effectiveness.

"As majority leader of the opposite party, Lyndon was certainly of tremendous help to Eisenhower during his terms," Shivers declared. "I asked him [Johnson] while he was in office as president if he didn't wish he had an opposition leader who was supporting him as strongly as Ike had had."

"It would be a blessing," Johnson replied. But he would add a historical footnote that his support of Eisenhower was only on programs on which he thought Ike was right.

Johnson and Shivers talked once at the LBJ Ranch in 1956 about the decision by Senator Daniel to leave the Senate to run for governor.

"He told me one time out at the ranch that Daniel was the only one who could beat Ralph Yarborough in that race," Shivers recalled. "Lloyd Bentsen was threatening to run for governor, as were several others. (Senator Jimmy Phillips was perhaps the leading conservative actually in the race.) But Lyndon told me himself that he thought Daniel was the only one who could beat Yarborough."

He was barely right. Daniel won by the grace of the hefty Duval County majority.

Johnson stayed out of Texas primaries, although he was often suspected of having a hand in one or another. Perhaps the most famous one was the primary race that never came to pass between former Congressman Joe Kilgore and Senator Ralph Yarborough in 1964.

Shivers and Johnson viewed Kilgore's decision to stay out of the race differently.

"I think because of his own race Johnson didn't want a race against Yarborough going on because it would be a heated contest and would divide up the state again," Shivers surmised. Shivers and John Connally were trying to get Kilgore to run, and they wanted Johnson's help. Shivers remembered it this way:

"He [Johnson] told me that he had promised George Meany that he would protect Yarborough, and that he was going to do it. I tried to tell him, and Connally did too, that he didn't need George Meany—Meany needed him. And that Kilgore would make a much better United States senator than Yarborough, that he could depend on Kilgore to really be of help to him and that he knew he couldn't trust Yarborough. I think now what he was planning for, and he accomplished it, was to get a tremendous vote for himself, and he did."

Kilgore was a close friend of Connally and of Walter Jenkins, Johnson's most trusted assistant. He was also a close friend of Johnson, although Kilgore was far more conservative than Johnson and would have been uncomfortable indeed voting for Johnson's Great Society programs.

Kilgore had a suite in the Driskill Hotel in Austin where he was having meetings about his possible candidacy. Johnson was in a meeting of the National Security Council when Jenkins brought in a note. Kilgore was on the phone, and had said he was going to the State Capitol to announce for the Senate unless Johnson objected or refused to go along with him.

"Walter, you know I don't get involved in primaries," he said after glancing at the note. "You tell them I'm not going to get involved in that."

As Johnson himself was to say at a meeting in Houston that year with Yarborough on the platform, Yarborough had a hundred per cent record of support for Great Society programs, and up to that point had been in support of Johnson's Vietnam policies.

Actually there was more going on than the abortive Kilgore candidacy. Friends of Senator Ralph Yarborough had been talking with friends of Johnson about a deal by which Don Yarborough (no relation) would be discouraged from running against Governor Connally that year (1964), and in turn there would be no strong candidate like Kilgore against Senator Yarborough. Don Yarborough had run Connally a close race in 1962 and was burning to try again. Supporters like Walter Hall of Dickinson felt that such a race would be hopeless, and got substantial promises of support for Don Yarborough if he would run for Congressman-at-large and thus be in a position to run for the Senate in 1966 against Senator John Tower. Some of that support came from close friends of Johnson, who were also friends of Connally.

Like many such "deals," it fell through. Don Yarborough insisted on the abortive try against Connally's second-term bid. While Kilgore bowed out, a political unknown named Gordon McLendon of Dallas ran against Senator Yarborough. Shivers and many of his supporters helped McLendon.

That fall, Johnson endorsed Senator Yarborough and the rest of the Democratic ticket, and, late in the campaign, both Governor Connally and Senator Yarborough sat on the platform with LBJ in a display of party unity.

That was the year Shivers endorsed Johnson for president, but of course he supported Republican George Bush against Yarborough in November.

The respect between the two leaders, despite their strong political differences, remained mutual.

"I trust him as an ally or an opponent," Johnson once said of Shivers. "We're different politically, but I've never known two men on different sides who had better rapport."

Their differing views on federal-state issues created no problems for them.

"Did Johnson interfere in state matters—pressure members of the Legislature to vote certain ways?" Shivers was asked.

"Not at all," Shivers replied. "Not while I was in office."

They had little contact while Johnson was vice president and Shivers was getting his business career steadied down. Shivers was in Washington, attending a board meeting of the Chamber of Commerce of the United States, on Nov. 22, 1963, the day his friend became president. He had gone to his hotel room after lunch, and the phone rang. It was an Austin friend, telling him of the assassination in Dallas. Like everyone else, Shivers didn't believe it.

"Turn on your television and see it," the friend advised. He did. He sent Johnson a telegram pledging him help and support, and returned to Texas that evening. As he left the hotel, he overheard someone in the hotel lobby say: "Blame it all on Texas."

Some time later, the phone rang at Woodlawn one evening while Shivers was at home. It was the White House calling.

"I'm sitting here with an old friend of yours, and we just thought

SOMEBODY ANSWER THAT OR I WILL!

MONDAY, JANUARY 27, 1964 - FORT WORTH STAR TELEGRAM

Courtesy, THE FORT WORTH STAR-TELEGRAM

we'd call you up and say hello," President Johnson said. The friend
was Jake Pickle, the new Congressman from the 10th District who
had been elected a few days after the Kennedy assassination. Pickle
had worked in Shivers' organization as well as Johnson's and Price
Daniel's, until he decided to be the candidate himself instead of the
organizer.

"I know you're in Washington a lot, and I want you to come by
whenever you're up here," Johnson told Shivers. "If you start coming up here and don't come to see me, I'm going to send the FBI
after you."

This revived the relationship between Johnson and Shivers
which had been dormant since 1960. As Shivers moved up in the
Chamber of Commerce hierarchy and made more trips to Washington, he was invited to the White House often. Sometimes it was for

a private dinner in the second-floor family dining room with one or two other couples. Once, Shivers was having dinner in Washington with some Austin people, and a presidential aide tracked him down.

Shivers was called to the phone, and found it was LBJ calling. He was having a briefing of Congressional leaders, and wanted Shivers to sit in.

"I'm sending a White House car for you," Johnson said, eliminating the possibility of a "no" from Shivers. Shivers went, and sat in on the briefing.

"He hit on what was a great idea, not inviting Congressional leaders over for a white-tie function, all at one time, but inviting them over in groups and having the Secretary of Defense or the Secretary of State talk to them, and explain some things," Shivers said, adding: "And he also gave them a drink—punch, of course—which they liked."

In 1967, when Shivers was chosen to be president of the Chamber of Commerce of the United States, he called LBJ and asked for an appointment. He was told to come over at 6 o'clock.

"I wanted to tell him myself that I was going to become president of the Chamber," Shivers explained. "Organizations like the U.S. Chamber are often critical of government. I said that I thought I would probably understand government better than any former president of the U.S. Chamber, and I would like to have a closer relationship with him and the government."

That relationship worked out well, as will be shown later.

But Johnson gave Shivers no inkling of his decision not to run again in 1968.

"I can appreciate his decision," said Shivers, who had made several such attempts to get out of public life. "But I certainly had no indication."

He was, with most Americans, surprised when Johnson said in 1968 that he would not run again in a race which history has shown that he probably would have won, just as Shivers would have won a U.S. Senate seat had he run for it in 1952 or 1957.

The Johnsons and the Shiverses, in "retirement," met on various occasions in and around Austin. The Johnsons attended the wedding of Cissie Shivers in 1970 and the reception which followed. The Shiverses attended the dedication of the LBJ Library in Austin, and Shivers went to an economic seminar Johnson held at LBJ State Park. Not long before his death, Johnson was in Austin at his barber shop, and had a Secret Service agent call to ask if Shivers would be

Governor Shivers and President Lyndon B. Johnson had their closest relationship when Shivers was president of the Chamber of Commerce of the United States during Johnson's elective term. They are shown in the White House.

in his office. He would be, so Johnson went to the Austin National Building for an hour of visiting. "What did they talk about?" we asked.

"Just visiting and recalling things," Shivers said. "Nothing really important. Just talking about things we've been through."

And both of these important Texans had been through a lot.

Shivers thought that Johnson's career as majority leader, vice president and president did something to erode the sectional prejudice that a man from the South or Southwest cannot be a president. If so, it was one of Johnson's major contributions, in his opinion.

Chapter 25

A New Way of Life

"This boy is in real bad shape," the strange doctor reported to the former governor late on June 6, 1968.

He was calling from Eufala, Alabama, and was talking about Robert A. Shivers, Jr.—known as "Bud" for most of his life.

Bud had dived off a pier at Lake Eufala just as waves from a passing motor boat jostled an aluminum skiff beneath the pier and moved it into the open a bit. He hit it full force.

A Coast Guard friend called Shivers and told him Bud had been in an accident and might have a broken collar bone but he thought it was nothing serious. Shivers asked the youth to have the doctor call after he finished an examination. Then he began arranging a plane flight for himself and Mrs. Shivers.

They had been to Eufala only a week before and knew the lake where the accident occurred. Bud had finished Coast Guard basic training and had been sent there a short time before. All of them joked about the Coast Guard having a station inside Alabama, but Bud explained that about half a dozen men were stationed there to police the heavy barge traffic.

The second trip was anything but pleasure, with the parents flying while officials and doctors were debating what procedure should be followed. The Coast Guard wanted to send Bud to the base hospital at nearby Fort Benning but the doctor who made the initial examination wanted him moved to a hospital in Columbus, Georgia, which had a good neurosurgeon. The doctor said he wasn't sure the patient could survive the trip but that it was urgently necessary to get him to a neurosurgeon because it appeared his spinal cord had been severed.

Attendants put him in an ambulance and packed sand bags around him so the motion wouldn't cause further damage to his spine. An Episcopal rector made the trip with him and helped get him located in the hospital.

He was awake and alert when the parents arrived about 11 p.m., and he said, "Daddy, I've dived off that place a hundred times."

Dr. Charles LeMaistre, later to become chancellor of The University of Texas System, called Shivers and volunteered to bring the head neurosurgeon from Southwest Medical School at Dallas, which LeMaistre then headed. The two of them recommended moving him to Wilford Hall Hospital at Lackland Air Force Base in San Antonio. He was flown there in an Air-Evac plane with nurses and most hospital facilities aboard. Shivers went with him.

They learned the fourth and fifth vertebrae were shattered and the spinal cord probably severed. Surgeons took some bone from his hip and attempted a repair, but it didn't hold and had to be done over. He stayed in Lackland until October, getting messages from all over the country and having a list of visitors that included President Johnson.

Bud went to the Texas Research and Rehabilitation Hospital in the medical center at Houston for treatment and training in movement. He got home for Christmas briefly, then returned on a permanent basis in January, 1969. He was confined to a wheel chair, with small prospect of getting out of it.

The whole family joined in the effort to make things as normal as possible for the patient, who made it easier for all by maintaining an outlook described as "excellent." Always a joker, Bud never lost his sense of humor or his morale—or, if he did, he didn't show it.

He enthusiastically helped outfit the bus he bought and named "Ironside" for the television character confined to a wheelchair. His father got the plans for the "Ironside" bus from the producers of the show, and Bud modified the plans to suit his own needs, including air-conditioning and a convenient bathroom. When it was finished, he could go to parties and take friends along with him on trips to the country, to shows or even to Houston, where he went to be best man at a schoolmate's wedding.

While his parents were adjusting to "the biggest change in their lives," Shivers one day mentioned to Jack Hayman, a Negro employee who lived on the grounds, that he had to find someone who could care for Bud and stay with him nearly around the clock.

Hayman asked if he might go to Austin's Seton Hospital and take the necessary course in patient care and then look after Bud at home. He completed the courses and took over.

Later his parents talked Bud into going to New York to see a specialist at New York University Hospital. He wasn't particularly interested or optimistic about the results, but he went. He came home after four or five weeks.

His life since then has been restricted to the wheelchair and bed but he is able to join the family for meals and go to parties small enough that his chair would not be in the way. An avid reader, he spends a lot of time with books. He went to Cissie's wedding in his chair, escorted a bridesmaid and sat in the receiving line.

As his father remarked, Bud leads a relatively normal life except for the wheelchair, "getting along as well as anyone could under the circumstances."

For him and his parents, there was help from hearing from friends all over the world. And they don't complain or worry. "There's not much you can do but live with it," Shivers says.

But for all it was a new way of life.

It meant that most visits with kinfolk were at Woodlawn. John, eldest son and only sire of grandchildren, has two sons and three daughters who frequently drop in. So does Brian, a student at The University of Texas at Austin. At greater intervals come visits from Marialice Sue or "Cissie" who is Mrs. Dillon Ferguson of Houston.

"Grandma" Shivers, who lives in Port Arthur, has a habit of spending alternate Christmas and New Year holidays with the former governor and his sister, Mrs. Maurine Wilson, who lives in Dallas. Sometimes she shows up for other holidays. But when she has finished her visit she wants to be driven home. That's her only concession to being driven.

"I've got a lot to attend to at home," she says when they beg her to stay over another week.

Mrs. Shivers comes from long-lived stock. Most of her brothers and sisters have made it to their 90s. She has twin sisters younger than she, and in 1973 had an older sister still living.

WASHINGTON REPORT
PUBLISHED BY THE CHAMBER OF COMMERCE OF THE UNITED STATES

World spotlight on Annual Meeting

National Chamber gears for action under Shivers

■ **WORLD SPOTLIGHT** was on the National Chamber this week as the 55th Annual Meeting grappled with national problems and Secretary of State Dean Rusk used its platform for a major address on world affairs and Viet Nam.

Everything was "go" from the Opening General Session in Constitution Hall, where more than 4,000 delegates and guests heard Secretary Rusk's dramatic indictment of Hanoi for responding "no" to 28 peace proposals, until Dr. Norman Vincent Peale delivered his stirring challenge at the closing luncheon.

In between, Allan Shivers of Austin, Tex., took over the presidency from M. A. Wright; world, national and community problems were discussed, debated and acted upon, and Jack Benny played the violin. (Details can be found on other pages and will be reported in future issues of WASHINGTON REPORT.)

SOCIAL HIGHLIGHT was The Dinner, at which President Shivers and an impressive headtable of business and government leaders were introduced to more than 2,500 diners before they were entertained by Jack Benny with his 11-year-old violin prodigy, Doris Dodge, and Songstress Jane Morgan.

Causes for which the National Chamber stands "are beacons in a stormy world," the former Texas governor said in his first formal remarks as the 40th president.

"The more rapidly life changes and the more complex it grows," Mr. Shivers said at the elegant dinner, "the more validity do our free market principles and voluntary methods acquire, and the more essential they are to maintain—but also more difficult."

He cited our foremost task to preserve human individualism, "without which the voluntary spirit cannot live, nor any voluntary organization exist." *(continued on page 2)*

NEW PRESIDENT ALLAN SHIVERS accepts gavel from predecessor, M. A. Wright, in front of painting of first president, Harry A. Wheeler, in Board Room, Chamber headquarters.

Building on his earlier news conference pledge to work during his administration for greater participation by businessmen in solving local and state problems, Mr. Shivers said:

"Every effort we make to become better citizens; every increase in our understanding and appreciation of the free market system; every new responsibility we accept in a community cause, is our further contribution to human progress."

He pleaded for ever better communications with government at all levels, and a positive attitude, one in which "we work constructively together and at the same time use positively our right to express criticism or concern or recommendations as the situation may call for."

"Let's move ahead on the course we know is right," he concluded.

Courtesy of the Shivers Museum Collection

Start of his year as the nation's top business spokesman was heralded in this news letter of the Chamber of Commerce of The United States.

Chapter 26

The No. 1 U.S. Businessman

Jack Benny had played his violin, and the 2,500 American business leaders and their wives settled back in their chairs in the International Ballroom of the Washington Hilton to hear, that May night in 1967, what sort of man was this Texan, Allan Shivers, who had just received the gavel as president of their organization.

They learned what this man who had been successful in both politics and business was going to make the major goal of his year as president of the Chamber of Commerce of the United States:

"We can make a contribution by developing ever-better communications with government—local, state and national. Our contribution will come from a positive attitude in dealing with government—in which we work constructively together and at the same time use positively our right to express criticism or concern or recommendations as the situation may call for. Let's move ahead on the course we know is right."

His brief "inaugural address" that night launched Shivers on a busy year during which he ruefully said he "had to neglect both my own business and the Chamber's business, because there simply isn't enough time."

Long-time observers of the Chamber's activity have suggested that Shivers' most significant actions during the year after he accepted the gavel from M.A. Wright, chairman of Humble Oil and Refining Company, was a long series of quiet meetings with top business leaders in all the major cities. Some twenty to thirty executives were invited to each meeting, to discuss with Shivers the need for business to play a more active role in public affairs. Shivers' goal at these and other meetings was:

"To get the average businessman more interested in the problems of his community and state, and more active in the political party of his choice. To do this, businessmen must take part in the selection, nomination and election of the best-qualified persons to public office at local, state and national levels."

"The meetings were action-oriented," one observer said. "Governor Shivers would open the meetings, effectively presenting the case for business action in public affairs with brief, extemporaneous remarks, and then lead what invariably turned out to be a wide-ranging yet penetrating and analytical discussion of the pros and cons of the problem. The meetings resulted in a number of companies organizing and/or expanding public affairs activities."

So the techniques by which Shivers had organized Texas businessmen for his campaigns and for his legislative programs were moved onto the national scene during that year. The program has continued as a part of the Chamber's policy.

It is just a block from the Chamber's offices on H Street, N.W. to the White House, where another Texan was living at the time.

The night after Shivers became the fortieth president of the Chamber, he and Mrs. Shivers had dinner with the Johnsons at the White House. They talked of how Shivers wanted business and government to work together, and Johnson joshed him about the *New York Times* story the day before which had called Shivers "a political charm boy."

"I think it is a good idea for businessmen to serve in government," Shivers said. "It gives them some knowledge of what government is all about."

The results of that dinner were quite apparent. Shivers' first official action was the appointment of a committee to appraise the impact on the economy which peace in Vietnam would have. This Chamber committee was to work closely with a committee within government created by President Johnson.

When dinner was over, Lady Bird Johnson reminded her husband that he had his "night work" to do. One of the manila folders in the foot-high stack of "things to decide" was a message to Congress urging an expanded training and job opportunities program for youth, and asking for $75,000,000 to finance it. Two days later, Shivers issued a statement supporting Johnson's request for money. It encouraged employers to create jobs for young people. But it also held government at arm's length by pointing out that the capital investment which business would make to create jobs would exceed by many times the $75,000,000 Johnson was asking government to spend.

The concern of the nation, as it focused on those two men as they talked that night around the family dining table on the second floor of the White House, was about the possibility of trouble in the streets during the coming summer. It resulted in an appeal to government and business policymakers to take actions in their own separate ways, to help solve the rising problems of unemployment of the young.

In this, and many other ways, the distance from the White House to the Chamber's offices was shortened during that year of close cooperation between the two Texans. When he was in Washington, Shivers would go by to see Johnson, to make suggestions and to get them.

One day when he went by, Johnson was having a meeting with a group of senators, budget officials and others. Marvin Watson of Daingerfield, Texas, Johnson's doorkeeper and appointments man, buzzed the President to tell him Shivers was there.

"The President asked Marvin Watson to bring me in, and I sat with them for awhile," Shivers recalled. "He introduced me, although I knew all of them except one.

"When the introductions had been finished, the President said, 'I want you all to know that Governor Shivers and I haven't always been together on everything. I have had him against me and for me, and I would much rather have him for me.'

"I felt the same way about him. I also believe that as President of the United States, particularly on foreign policy, he was entitled to my strong support on the basis that he had, or was in a position to obtain, the facts to support his position. He was the only man who could really speak for the United States in foreign affairs. My difference with him would be on domestic affairs."

Shivers had been a director of the Chamber since 1960 and was its treasurer when he was elevated to the presidency and began a most eventful year of travel, talk, visiting and working as the No. 1 spokesman for United States business.

While he supported Johnson's programs in some fields, he was quick to speak on Chamber policies. A week after he endorsed the youth jobs program, he voiced a warning that the federal government should not be taking over the transportation system.

"Let's dedicate National Transportation Week to proving that businessmen, in cooperation with all levels of government, can keep our transportation system moving ahead as a productive, taxpaying economic force."

On the railway labor dispute then under way, Shivers attacked a union for "using the public as hostages to enforce its demands on an employer," and used it as a springboard for a call for Congressional investigation of industry-wide bargaining, which he felt was a challenge to free enterprise.

A free trader, Shivers praised the outcome of the Kennedy Round of trade negotiations in general, and suggested that the promotion of exports by both business and government should be concentrated in industries in which imports were having heavy impacts. He was shortly appointed to the National Export Expansion Council by Secretary of Commerce Alex Trowbridge, to give him a way to make that proposal come to pass.

And, a few weeks later, Shivers was chairman of the National Conference on the Kennedy Round, called together to explain to businessmen the advantages of the removal of some significant trade barriers by those government negotiations.

Shivers started getting around the country that summer, beginning a series of 25 major speeches, a great many of them on the push for businessmen in politics. He had solid backing from delegates to the Chamber convention at which he had become president. A poll, taken on new-fangled voting machines, had shown that 99 per cent of the delegates felt that businessmen should involve themselves in helping to solve community problems such as education, welfare, race relations, unemployment, crime, pollution and slums. They also had voted that local taxes were inadequate to meet local needs and that business should support federal revenue-sharing. But 76 percent felt that businessmen in their communities were not as well informed on local problems as they should be.

Shivers set out to remedy that, not only with a series of small meetings with heads of major business, but also with public speeches at conventions, seminars and other events.

Three big leather-bound scrapbooks in his office show the attention Shivers got during that year. There are no clippings, of course, on the series of closed meetings. But many of his public speeches drew wide attention. That was indeed a year of travel for the Shivers family. Mrs. Shivers went with him on some of his trips, which included visits to Switzerland, Italy, Spain, Japan, Mexico and Canada.

In Detroit, at the National Association of Counties, Shivers said that outmoded state constitutions must be revised, to allow counties and cities to meet the demands of modern times. He said that specialists from the U.S. Chamber had met with business and government leaders in 45 states to get the reform movement moving.

"There is a ring of reform in the air," he told the county judges and commissioners, "the appearance of an idea whose time has come."

A series of 24 conferences on "Congressional Action" was held over the nation by Chamber executives, to show businessmen how to communicate their desires to Congress.

In San Francisco, Shivers told a tire dealers' gathering that the Social Security program should be kept, and that efforts to turn it into a welfare program should be fought.

In Dallas, he told a life insurance convention that the "rising concern for human rights should be extended to taxpayers, savers and pensioners" who are damaged by proposals for higher taxes for guaranteed annual wages, spending for the war on poverty and other programs which might not have been examined carefully enough.

He got a lot of editorial support for a speech in Houston to the Independent Petroleum Association in October, calling on unions to "grow up." He said that special privileges given unions in the Depression days are being hung onto "like an insecure child hanging onto a familiar toy."

At a Denver Chamber of Commerce luncheon, Shivers took a swing at President Johnson's consumer protection policies. "The federal government's labor and fiscal policies, not the business practices government is trying to regulate, are the real harm to the consumer," Shivers declared. This was his "Brother, you may be next" speech in which he told businessmen they should stand together against government encroachments in any industry.

In Columbia, South Carolina, Shivers said business must establish contact with the younger generation which, polls showed, was not convinced that business was concerned with social problems.

Shivers urged the use of force to recapture the *Pueblo* when the North Koreans captured it, took on the consumer protection movement as "political," and urged educators to take advantage of technological advances available to them from industry.

In February, he announced the "Forward America" program, an effort to fuse business, labor, civil rights and women's organizations into an attack on poverty. When President Johnson urged the finding of jobs for 500,000 hard-core unemployed, Shivers approved, saying that business was already at work on that problem, and would cooperate with any realistic plan advanced by the administration.

But Shivers was attacked by a writer in the *Chicago Tribune* for the "Forward America" plan, saying it was proposed by the Texas "in-group in Washington" and was "just an office to give advice, rather than a real program."

At a "growth cities seminar" at Tulsa, Shivers declared that civic leaders are too often concerned only with growth, not with keeping up "with the problems growth creates." He urged block grants to the states for the new law enforcement assistance program, because it would encourage states to take a stronger role in law enforcement. That view prevailed and became the law.

In March, Shivers took time off from business to practice what he had been preaching—at home. He testified to the Texas Constitutional Revision Commission that state government should be modernized by giving the governor the power to appoint key executives, so he would be responsible for what they did. But the prophet was not honored in his home state, and the commission produced a "nothing" set of recommendations.

In April, he and Mrs. Shivers went to Beaumont, where Lamar State College of Technology dedicated "Shivers Hall" and "Brooks Hall," the latter named for Congressman Jack Brooks who, as a Texas House member, had helped create the college 21 years before.

Shivers "turned to preaching" at the Executives Club in Chicago when he moralized on the need to say "no" instead of "asking government to do everything for you." His attack on greed led to an attack on him by the *Arkansas Gazette*, which said he shouldn't be talking about greed when he was "one of the principal architects of the tidelands oil grab."

Lyndon Johnson was coming up with a balanced budget for 1968, and of course Shivers praised that novel idea. He said it was time to be smarter about spending our national wealth, and came out for being more selective on spending programs.

"The man of mature spending habits sees an object lesson in someone lying in the gutter," Shivers went on. "The free spender sees a case for a new aid program."

By the time May arrived, and he handed on the Chamber gavel to Winton Blount, the Alabama contractor who was later to become Postmaster General in President Nixon's cabinet, Shivers was ready to get back to his private business.

The convention which ended his term bore the Shivers brand. Almost the entire program was devoted to political problems. Shivers had switched the traditional cocktail party and social reception to a workshop program on mutual understanding and mutual responsibility.

(He was soon to make the same sort of change in policies of the Austin National Bank. Instead of a dinner or a football party for customers and correspondent banks, Shivers had the bank sponsoring a speech by an interesting economist, followed by a cocktail party.)

But while his year as president of the Chamber has long since been ended, Shivers is still active in its work. In the spring of 1972 he was chairman of a Chamber conference at Litchfield Park, Arizona. The then Secretary of Defense, Melvin Laird, and a number of other speakers talked with fifty leading corporation executives.

You could almost guess what the subject was. It was a discussion of business responsibility, the current attacks on business, and analysis of where business is at fault and where the attacks are at fault, but in either case—what's to be done about it?

That remained his theme as he became Citizen Shivers but continued travelling over the nation.

At an age when most men think of, hope for or try retirement, he kept a schedule that would have taxed his sons and most men within 25 years of his age.

A typical six-weeks itinerary shows him with some Saturdays and Sundays at home, but not all of them.

Some of his travel involves trips to Washington for his job as chairman of the advisory Board of Directors of the Export-Import Bank of the United States. This carries on his interest in foreign trade shown during his Chamber of Commerce career, when he headed a delegation to Japan for conversations with Japanese business leaders.

The Export-Import Bank was created by Congress to promote exports of American goods by arranging for credit, with the principal requirement being that the loan will be used to buy U.S. made goods.

Other members of the board of directors in 1973 were: Stephen D. Bechtel, Sr., senior director of Bechtel Corp., San Francisco; William Blackie, chairman of the board of the Caterpillar Tractor Co., Peoria, Ill.; Walter L. Cisler, chairman of the board of the Detroit Edison Co., Detroit; Paul L. Davies, senior director of the FMC Corp., San Jose, Calif.; J. Victor Herd, director of the Continental Corp., New York; Mrs. Elizabeth R. Jager, economist for the AFL-CIO, Washington; Arthur L. Reisch, senior vice president of the First Western Bank and Trust Co., Los Angeles, and president of the Bankers Association for Foreign Trade, and Victor E. Rockhill, executive vice president of the Chase Manhattan Bank, New York.

If a steel mill was to be built in France, French banks would finance part of it, and the Ex-Im might finance the portion needed to buy mill equipment in the United States.

"It is one of the forces working to improve the balance of payments and the balance of trade for the United States," Shivers explained. "It has hundreds of millions in assets, and it has shown a profit every year."

When he was at one meeting during the fighting in East Pakistan, he noted that a big hotel in Dacca had been financed by the Ex-Im Bank.

"Fortunately, both sides agreed to spare as much of the city as possible."

Shivers mixes work with the Masonic orders, business corporations on which he is a director, banks on which he is board member or chairman, affairs of the First Baptist Church of Austin, Chamber of Commerce of the United States and events related to his favorite hobby—golf.

He is active in the business of the Scottish Rite Hospital and other interests; of the Headliners Club in Austin; of the Austin Club stockholders; and his own Austin National Bank. But he also puts on his calendar the important birthdates in his own family and special events for special friends.

He goes to meetings of the board of Texasgulf of New York; of the M.D. Anderson Cancer and Tumor Research Institute; of banks in Woodville, Houston and Austin; of Pacific Pumps, a subsidiary of Dresser Industries of Dallas; of Global Marine, Inc.; of the Augusta National Golf Club; of Celanese Corp.; and numerous Scottish Rite gatherings. He is leading a drive to raise $34,500,000 for the M.D. Anderson Institute. He has been named a distinguished alumnus of The University of Texas, and in 1973 was appointed to the UT System Board of Regents.

He is big business and philanthropy now, where he once was a barefoot working boy in East Texas and as eligible for aids as many of the folks he now tries to help.

Shivers has been called right some of the time and wrong some—and probably he was in both categories some of the time. But history probably will record that he was right oftener than wrong, and that should be good enough for any mortal man.

Shivers also has been called cold, harsh, and even, by some of his less charitable critics, ruthless. And possibly he fell at one time or another into one or all of those classifications.

Yet Weldon Hart, probably his closest political friend as well as employee, calls him one of the most gracious about saying "no." Hart says he did not hesitate to say "no" when that was his feeling. No one ever called him wishy-washy. But Hart contends he did it in such a way that almost no one went away with the feeling he had been trampled upon. To use Hart's words, he "made those he turned down think they had gotten fair consideration."

In many ways, he was—in the manner of Franklin D. Roosevelt—a product or a victim of his times, depending on the point of view.

No one can deny that he did many things for Texas that had to be done at particular times. Many were not times of his own choosing. Many were things a weaker or less aggressive man might not have achieved.

But, as far in retirement as he probably will get, he maintains the same belief he had as governor.

"Businessmen," he says, "must get into politics."

"The very existence of business depends on it," he contends.

"Like it or not, they are involved. They have to be."

And that is the Allan Shivers who, back when magazine writers were saying that he "held Texas in the palm of his hand," taxed business more heavily than anyone had up to that time, and who talked businessmen into liking it.

He never stopped piping.

Index

NOTE: Since the name of Allan Shivers appears on almost every page, it has not been indexed. And as the titles of many persons changed during the course of the book, "Mrs." is the only title used in this index.

A

Abshire, Mr., 26
Abshire, Virginia, 25
Acers, Maurice, 93, 94, 138, 164
Acheson, Dean, 109
Adams, Gilbert, 25
Adams, Sherman, 143
Adams, Tod R., 160
Aikin, A. M. Jr.,22, 131, 150
Aleman, Miguel, 65, 85
Allison, Dwight, x
Allred, James V., 5, 16, 18, 20, 22, 23, 28, 212
Allred, Renne Jr., 174
Anderson, R.B., 18, 74, 200, 213
Anderson, Robert, 129, 143
Armour, Tommy, 203
Armstrong, G.W., 203
Ashburn, Ike, 103
Ashley, Carlos, 161, 174

B

Bailey, Joseph Weldon, 7, 8
Baldwin, Robert B., 93
Banks, Jimmy, ix, 93, 96, 97, 98, 131, 134, 138, 213
Barkley, Alben, 54, 77
Battle, John S., 137
Baum, Harvey, 142
Bean, Woodrow, 187
Bechtel, Stephen D. Sr., 237
Beck, Harold, 16
Beck, J.E.H., 16
Bell, John, 132
Bell, Marshall O., 46
Benedum, Mike, 87

Benny, Jack, 231
Benson, Ezra Taft, 135
Bentsen, Lloyd Jr., 57, 185, 219
Bentsen, Lloyd Sr., 63, 88, 89
Betts, Charles O., 175
Blackert, E.J., 16
Blackie, William, 237
Blakley, William A., 93, 190, 215
Blount, Winton, 236
Blundell, Jim, 186, 189
Box, John C., 11
Braly, Earl, 93, 96, 97
Brees, H.J., 48
Brennan, Spike, Mrs., 186
Briscoe, Dolph Jr., 76, 96, 103, 104, 105, 128, 132
Broadfoot, A.S., 149
Broeter, Lorenz, 63
Brooks, Jack, 236
Brooks, Marietta, Mrs., 186
Brooks, P. Pierce, 179
Brown, Nelson, 93
Brown, Noel, 39
Brown, Paul H., 63, 99, 175
Brownell, Herbert, 185, 208
Browning, Gordon, 119, 129
Bryan, William Jennings, 26
Buchanan, D.S., 48
Bullington, Orvil S., 48
Burleigh, Harry, 137
Burris, Ed, 71
Bush, George, 221
Butler, George, 111, 175
Butler, Paul, 164, 168
Byrd, Harry, 112
Byrnes, James E., 1, 164, 165, 167

242